CAMBRIDGE LATIN AMERICAN STUDIES

EDITORS
DAVID JOSLIN   JOHN STREET
TIMOTHY KING   CLIFFORD T. SMITH

12

POLITICS AND TRADE IN
SOUTHERN MEXICO
1750–1821

THE SERIES

POLITICS AND TRADE
IN SOUTHERN MEXICO
1750–1821

BY

BRIAN R. HAMNETT

Assistant Professor of History
State University of New York at
Stony Brook

CAMBRIDGE
AT THE UNIVERSITY PRESS
1971

Published by the Syndics of the Cambridge University Press
Bentley House, 200 Euston Road, London N.W.1
American Branch: 32 East 57th Street, New York, N.Y.10022

Library of Congress Catalogue Card Number: 70–116 839

ISBN: 0 521 07860 1

To my Mother and Father

Printed in Great Britain
by Alden & Mowbray Ltd
at the Alden Press, Oxford

CONTENTS

ACKNOWLEDGMENTS

I should like to express my gratitude to the various persons in Mexico, Spain, England, and the United States, who have contributed in no small way to the realisation of this work. Dr. John Street at the Centre of Latin American Studies, Cambridge, kindly undertook the task of directing the original dissertation which gave rise to the present book. I should also like to thank Professor David Joslin at Pembroke College, and Professor Woodrow Borah at Berkeley, for their valuable advice and criticism. I am grateful to the Master and Fellows of Peterhouse for their support of my research project, and to the Department of Education and Science in London and the Astor Foundation for financial support. I am indebted to Dr. John Vincent for his sustained encouragement of this work during all its phases. In Spain, the kindness of Señorita Rosario Parra, director of the Archives of the Indies in Seville, and her staff, greatly aided my work in that magnificent depository. In Mexico, Dr. J. Ignacio Rubio Mañé, director of the National Archives, and his staff, received me with grace and courtesy.

Stony Brook   B. R. H.
July 1969

ARCHIVAL ABBREVIATIONS

ACO   Archivo de la Catedral de Oaxaca

AEO   Archivo del Estado de Oaxaca

AGI   Archivo General de Indias (Seville)

AGN   Archivo General de la Nación (Mexico City)

AHH   Archivo Histórico de Hacienda (Mexico City)

AHN   Archivo Histórico Nacional (Madrid)

AMO   Archivo Municipal de Oaxaca

BN   Biblioteca Nacional (Mexico City)

BM   British Museum (London)

BSMGE   Biblioteca de la Sociedad Mexicana de Geografía y Estadística (Mexico City)

WEIGHTS, MEASURES, AND CURRENCY

1 Cochineal was weighed before shipment to Spain in *cargas* of 9 *arrobas*:

    1 arroba = 25 Spanish pounds = 25 English pounds
    1 carga = 225 pounds

2 A *zurrón* was approximately 100 pounds

3 Maize, wheat, and beans were weighed as follows:

    4 cuartillos = 1 almud = 7·568 litres
    12 almudes = 1 fanega = 22·704 litres
    2 fanegas = 1 carga = 181·630 litres

4 A *vara* was the linear measure for textiles:

    1 vara = 0·838 metres = 32·99 inches

5 Currency:

    12 granos = 1 real
    8 reales = 1 peso
    1 peso = 4 shillings sterling *c.* 1780

INTRODUCTION

On to the indigenous civilisations of the Zapotecs and Mixtecs, the Castilian conquerors grafted the political and religious experience of Spain. The Aztec outpost of Huaxyacac became the centre of Spanish power and influence in the fertile Valley of Oaxaca. Through the course of the later sixteenth and seventeenth centuries, many of the indigenous areas of the province of Oaxaca fell under the spiritual control of the Dominican Order, which, from its Baroque convents and churches, exercised a theocratic authority that virtually excluded the power of the Crown. The Crown's authority emanated from the capital, the city of Antequera de Oaxaca, named after Antequera in Andalusia, which it was supposed to resemble; but in these religious centuries, often the authority of the Bishop of Oaxaca evoked a more immediate response in consciences.

Oaxaca was one of the main centres of Spanish power in the colonial period, a power whose bases were fixed more firmly into the centre and south of New Spain than in the modern Mexican Republic, which tends more strongly to the north and north-centre. The colonial Oaxaca was a region comparable with Guatemala, with Quito, and the highland regions of Peru, centres where Castilian authority influenced and permeated already well-formed indigenous cultures, and where, gradually, not without resistance, and often by means of symbols and demonstrations, the religion brought by the friars exercised a mystical fascination for the former subjects of the Aztecs, Mayas, or Incas. Within New Spain itself, Oaxaca was one of the great episcopal sees like Puebla, or Valladolid de Michoacan, under the authority of the archiepiscopal see of Mexico.

Many of the indigenous crafts of the pre-conquest era continued in Oaxaca, the cotton-mantle industry of Villa Alta, Teotitlán del Camino, and other towns, and the gathering of the cochineal insect to produce the indispensable scarlet dye, for example. After the expansion and decline of the silk industry in Oaxaca in the course of the sixteenth century, the cochineal, cotton, and cotton-mantle trades assumed the role of the central activities of the indigenous population, upon whose labours the Spanish element depended for their prosperity and political supremacy.

Oaxaca, because of these activities, was often considered by the Spanish Peninsular merchants and the Royal administrators there to be next in importance to the silver-mining regions of Guanajuato and Zacatecas. For, the export of the scarlet dye to the European textile industries contributed to the lessening of the bullion drain from the Indies, which so much plagued and perplexed the Spanish Metropolitan Government. The cotton of the Pacific coast region, especially around Jamiltepec, supplied the cotton textile *obrajes* (workshops) of both Puebla and Oaxaca, emerging in the course of the eighteenth century.

Foreign commentators also frequently alluded to the Oaxaca cochineal dye.[1] For, prior to the invention of chemical dyes in the middle of the nineteenth century, the chief source of the scarlet dye was Oaxaca, and of the purple and blue dye, the indigo of Guatemala and later Venezuela. These, and to a lesser degree, the dye-woods from Yucatán and Central America, attracted merchants from Spain, and aroused the competition of the Dutch, British, and French. These rival merchants would operate through the Cádiz and Seville trades, through their bases in the Caribbean islands, or by contraband directly from the shores of the Spanish Indies. In Spain, great merchant houses, such as the *Cinco gremios mayores de Madrid* and the Casa de Uztáriz dealt both in the cochineal of Oaxaca and the indigo of Guatemala in the eighteenth century. Houses with bases in Cádiz and Veracruz, the Casas de Cos, Muñoz, and Cosío, and a house with connexions also in London, the House of Gordon, Reid, and Murphy, with Tomás Murphí as its representative in Veracruz, all traded in dyes and bullion in return for manufactured goods or the primary products of the Peninsula.

The predominance of such primary products as olive oil and wines in Spain's trade to the Spanish Indies was evidence of her incapacity to become the industrial metropolis for her American market. Such an endemic and strategic weakness favoured both foreign manufacturers and

---

[1] The French botanist, Thierry de Ménonville, described in his *Travels to Guaxaca in 1777* how he succeeded in smuggling examples of the cochineal insects and the cactus on which they throve out of Oaxaca to the French part of the Caribbean island of Santo Domingo, where the French hoped to produce the dye for themselves: see M. Nicolas Joseph Thierry de Ménonville, *Travels to Guaxaca, Capital of the Province of the same name, in the Kingdom of Mexico*, contained in John Pinkerton, *A General Collection of the Best and Most Interesting Voyages and Travels in All Parts of the World* (17 vols.; London 1808–14), xiii, 753–876.

The Abbé Raynal described the importance of the cochineal dye and New Spain's export of it along with silver to the Philippines for exchange with Chinese silks, in his, *Histoire philosophique et politique des établissements et du commerce des européens dans les deux Indes* (Paris 1820 edition), tome III, bk. 5, 89; bk. 6, 352–60.

The German traveller and scientist, Baron Alexander von Humboldt, wrote of it, after his visit to New Spain in 1803, in his *Essai politique sur le royaume de la Nouvelle Espagne* (5 vols.; Paris 1811), II, 324; III, 262.

Introduction

domestic producers within the Indies itself.[1] In New Spain, both the *obrajes* and the indigenous village textile crafts employed the cochineal of Oaxaca and the indigo of Guatemala for silks, cottons, woollens, and linens.[2] These products were in considerable demand among the mestizo and Indian population of the Viceroyalty, as they were generally of an ordinary quality and low price. The indigenous production from Oaxaca, in particular the town of Villa Alta, reached markets as far and diverse as Mexico City, Puebla, and the silver-mining communities of Taxco, Guanajuato, and Zacatecas.[3]

In contrast to the Bajío, the province of Oaxaca was not so much dominated by the Creole landowners as by the Alcaldes Mayores and the Spanish Peninsular merchants. The former, also chiefly of Peninsular origin, were notorious for their abuse of the indigenous population and for their peculation of the Royal revenues. These Alcaldes Mayores occupied the function of civil administrators of the towns in the indigenous areas of settlement.[4] They resided in the head-towns of the regions, the *cabezera*, in the local Royal residence, the *Casas Reales*. Their faculties included the cognizance of civil and criminal jurisdiction in the first instance in Indian areas, in contrast to the Alcaldes Ordinarios of the Cabildos, who undertook the same function for the areas of Spanish and

---

1 See Ricardo Cappa, S.J., *Estudios críticos acerca de la dominación española en América* (Madrid 1888–97), vii; Humboldt, *Essai politique*, iv, bk. 5, 284 *et seq.*; 'État des manufactures et du commerce de la Nouvelle Espagne'; Jan Bazant, 'Evolución de la industria textil poblana 1544–1845', *Historia Mexicana*, 52 (April–June 1964), 473–516; John L. Phelan, *The Kingdom of Quito in the Seventeenth Century: Bureaucratic Politics in the Spanish Empire* (Wisconsin 1968), 66–85.

2 For the *obrajes* see M. Carrera Stampa, 'El obraje novohispano', *Memorias de la Academia Mexicana de la Historia*, xx (April–June 1961), no. 2, 148–71; *ibid.* 'Los obrajes de indígenas en el virreinato de la Nueva España', *Vigésimo-séptimo Congreso Internacional de Americanistas*, ii (Actas de la Primera Sesión celebrada en la Ciudad de México en 1939), 555–62.

3 Biblioteca de la Sociedad Mexicana de Geografía y Estadística (BSMGE), Mexico City, MSS José María Murguía y Galardi, *Estadística del estado de Oaxaca 1826–28* (5 tomes containing 9 vols.), vol. i, app. to pt. 2, f. 29 *v*.

4 There was little difference between the functions of Alcaldes Mayores and Corregidores. Theoretically, the latter governed a town, while the former administered a territorial division in the countryside, known as a *provincia*, and later, after the replacement of Alcaldes Mayores by Subdelegates under the Royal Ordinance of Intendants of 1786, as a *partido*. Territories within the jurisdiction of the Audiencias of Quito, Lima, and Charcas had no Alcaldes Mayores, only Corregidores. Unlike the case of the Spanish Peninsula, the Corregidores in the Indies were not required to have qualified at law, but might be laymen, i.e. *de capa y espada* as opposed to *letrados* or *togados*. José María Zamora y Coronado, *Biblioteca de legislación ultramarina en forma de diccionario alfabético* (6 vols.; Madrid 1844–49), i, 180–84; J. Ignacio Rubio Mañé, *Introducción al estudio de los virreyes de Nueva España 1536–1746* (4 vols.; Mexico 1959–61), i, 77–79; C. H. Haring, *The Spanish Empire in America* (Oxford 1947), 138–42; L. B. Simpson, *The Encomienda in New Spain, The Beginnings of Spanish Mexico* (California 1950), 191, n. 18.

3

Creole residence. The Alcaldes Mayores, often military men, were entitled to appoint lieutenants who were expected to be qualified at law (*tenientes letrados*), in order to advise them on matters of legal procedure. Both officials were required to offer the Crown a *fianza*, an advance guarantee, which would ensure the Crown's receipt of the revenues it had trusted its administrators to collect. The presentation of *fiadores*, who would reimburse the Crown in the Alcalde Mayor's default, was the condition of receipt of office from the Superior Government in Mexico City.[1]

In the city of Oaxaca, another local representative of the Royal authority resided, the Corregidor.[2] As a Royal magistrate the judicial functions of this official involved the exercise of full jurisdiction in the area to which he had been assigned. Like the Alcalde Mayor, he enjoyed the right to appoint a lieutenant. The Corregidor also acted as president of the Cabildo and the Royal representative on that municipal corporation.[3] Both the Alcaldes Mayores and the Corregidores were forbidden by the Crown to hold estates or to engage in trade either in person or through agents during their five-year term of office.[4] They were not allowed to marry any resident of their area of jurisdiction while they still occupied public office unless they received a special dispensation from the Crown.[5] While ensuring that the Indian tribute revenue was duly collected, the Alcaldes Mayores and Corregidores were especially entrusted with the task of protecting the Indians. Both officials were to make regular visits to the Indian towns with their rod of justice (*vara de justicia*), in order to hear complaints of injustice against local landowners, estate managers, Indian caciques, or parish priests.[6]

[1] E. Ruiz Guiñazú, *La magistratura indiana* (Buenos Aires 1916), 295.
[2] Carlos E. Castañeda, 'The Corregidor in Spanish Colonial Administration', *Hispanic American Historical Review [HAHR]*, ix (1929), 446–70.
[3] *Ibid.* and Ruiz Guiñazú, *Magistratura indiana*, 292–300.
[4] *Recopilación de leyes de los reynos de las Indias* (Madrid 1943 edition), bk. 5, title 2: law xxv, 'Que los gobernadores no apremien a los indios a que les labren ropa'; law xlvi, 'Que los virreyes procuren remediar las ganancias ilícitas de los gobernadores'; and law xlvii, 'Que la prohibición de tratar, y contratar comprehende a los gobernadores, corregidores, alcaldes mayores, y sus tenientes'.
[5] *Ibid.* law xliv, 'Que los gobernadores, corregidores, alcaldes mayores, y sus tenientes letrados no puedan casar en sus distritos'; and law xlv, 'Que los gobernadores no tengan ministros, ni oficiales naturales de la provincia, ni parientes dentro del quarto grado'. See Archivo General de Indias [AGI] *México* 1128, *Consultas, decretos, y reales órdenes* (1769–1770). On 31 May 1770, the Crown conceded license to Joseph Rodríguez del Toro, Oidor of the Audiencia of Mexico, to marry his daughter, born in New Spain, to the Corregidor of Oaxaca Pedro de Pineda. The prohibition, then, was not absolute. It served as a reminder to the parties concerned to consult the Crown before they acted.
[6] *Recopilación*, bk. 5, title 2, law xv, 'Que los gobernadores y corregidores visiten los términos,

4

Introduction

While the Laws of the Indies assigned certain specific salaries, for example the sum of 2,500 pesos per year for the Corregidor of Mexico City, the average salaries for the Alcaldes Mayores and Corregidores in the locality were too small to cover their administrative expenditure. The Crown could not afford to pay its extensive bureaucracy. Prior to Philip II's *Real Cédula* of 1582, which provided for the payment of salaries from the Indian tribute revenues, the Crown had charged them to the account of the Indian communal funds. The tribute levy, however, was no solution, owing to the fluctuating and undependable nature of such revenues, and the collapse of the indigenous population figure in the course of the sixteenth and earlier seventeenth centuries in New Spain. Therefore, the issue of salaries for the representatives of the Royal authority in the locality and in the Indian towns plagued the Metropolitan and Superior Governments throughout the colonial period.[1]

This lack of proper salaries forced the Mexican Alcaldes Mayores and the Peruvian Corregidores to contravene the Laws of the Indies by indulging in illicit trading practices so stringently forbidden by the Crown. In most cases the goods or cash in which they traded would be supplied through a contract with a private merchant, a member of the mercantile corporation, the juridically constituted Consulado of Mexico. In return for agreeing to such a contract, the merchant would offer to cover the administrator's *fianza*.[2]

The ingoing administrators were generally small men of low position, or military persons of small fortunes. Newly arrived in the Indies, they expected to gain rapid wealth, and return to Spain to live in style. However, since the Crown's exigencies required them to pay their own fare across the Atlantic, and expected them on arrival to meet the obligations of the *fianza*, they were faced with financial burdens far beyond their limited capacity. Their plight was described by Viceroy Amarillas of New Spain in a letter to the Crown written on 9 April 1759 from Mexico City. He explained that the Alcaldes Mayores sent by the Metropolitan Government would often arrive in Veracruz burdened with family obligations as well as their duty to offer the *fianza*, and to pay the shipping companies which had brought them. Some of the justices did not even know of the

---

y de lo que resultare avisen a las Audiencias'; G. Lohmann Villena, *El corregidor de indios en el Perú bajo los Austrias* (Madrid 1957), 403–49; Constantino Bayle, *El protector de indios* (Seville 1945), 125–8.

1 *Recopilación*, bk. 5, title 2, law i; Castañeda, 'The Corregidor', 463; Lohmann Villena, *El corregidor*, 428, 431 n. 23; Bayle, *El protector*, 127, 143.

2 Zamora y Coronado, *Biblioteca*, III, 244–7; Lohmann Villena, *El corregidor*, 436.

fianza requirement, and actually expected to take up office immediately upon arrival.[1]

Similar complaints were expressed by Villarroel, Alcalde Mayor of Tlapa, to the Viceroy on 16 April 1774. As a result of their debts, the *fianza*, and the 1,000 pesos for the equipment of their offices, the Alcaldes Mayores were reduced to begging favours from door to door. In their everyday administration right down to the very official sealed paper on which all business was to be written they had to offer *fianzas*. Therefore, in order to pay their way, they were constrained to commit all manner of extortions and injustices in the smaller and poorer provinces. In the richer provinces they would be obliged to form a contract, generally with a Spanish Peninsular merchant, for the coverage of the *fianzas*, in return for which the Alcaldes Mayores would undertake to manage the *fiador's* trading activities with the Indians. Such an operation, in which the Alcalde Mayor issued cash or basic equipment or commodities to the Indians on the account of the merchant, was known as the *repartimiento*. This form of trading, always denounced by Crown and clergy (at least at the level of the episcopacy) and contrary to the Laws, occurred frequently in the province of Oaxaca, because of the demand for its products. The merchant who financed the *repartimiento* was known as the *aviador* or *habilitador*, and the process of outside financing as *avío* or *habilitación*. Ingoing administrators would solicit such *avío* from the merchants to the sums of, for example, 15,000–20,000 pesos in silver reales or in commodities for issue to the Indians. In return, the Indians would be required to pay back their debt in the finished product of their region, such as cochineal, cotton, cotton mantles, and other ordinary cotton garments for use amongst the indigenous and mestizo population.

It would not so much be the Alcalde Mayor himself who occupied the central role in such trading operations but his legal lieutenant. This official, instead of being qualified at law as the Laws of the Indies specified, would be a nominee of the merchant-*aviador*. Villarroel complained that the Alcaldes Mayores were powerless to prevent the abuse of their authority by such lieutenants in the collection of Indian debts to the *repartimiento*. In any case the lieutenant usually could not be removed without the prior consent of the *aviador*. Moreover, at the end of his term of office, the Alcalde Mayor was expected to divide the profits of his trade among all interested parties, including both his *aviador* and the lieutenant.[2]

---

[1] Archivo General de la Nación [AGN] Correspondencia de los virreyes (serie 1), 1 (Amarillas 1755–6), exp. 123, f. 185.
[2] Biblioteca Nacional [BN] (Mexico) MSS 1378, f. 211, Hipólito Ruiz y Villarroel, 'Sobre

Introduction

Only the Corregidores and Alcaldes Mayores were able to manage the *repartimiento*, because only they were endowed with full Royal jurisdiction, which they employed to coerce the Indians to trade in commodities they might not otherwise be inclined to produce in bulk. The Royal power of justice, then, was used to violate the freedom of trading prescribed for the indigenous communities by the Laws of the Indies. By creating commercial monopolies within the locality, and by expelling any intruding merchants, the Alcaldes Mayores sought to keep the local trade confined to their *aviador's* interests.[1]

Similar *aviador* functions were assumed by the Spanish Peninsular merchants of the Consulado of Lima in the Viceroyalty of Peru. The merchants undertook to finance both Corregidores in their *repartimientos* and mine-owners in their operations.[2] Like Peru and New Spain, the Captaincy-General of Guatemala contained large groups of indigenous communities living at subsistence level. There, too, the *repartimiento* functioned in connexion with the indigo monoculture. The merchant-*aviador* occupied a central role. For, the indigo planter received the basic commodities necessary for his subsistence and operations through the contracts made between the Spanish Peninsular *aviador* and the local Alcalde Mayor or Corregidor. In return for such a contract, the merchant would pay into the Royal Treasury in Guatemala City the revenues due to the Crown from the administrator's area of jurisdiction.[3]

The present work traces the struggle of the Spanish Crown and the episcopal authorities in Oaxaca to secure the observation of the law in the trade and government of the region. The importance of the products of Oaxaca for both New Spain itself and for the wider world market provided the main explanation of the difficulty of achieving such a regulation, and the main incentive for the adoption of such a thorough reform as that advocated by Visitor-General to New Spain, José de Gálvez. The interests of the merchant-*aviadores*, in both Mexico City and Oaxaca, and of the Alcaldes Mayores, naturally made them bitter opponents of the administrative and commercial reforms enacted by the Spanish Crown between

el modo de servirse las Alcaldías mayores, y perjuicios que sufren de los oficios de México' (1774).

1 *Recopilación*, bk. 5, title 6, *De los indios*; Lohmann Villena, *El corregidor*, 431–5.

2 *Ibid.* and G. Céspedes del Castillo, 'Lima y Buenos Aires. Repercusiones económicas y políticas de la creación del virreinato del Plata', *Anuario de Estudios Americanos*, iii (1946), 669–874.

3 Robert S. Smith, 'Indigo Production and Trade in Colonial Guatemala', *HAHR*, xxxix (1959), 181–211; Troy S. Floyd, 'The Guatemalan Merchants, the Government, and the "Provincianos" 1750–1800', *HAHR*, xli (1961), 90–110.

1778, when the system of freer trade within the empire was first definitively codified, and 1795, when two new Consulados were incorporated at Veracruz and Guadalajara. Their opposition meant a political split within the ranks of the Spanish *Peninsulares* within New Spain. This was especially serious because, firstly, the government in Spain during the reign of Charles IV (1788–1808) was at its most unpopular both in Spain and the Indies, and, secondly, the split occurred against the background of mounting Creole demands for self-government.

CHAPTER I

OAXACA—ENVIRONMENT AND TRADE

During the course of the first century after the Conquest, the dye trade of Oaxaca secured a position in New Spain's export trade second only to that of silver. The scarlet cochineal dye, produced almost exclusively by the Indian population, maintained this role until well into the nineteenth century, when competition from Guatemala after 1821, and the invention of chemical dyes after the 1850s combined with the effects of the wars of Independence after 1810 to damage the Oaxaca economy to the degree that the indigenous dye trade was practically eliminated.[1]

Prior to the discovery of the Mexican-Indian cochineal, the chief source for the scarlet dye had been the kermes insect, which had thrived in the Mediterranean basin, and had provided the European powers with their needs. The entrepôt had been Venice. However, the exploitation of the Mexican dye, produced in the early years in Tlaxcala, Huejotzingo, and Cholula, as well as Oaxaca, put on the world market a dye with ten or twelve times the propensities of the kermes.[2] The first shipment of the Tlaxcala–Oaxaca dye into Spain occurred in 1526, and by the late 1540s cochineal was being sold in quantity in the market of Tlaxcala. In response, the local cabildo (municipal council) sought to encourage plantation of *nopaleras*, the cactus groves on which the cochineal insect throve. By the middle of the sixteenth century, Tlaxcala's Indians were reputed to be earning over 100,000 ducados annually from their dye sales.[3]

Most European merchants took active interest in the fortunes of the dye trade. The powerful Fugger banking and commercial house maintained agents in the major ports and capitals, between 1550 and 1600, in order to report the crucial movements and unfortunate vicissitudes of Spain's trades in bullion and dyes.[4] The first cochineal cargoes arrived in

[1] See Raymond L. Lee, 'Cochineal Production and Trade in New Spain to 1600', *The Americas*, iv (1947–8), 449–73; and, 'American Cochineal in European Commerce, 1526–1625', *Journal of Modern History*, xxiii (1951), 205–24.

[2] Lee, 'American Cochineal', 205–6. For remarks on the sixteenth-century areas of production, see Charles Gibson, *The Aztecs under Spanish Rule. A History of the Indians of the Valley of Mexico, 1519–1810* (Stanford 1964), 354.

[3] Lee, 'Cochineal Production', 457; Charles Gibson, *Tlaxcala in the Sixteenth century* (Yale U.P. 1952), 149–50.

[4] Victor von Klarvill (ed.), *The Fugger News-Letters, Being a Selection of unpublished letters*

Antwerp in 1552 and 1553, and in 1569 records began of the dye's import into England, where it came to assume considerable importance in the English cloth industry. The Amsterdam exchange received its first trading quantities of the dye in 1589.[1]

The increasing demand for the product, and the heavy profits received from it, encouraged extremes of fraud and speculation within New Spain itself. As early as 1548, the Cabildo of Tlaxcala had been appointing Indian officials to supervise the administration of the cochineal trade.[2] However, anxious to assert for the Crown this supervisory role, Viceroy Martín Enríquez established the office of *juez de granas* (cochineal magistrate) in the city of Puebla in 1572. At such a clear emphasis of Royal right, the Cabildo of Puebla naturally protested, seeing its corporate privilege threatened. This response, nevertheless, revealed the intensity of private interest in the trade. For, the very Alcalde Mayor of Puebla himself had severely compromised his position by becoming one of the city's chief dye merchants, along with the Regidores (city councillors) of the cabildo. For such reasons, Martín Enríquez justified his actions. Moreover, the merchants of Seville were reporting that the present year's cargoes of cochineal had been adulterated with soil.[3]

In 1575, the Viceroy reported to the Crown that the cochineal trade was a much greater activity than any other in the Realm. Mestizos and other castes would pass with ease among the Indian towns, despite such blatant violation of the Laws of the Indies, persuading the inhabitants to cultivate the dye. In the province of Oaxaca, the Dominican Order controlled most of the Indian towns, and the Franciscans exercised similar authority elsewhere. In certain of the Oaxaca towns, cochineal assumed such importance that about 7,000 arrobas would be gathered in an average year at the rate of 12 reales of silver per pound. In this way, the average annual value of the trade was reaching 259,000 pesos, a very considerable sum in those early decades.[4] Around 1600, the estimated cochineal import into Spain reached between 10,000 and 12,000 arrobas, valued at 600,000 pesos. By the 1620s, then, a substantial trade was developing in Mexican cochineal at the port of Seville.[5]

from the Correspondents of the House of Fugger during the years 1568–1605 (2 vols.; London 1925–6) ii, 231–2; for example, the Fugger agent in Lisbon reported on 19 October 1591 that the fleet from New Spain, about seventy ships, carried 14,000 arrobas of cochineal.

[1] Lee, 'American Cochineal', 207, 209, 210.   [2] Gibson, *Tlaxcala*, 150, n. 84.

[3] AGI *Mexico* 19, *Correspondencia de los virreyes de Nueva España (años 1574–5)*, ramo 1, no. 132: Martín Enríquez–Crown, 5 April 1574.

[4] *Ibid.* no. 157: Martín Enríquez–Crown, 21 Sept. 1575.

[5] Lee, 'American Cochineal', 206, 208.

Such a development was recognised in Philip III's Cochineal Ordinance of 1620, which described the dye as, 'one of the most precious products that is raised in our Western Indies . . . a merchandise equal in estimation to gold and silver'.[1]

This Ordinance aspired to restrain the still frequent frauds in the trade by authorising the *jueces de grana* to visit the cochineal markets regularly. However, as Viceroy Marqués de Guadalcázar reported in 1618, it was these very officials who were equally perpetrating such abuses.[2]

For, owing to the traditional and frequent practice of obstructing Royal policies which conflicted with their economic interests, Crown and Viceroy were experiencing great difficulty in persuading the merchants and administrators involved to conform to the letter and spirit of the Laws of the Indies. Most of the time, the Crown was fighting a losing battle. Consequently, the Indian communities concerned, especially in the cochineal and related trades in Oaxaca, did not cease to be subject to abuse.

As a result, the Visitor-General of New Spain, Bishop Juan de Palafox y Mendoza of Puebla, in June 1641, denounced the Alcaldes Mayores of the Viceroyalty as 'forces of desolation' in the largely Indian, mestizo, mulatto, and negro-populated areas outside the great Hispanic cities, such as Mexico and Puebla. For, so far from representing the presence of Royal Justice in the locality, they were generally members of the Viceroy's entourage. Even the esteemed Viceroy Marqués de Cadereita had filled offices in that way. Palafox regarded the Alcaldías Mayores as nothing better than sources of entertainment for the Conquerors. Moreover, in view of the Alcaldes Mayores' receipt of a pittance of between 300 and 500 pesos as their annual salary, it was no surprise that they were obliged to *tratar y contratar* with the Indians, in gross violation of the Laws of the Indies, in order to maintain themselves.[3] Since, in any case, they were creatures of the current Viceroy, no redress of grievances was ever possible. Palafox went so far as to claim that all conception of justice was relative to the particular policies of whichever Viceroy happened to be in office. Even the *residencia* was useless as a deterrent. For, it would be taken during the term of office of the administrators' patron, the Viceroy. Moreover, outgoing Alcaldes Mayores would usually leave a donation of

---

1 Barbro Dahlgren de Jordán, *Nocheztli, La grana cochinilla* (Mexico 1963), 9.
2 *Boletín del Archivo General de la Nación, Mexico*, tomo II, no. 4, primera serie (July–August 1931), 493–506.
3 *Recopilación de leyes de los reynos de las Indias* (Madrid 1943), bk. 5, title 2, law 47, 'Que la prohibición de tratar, y contratar comprehende a los gobernadores, alcaldes mayores, y sus tenientes'.

around 800 pesos to their successors entrusted with taking the *residencia*.[1]

Responding to the profits from the cochineal trade, these administrators' main concern was to enclose a trade monopoly within their areas of jurisdiction, to the complete exclusion of other Royal vassals, and in contradiction to the Laws of the Indies.[2] This restriction of trade into few hands contributed to the general impoverishment of the Realm. At the same time as they violently expelled their trade rivals, the administrators failed to pay the Royal sales-tax on their illicit trade. For, since it was the Alcalde Mayor who was both Royal tax-collector and illegal trader, it was unlikely that he would either incriminate or inconvenience himself by exacting such a tax upon himself. This disorder and illegality was bad enough, but, 'the Alcaldes Mayores do not trade for themselves, but as factors for those who supply them'. Therefore, recourse was fruitless. For the Alcaldes Mayores would be protected by their sponsors, men with friends in high places in the administration in Mexico City. As a result, Palafox concluded, there was no one to execute the provisions of the *Reales Cédulas* and the Laws of the Indies.[3]

Neither Palafox's request of September 1642, that criminal proceedings should be taken against Alcaldes Mayores who usurped Royal financial rights, nor the Crown's *Real Cédula* of 12 August 1649, in response to the excesses reported, seem to have had any effect.[4] For the subsequent Bishop of Puebla, on 29 October 1660, denounced the same trade monopolies, the same coercion, and the same exorbitant prices. In the province of Puebla, for example, the Alcaldes Mayores were issuing subsistence products and livestock from the haciendas to the Indians at exorbitant prices. In Oaxaca, where they traded in cochineal, tobacco, cotton, cotton mantles, and various other indigenous textiles, excessive prices were being offered in sales to the Indians in order to undervalue the indigenous products. The Bishop explained that, 'to arrange this trade, as soon as the Alcaldes Mayores are nominated, they look for a merchant who can finance them (*aviar*)'.[5]

Since private interests prevented the Crown from implementing its laws, and curbing the problem of the Alcaldes Mayores' illegal *repartimientos* to the Indians, the lower classes thus adversely affected began sporadically to take matters into their own hands in the spring of 1660. A series of peasant risings—a Oaxaqueño *jacquerie*—began on 22 March 1660

---

[1] AGI *Mexico* 600, *Expediente sobre el punto de reforma de los alcaldes mayores é inquietudes en Tehuantepec, años 1642 a 1678 intercalados.*

[2] *Ibid.* See also *Recopilación*, bk. 6, title 1, laws 24 and 32.

[3] AGI *Mexico* 600.   [4] *Ibid.*   [5] *Ibid.*

in Tehuantepec. There, the Alcalde Mayor, whose *repartimientos* had reputedly been valued at over 20,000 *pesos de oro*, was killed by the Indians, and the *Casas Reales* burnt down. The movement spread across to Nejapa against the Alcalde Mayor's *repartimiento* for cochineal and cotton mantles. In Ixtepeji, the Alcalde Mayor was forced to flee as a result of a rising against his *repartimiento* for cochineal. Similar risings occurred in Teutila and Teococuilco, in Villa Alta, and across to Huajuapan. From there they spread to Huamantla, Tlaxcala, Zimapan, Otumba, and Tancítaro.[1]

Several of the areas in rebellion in Oaxaca, a total of twenty towns, were pacified by the personal intervention of the Bishop, a Creole, Alonso de Cuevas Dávalos, who preferred a lenient course of action with the rebels. For they themselves had professed their uninterrupted loyalty to both the Crown and the Bishop.[2]

The investigation of the causes of the rebellion, and the punishment of the guilty were entrusted to an Oidor of the Audiencia of Mexico, Montemayor de Cuenca, who duly left Mexico City in February 1661. He reported that, in the case of the cotton-mantle producing jurisdiction of Villa Alta, not even the pressure of the Dominicans had been able to remedy the abuses. For, there, the Alcaldes Mayores would secure the cochineal dye from the Indians at the price of 16 reales per pound, while they would sell it at 30 and 32 reales. At the same time, they were able to commission the Indians to weave the cotton mantles, so much in demand among the lower classes of the Realm, through their control of a large part of the cotton supplies. The raw material they would then issue in lots to the Indians. In Yaguila, for example, there would be two *repartimientos* of cotton per month, in which eight pounds of cotton would be issued to each family, deducting the cost from the price of each finished cotton mantle of five yards (*varas*) in length and one in width. In general, in Villa Alta, one mantle was to be finished in twenty days. This mantle

---

1 *Ibid.* See also Luis González Obregón, 'Las sublevaciones de indios en el siglo XVII: *iii*. Las sublevaciones de indios en Tehuantepec, Nejapa, Ixtepeji, y Villa Alta', *Annales del Museo Nacional* (Mexico), segunda época, tomo iv, (1907), 145 *et seq.*, and Basilio Rojas, *La rebelión de Tehuantepec* (Mexico, 1964).

2 The Indians of Tehuantepec, who in armed bands had occupied the chief town of the jurisdiction and exhorted the other towns to rise up and kill their opponents, went out to meet the Bishop while still under arms. The Bishop rode through the town in full pontifical robes. In awe, the Indians prostrated themselves on the ground, or led the reins of his mule. Women, previously active in the rebellion, took their mantles from their shoulders, and spread them over the street so that the Bishop's mule could pass over them. This occurred to the accompaniment of trumpets, horns, and chirimías. See González Obregón, 'Las sublevaciones'.

would bring a market price of 16 reales. However, the Indian weavers would receive a price of only 8 reales from the Alcalde Mayor. Besides this abuse, the Indian population, which manufactured its own clothing, would be required to receive imported clothing issued in the *repartimiento*. For such clothing, it was obliged to pay in the products of the region.[1] In such a way, the activities of the Alcaldes Mayores forced the Indians to be both producers and consumers of commodities from which the justices and their financial backers derived a large measure of their wealth.

The Metropolitan Government took the lessons of the 1660 risings so seriously that the Council of the Indies, on 29 May 1662, recommended the issue of a *Real Cédula* declaring the confiscation of all goods involved in the *repartimiento*, and their reversion to the Crown in forfeit. At the same time, all debts to the Alcaldes Mayores were to be declared annulled.[2] The law, if it was ever issued, apparently had no effect. For on 20 April 1686, the Bishop of Puebla wrote to the Crown complaining of the perjury of Alcaldes Mayores who violated their oaths of office by trading with the Indians. The Bishop, however, saw to the core of the problem when he pointed out that if ever the laws against trading and contracting with the Indians should be enforced, there would not be a single person willing to assume the office of either Corregidor or Alcalde Mayor.[3] In response to the Bishop of Puebla's remarks, the Crown issued the Royal Despatches of 1687 for the rigorous punishment of violations of the law. This once more proved to be of no avail, and the whole matter had to be repeated—with equally strong language—in the *Real Cédula* of 10 February 1716.[4]

The preoccupation in Oaxaca with the cultivation of the *nopaleras* for the production of the cochineal dye tended to lead to the neglect of maize and other subsistence crops by the Indians. The ingoing Bishop of Oaxaca at the turn of the century, Fray Ángel de Maldonado, became especially concerned that such neglect would give rise to periodic shortages of food-stuffs amongst the indigenous population. He, therefore, recommended that, as a deterrent to the further extension of cochineal cultivation, the Crown should allow the Church to exact a tithe on the dye produced by the Indians.

---

[1] AGI *Mexico* 600. [2] *Ibid.*

[3] AGI *Mexico* 634, *Expedientes sobre alcaldías y alcaldes mayores del distrito de aquella Audiencia, años de 1701 á 1717.*

[4] *Ibid.* See also R. Konetzke, *Colección de documentos para la historia de la formación social de Hispanoamérica, 1493–1810*, vol. iii, tomo I (1691–1799), doc. 91.

The Bishop's report, sent to the Council of the Indies on 26 December 1702, opened the whole complicated question of whether the Indian producers should pay a tithe, an issue that was not resolved until the beginning of the nineteenth century. Fray Maldonado, on visitation in Villa Alta, requested that the Indians should pay on both cochineal and cotton. For, in view of the great demand for the dye among the nations of the world at the present time, the Indians directed their attention to its production, in such a way that over half the agricultural labouring population of Oaxaca were occupied in its cultivation. In consequence, the Indians had left the greater part of their fields uncultivated for products of alimentation. The Bishop concluded from this that the Indians should be removed from their status of exemption from tithe payment on the dye, and given a similar status to that of the tithe-paying Spanish producers.

Like all previous commentators on the situation in Oaxaca, the Bishop singled out for attack the abuses committed by the local Alcaldes Mayores. Like Palafox, Maldonado pointed to the complexity of interests behind those justices. 'The Alcaldes Mayores have in Mexico City one or another minister of the Audiencia at their entire disposition. As a result of such a dependence, they have the Royal Audiencia in their defence.'[1]

The Real Acuerdo of Mexico discussed the tithe issue, on 9 April 1703, side-stepping the matter of complicity with the Alcaldes Mayores. The Acuerdo reported to the Crown that an imposition of the cochineal tithe on the Indians would have disastrous consequences. The Laws of the Indies and the *Reales Cédulas* had exempted Indian cochineal growers, who, in any case, were sufficiently burdened by their payment of tribute to the Crown. The result of any attempt by the clergy to add to that an ecclesiastical tithe would only serve to burden the wretched Indians even more. From there the matter went before the Fiscal of the Council of the Indies in Madrid, who supported the views of the Audiencia of Mexico, on 14 November 1703. Moreover, he added that the Bishop had only just arrived in his diocese, and should not have considered introducing such far-reaching innovations. The Council of the Indies agreed.[2]

Nevertheless, the matter had to be discussed all over again when, in 1715, the *Cabildo Eclesiástico* (Cathedral chapter) of Oaxaca attempted to secure the Crown's approval for the collection of a cochineal tithe to supplement the ecclesiastical revenues. This time the clergy secured the Audiencia's approval. However, on 9 June 1718, the Council of the Indies

---

[1] AGI *Mexico* 877, *Cartas y expedientes del obispo de Oaxaca, 1651–1760*, Council of the Indies, no. 21, 9 April 1703, (no. 4).   [2] *Ibid.*

refused to ratify that decision. In conformity with the opinion of their Fiscal, the Council emphasised the principle of non-exaction. Immediately, there followed a protest from the Bishop of Oaxaca. The Council responded with a further discussion of the issue, in which the Fiscal explained that the brunt of the payment of such a tithe would fall on those least capable of paying, the Indian growers. As a result, the Council reaffirmed its former decision on 12 June 1719.[1]

Table 1. *Value of offices of Alcalde Mayor/Corregidor*

		(pesos)
Jicayan (Oax.)	7 December 1718	7,500
Villa Alta (Oax.)	29 June 1718	7,000
Salvatierra–Celaya	20 January 1719	5,500
Cuernavaca	7 December 1718	5,000
Huejotenango	14 February 1719	5,000
Cuicatlán–Papalotipac (Oax.)	23 June 1718	4,500
Teposcolula (Oax.)	24 June 1718	4,200
Chichicapa (Oax.)	26 June 1718	4,200
Taximaroa–Maravatío	21 December 1718	3,500
Corregimiento of Oaxaca (Oax.)	20 December 1718	3,000
Huajuapan, Tonalá, Minas de Silacayoapan (Oax.)	10 December 1718	3,000
Tehuacan	20 December 1718	3,000
Teozacoalco–Teococuilco (Oax.)	7 December 1718	2,800
Michoacan	31 January 1719	2,800
Malinalco	31 January 1719	2,800
Querétaro (Corrto.)	20 September 1719	2,500
Teutila (Oax.)	9 February 1719	2,400
Córdoba	9 February 1719	2,400
Zacatlán (Corrto.)	31 December 1718	2,250
Izúcar	7 December 1718	2,000
Chalco	5 January 1719	2,000
Old Veracruz	9 February 1719	1,500
Guanajuato	14 October 1719	1,200
Cholula	21 March 1719	1,000
San Andrés Tuxtla	9 February 1719	1,000
Chihuahua	4 March 1719	800

It was not only the clergy but also private individuals who sought to profit from a share of the trades of Oaxaca. The importance attached to the possession of public office in Oaxaca can be seen from the price at which they were valued. At the top of a list containing the values of the

[1] AGI *Mexico* 2693, *Expedientes inventariados (1807)*, Diferentes Cosecheros de grana de la intendencia. . . . Oaxaca, 22 July 1806.

offices of Alcalde Mayor and Corregidor in New Spain for the years 1718 and 1719, came the two Oaxaca jurisdictions of Jicayan and Villa Alta. These areas were extremely remote, even from the city of Oaxaca, but were, nevertheless, valued at the supreme prices of 7,500 and 7,000 pesos respectively, more, that is, than Cuernavaca, Querétaro, Valladolid de Michoacan, Guanajuato, Tehuacan, or Cholula.[1] Jicayan, on the Pacific coast of Oaxaca, produced both the cochineal dye, and cotton, chiefly for employment in the cotton textile *obrajes* in the province of Puebla and in the city of Oaxaca. Villa Alta, in the sierra north of the Valley of Oaxaca, produced both cochineal, and the cotton mantles so frequently worn by the mestizo and indigenous elements of New Spain's population.[2]

Table 1 illustrates this scale of values throughout New Spain.

As the table indicates, the most highly prized Alcaldías Mayores were precisely those situated in the main areas of indigenous population, namely in the provinces of Oaxaca, Puebla, Mexico, and Michoacan. In such areas, the various forms of the *repartimiento* would have offered the Alcalde Mayor or Corregidor and his *aviador* considerable profits.

The importance of the economic activities of Oaxaca was also reflected in the increasing sale price of the lease of the Royal sales-tax, the alcabala, in the collection areas of the city of Oaxaca and the Cuatro Villas del Marquesado. This lease, '*en lo antiguo*', had been valued at 3,620 pesos annually. In the year 1680, the price rose to 7,350 pesos, when the lease was auctioned for nine years to Francisco Matilla, presumably a merchant or chief citizen of Oaxaca, Puebla, or Mexico. Between April 1691 and April 1700, Ignacio de la Herrán Terán secured the lease for 12,000 pesos annually, in years when the Fleets arrived from Spain, and 10,000 pesos, when they did not. He ceded his lease to a group of army captains, of whom Rodrigo de la Chicas and Joseph de Ibaeta were citizens of Oaxaca city, in 1693.[3]

Even so, the Crown was especially preoccupied with losses sustained in the process of auctioning the leases of alcabalas. The *Real Cédula* (*por la vía reservada*) of 10 January 1718 ordered, therefore, that all leases sanctioned in New Spain should be placed under the direction of the

---

1 AGI *Mexico* 635, *Expedientes sobre alcaldías y alcaldes mayores, etc. 1718–1737*, Relación de los Empleos, 17 November, 1719.
2 Biblioteca de la Sociedad Mexicana de Geografía y Estadística [BSMGE], MSS Murguía y Galardi, José María, *Estadística del estado de Oaxaca* (5 tomes containing 9 vols.; 1826–8), vol. i, app. to pt. ii, f. 29 *v*.
3 AGI *Mexico* 871, *Expediente sobre el ramo de alcabalas de aquella ciudad (Antequera de Guajaca), 1693–1728*.

Viceroy. At the same time, the prices of the leases were to be set as high as possible, and there was to be greater security of payment to the Royal officials concerned. The Crown was anxious to prevent the lessees from securing great profits on their transactions to the detriment of the Royal finances. Subsequent *Reales Cédulas* of 2 September 1726 laid down the form of the proceedings.[1]

The lease of November 1719 to November 1727 was set at the rate of 12,600 pesos, not especially higher than the 1691–1700 period, probably owing to the slackening of trade during the War of the Spanish Succession. Towards the end of 1727, a citizen of the city of Guatemala, Simón de Larrazábal, requested the lease for nine years of the Oaxaca and Cuatro Villas collection, which he said had traditionally been '*a cargo de los vecinos y mercaderes*'. The price he offered for the period November 1728 to November 1737 was 14,000 pesos. The Council of the Indies debated the matter against the background of its legislation of 1718 and 1726, and concluded that the lease should be granted, by the *Real Decreto* of 26 January 1728, but at the increased rate of 15,000 pesos.[2]

In conjunction with the visitation of the tribunals of justice in New Spain by Visitador Garzarón, the *Real Cédula* of 13 December 1721 was issued, declaring the abolition of the illegal contracts between the justices and their *aviadores*, and ordering the punishment of the guilty parties. Garzarón's visitation showed once more the lack of compliance with the Royal legislation, and the entire abandon in which lay the Laws of the Indies. Such a situation gravely reflected on the effectiveness of the Royal authority in New Spain. As a result, the *auto* of the Audiencia of Mexico, on 22 December 1722, banned the *repartimiento* even through intermediary parties. Severe punishments were prescribed for non-compliance, for the guilty were to be suspended from office and banished from the Realm.[3]

Nevertheless, the fulminations of the Royal authorities seem to have had little effect. For, in Veracruz in June 1728, the ingoing Alcalde Mayor of Tehuantepec, Felipe Conde y Calvo, who had consumed his patrimony in the expensive voyage to New Spain, agreed to a contract with an *aviador*. He was to receive the sum of 2,896 pesos 4 reales from the *Alférez* (Royal lieutenant) of the city of Veracruz, Joseph Suárez Camaño, for the *habilitación* of the Alcaldía Mayor of Tehuantepec, and especially for employment in the cochineal trade. The finished dye was to be sent

---

1 *Ibid.*   2 *Ibid.*
3 Museo Nacional de Antropología, Mexico City, *Microfilm Collection*, Series Oaxaca, roll 21, Archivo del Juzgado de Teposcolula, primer instancia, legajo 5, 1669–1881.

from the Isthmus up to the city of Oaxaca within six months from the date. Unfortunately, the Alcalde Mayor died that August, but, preoccupied with the obligation he had contracted, he had gone so far as to have suggested in his will that the Crown should appoint his son, a minor, to continue his term of office. A lieutenant would have administered the jurisdiction of Tehuantepec in the minor's name, ensuring that the terms of the contract were honoured. This, however, gravely disturbed the Audiencia. For, in January 1731, the Fiscal de lo Civil, opposing the implication that Royal offices were personal property, declined to put into effect the late Alcalde Mayor's suggestion.[1]

The outright disobedience of the law by the Alcaldes Mayores was denounced by the Bishop of Oaxaca, Santiago y Calderón, on 26 March 1732. The Bishopric, he reported, was reduced to an unhappy state by the violence of the justices, who had connexions with the principal merchants and citizens of substance in Oaxaca city. As a result, the Bishop said, he suffered great calumny against his person. In a further report, pursuing the same theme, he described how he wrote as if with tears of blood, lamenting the desolation of the province by its exploiters. Moreover, the Alcaldes Mayores involved were engaged in controversy with the local clergy over the legality of their operations. At the same time, many clergy were themselves seduced by the profits to be derived from illicit trading. They failed to expound the Christian doctrine, and they neglected the administration of the sacraments. There were no teachers to impart a knowledge of the Castilian language.[2]

The double preoccupation with the state of the Royal revenues and the abuses suffered by the Indians lay behind the comprehensive legislation of 1751 on the issue of the *repartimiento*. For, in response to reports from the Viceroys of New Spain and Peru on the backward state of the Royal revenues, and the disorder and violence caused by the illicit trading, the Crown, under the influence of the Marqués de Ensenada, issued the *Real Decreto* of 28 May, and the *Reales Cédulas* of 15 June and 17 July 1751.[3]

In essence, the problem was that the Crown could not enforce observance of the law. Added to that was the report from the Viceroys that several of the local justices were leaving their posts through lack of adequate salaries. Others were illegally supplementing their meagre wage by negotiating for contracts to issue *repartimientos* to the Indians. To the abuses stemming from such trading, the Viceroys attributed the decadent

1 AGI *Mexico* 635.
2 AGI *Mexico* 877, Bishop–Crown, 26 March and 3 November 1732.
3 AGI *Indiferente general* 1706; AGN *Reales cédulas* (origs.), 71, exp. 147, ff. 540–3 *v*.

state of the Royal income from Indian tributes. They warned that if the abuses were not corrected, the Crown would witness the final ruin of the indigenous population, and the total disintegration of its American dominions.[1]

However, there was a series of further problems, which would have vitiated any attempt at a quick and easy solution to the Indian problem. The Viceroys stated that it was a well-known fact that the Indians were lazy, idle, and degenerate, abhorring all forms of labour. By their nature they were inclined to drunkenness and vice. If they were not forced to work, the fields would be uncultivated, and the mines unexploited. If they were not forced to receive clothing, they would be content to live naked. Out of such repeated problems had risen the *repartimiento*. No one but an Alcalde Mayor was prepared to trade with the Indians, in view of the long delay and great uncertainty involved in the repayment of loans.[2]

The Viceroys, then, presented the Crown with two contradictory positions. On the one hand, they denounced the desolation produced by the *repartimiento*. On the other hand, they called the Indians idle and degenerate, fit only for forced labour in fields and mines. What the Viceroys wanted was for the Crown to work out a synthesis, which they could then apply. The implication of such a policy was the departure from the Crown's traditional firm prohibition of the *repartimiento*, in favour of tacit recognition of its inevitability. Such a policy, should it be adopted, would resolve the moral quandary of Crown and Church since the sixteenth century over the conflict between the force of the Laws of the Indies and *Reales Cédulas*, on one side, and the economic necessity of the system built up around the commercial activities of the Alcaldes Mayores, Corregidores and their financial backers, on the other side.

Therefore, for the first time, the Crown acknowledged the practicability of the *repartimiento*, which it had been unable to legislate out of existence, but, at the same time, the Crown was determined to impose a code of morality to regulate the conduct of the justices. The legislation of 1751, therefore, ordered the establishment of Juntas in each of the three Viceregal capitals, Santa Fé de Bogotá, Lima, and Mexico City. The Viceroys were to act as presidents. The Juntas were to watch over the levels of prices of commodities issued and collected. On the basis of information on the usual rates of such goods, they were to draw up a tariff of legal prices, which the justices would then be expected to observe. The penalty of violation was to be deprivation of office. In this way, the

---

[1] *Ibid.*   [2] *Ibid.*

Crown hoped to regulate the *repartimiento*, and avoid vexation. Moreover, the tacit consent to issue it would relieve the justices' consciences of the great burden of guilt involved in breaking the law. By recognising the profit incentive derived from the holding of public office, the Crown ensured that there would continue to be candidates ready to offer their services. Moreover, since the justices no longer would have to hide the fact that they were issuing *repartimientos*, there would no longer be any excuse to hide their non-payment of *alcabala* on sales involved.[1]

In response to this series of *Reales Cédulas*, the Viceroy of New Spain, Conde de Revillagigedo the Elder, reported on 10 April 1752 that as a result of the decision of the Mexico Junta, he was proposing to contact all the 153 justices of the Realm. They would be required to send the Superior Government lists of commodities and prices involved in the *repartimiento* in their locality.[2]

The information began to reach Mexico City after the late spring of 1752. It gave a detailed survey of economic conditions in the Alcaldías Mayores of Oaxaca. For example, the Alcaldía Mayor of Ixtepeji subsisted from the cochineal trade. The Alcalde Mayor supplied the Indians with the cash necessary for the conduct of the trade, and they repaid him in the finished dye at the rate of 12 reales per pound. This rate was low considering the market price for cochineal in the city of Oaxaca at 18 reales per pound. In past years, about 4,000 pesos had been distributed among the Indians for the production of the dye. The present justice explained that he depended on his own resources for this *repartimiento*, and had never acquired an outside backer (*aviador*). He added, however, that he knew of several other Alcaldes Mayores who had, in fact, taken *aviadores*, with whom they would divide the profits of their trade.[3]

There were three chief activities in the Alcaldía Mayor of Teutila: cotton cultivation, the weaving of ordinary textiles, and vanilla cultivation. In this way, the jurisdiction found itself incorporated into the main spheres of economic life in the Viceroyalty. In their *repartimientos*, the Alcaldes Mayores would make prior contracts with *aviadores*, with whom they would subsequently share 20 per cent of the profits of their trade. Included in the goods issued to the Indians would be both Spanish Peninsular and Viceregal commodities. Included in the latter were cloths of Querétaro, Cholula, and Texcoco. In exchange for such commodities,

---

[1] *Ibid.* See also G. Lohmann Villena, *El corregidor*, 427, n. 15.
[2] AGN *Reales cédulas* (origs.), 72, exp. 155, ff. 426–7.
[3] AGN *Subdelegados* 34, Superior gobierno 1752, Informes de curas y alcaldes mayores sobre la permisión de repartimiento en los partidos del reyno.

the Alcaldes Mayores would take from Teutila its cotton, vanilla, and cotton textiles. About 30,000 to 40,000 arrobas of cotton would be collected annually at the rate of 6 reales per arroba. From the lowland towns, like Chinantla and Tuxtepec, the cotton would be taken by river, until it would be collected by the muleteers of Orizaba for eventual transportation to the *obrajes* of Puebla and Mexico, where it would generally sell for 14 reales, and above.[1]

Chinantla and some other towns of Teutila spun cotton, and manufactured *huipiles* (a popular sleeveless blouse worn by Indian women), petticoats, and counterpanes. Between 12,000 and 15,000 of the ordinary quality *huipiles* would be taken by the Alcalde Mayor at the rate of 4 reales each, and sold elsewhere in the jurisdiction at 6 reales, or in Oaxaca city, Puebla, or Mexico at the current rate of demand.[2]

The total capital (*avío*) required for the various *repartimientos* of Teutila would come to between 40,000 and 50,000 pesos annually. The greater part of the ingoing products would be Castilian or Viceregal, including mules. Silver reales would also be issued, generally borrowed from chantries, pious foundations, or other such religious sources, at the interest rate of 5 per cent per annum. Once initially financed, the area could maintain itself, generating sufficient profits for reinvestment, except in years of scarcity.[3]

Despite the legislation of 1751, and the detailed examination of 1752, Revillagigedo the Elder still felt it necessary to write in his *Instrucción reservada* to his successor, in 1754, that the Indians were an easy prey to the oppressions of the Alcaldes Mayores, the parish clergy, and the hacienda owners. Most Alcaldes Mayores were poor, except the few and the fortunate who served in the province of Oaxaca, where the cochineal dye was gathered. These usually would not lack an *aviador*. Wherever a justice could not supplement his income by trading in *repartimientos*, he

---

[1] *Ibid.* The cotton would be cropped in April and May, before the rainy season hit the *pueblos bajos*. The proper development of the trade was greatly hindered by the enormous difficulty of transportation, and the consequent high cost of freight charges. Added to this was the fact that the cotton would not be unseeded at the place of production, but at that of its destination. This naturally kept prices high. As far as its collection by the Orizaba muleteers, the freight charge on 1 *carga* of cotton would be $2\frac{1}{2}$ reales. From there to Mexico City, a further 11 pesos per carga would be added. Given the price of 1 carga at $10\frac{1}{2}$ pesos, the total freight and extra costs would have increased this initial price to as much as 22 pesos 3 reales. In Mexico City, an *alcabala* of 8 per cent, a sum of 2 pesos, and an '*encomienda de venta*' of 4 per cent, at 1 peso, would be added, bringing the final price to over 25 pesos, giving very often little or no profit on the trade.   [2] *Ibid.*

[3] *Ibid.* For a discussion on the economic role of Church funds, see Asunción Lavrín, 'The Role of the Nunneries in the Economy of New Spain in the Eighteenth Century', *HAHR*, xlvi, no. 4, (Nov. 1966), 371–94.

would lay his hands on the Royal revenues he was entrusted with collecting.[1]

It was becoming obvious that once again the authority of the Crown was being ignored. At the same time, the Viceroy of Peru was reporting that the regulations drawn up there were not being observed. As a result, the Crown issued new orders, commanding that the previous ones should be obeyed. On 18 March 1761, the Crown produced a regulation for Peru, which it declared applicable to New Spain. On this basis, the Junta in Mexico City, set up in 1751, finally came to a decision in 1763, on what should be done. In the presence of the Viceroy, the Marqués de Cruillas, the Junta decided that the *repartimiento* should be allowed to continue, under the terms of the 1751 provisions. Ministers of the Superior Government were to begin its regulation by taking secret evidence concerning the type and quantity of goods issued.[2]

1 AGI *Mexico* 1506, *Gobierno del virrey conde de Revillagigedo* (1745–56), Mexico, 28 November 1754, copy of the elder Revillagigedo's *Instrucción reservada*, ff. 7–8.
2 AGN *Reales cédulas* (origs.), 71, exp. 147, and 72, exp. 155, and AGI *Indiferente general* 1706.

CHAPTER 2

THE STRUGGLE FOR CONTROL OF TRADE

Spain faced considerable foreign competition for the Mexican dye. For, England, France, and Holland possessed a greater capacity of consumption. As a result, the Viceroyalty of New Spain, in many respects, was a producer of bullion and primary products for the European countries with a more advanced industry than Spain. Their power, economic in character, operated behind the shadow of political control exercised by Madrid. In anxious reaction to such a detrimental situation, Spanish Governments since the constitution of the Junta de Comercio in Madrid in 1679 had been preoccupied with the recovery of national control over the Indies trade. Parallel to this commercial policy the Spanish Ministers and writers, especially after the accession of Philip V in 1700, advocated the advancement of Spanish industrial activities, especially textiles.[1]

Until such reforms could be brought to successful fruition, the wealth of the Oaxaca merchants and their seniors in the Consulado of Mexico was secured principally not so much by trading to the Spanish national textile factories, but to those of Spain's main competitors for the export trade to the Indies. Whether through the legitimate trade to Seville or Cádiz, or through the notorious contraband trade, the merchants of New Spain were the recipients of foreign manufactures. The merchants of Seville and Cádiz, for their part, often acted as the intermediary factors in the drain of both bullion and dyes through the Spanish Peninsular entrepôt to northern Europe.[2] In this way, the economy of New Spain must have been much more closely related to the trends of the world economy than has previously been supposed.

In England, for example, the import of dyestuffs assumed greater importance in the second half of the seventeenth century. For, more cloth tended to be dyed at home, rather than in the Dutch dyeing and finishing industries. A comparative table of values of all types of dyes from the

---

[1] For the Spanish background, see J. Carrera Pujal, *Historia de la economía española* (Barcelona 1943–7), vol. iii; Richard Herr, *The Eighteenth Century Revolution in Spain* (Princeton 1958); and J. C. La Force, *The Development of the Spanish Textile Industry, 1750–1800* (Berkeley 1966).

[2] See A. Christelow, 'Great Britain and the Trades from Cádiz and Lisbon to Spanish America and Brazil, 1759–1783', *HAHR*, xxvii (1947), 2–29.

world centres of production entering England between 1663 and 1774 has been presented in two articles by R. Davis, a version of which is placed in Table 2.[1]

Table 2. *Value of import of dyes into England, 1663–1774*

	1663–9	1699–1701 (London)	1699–1701 (England)	1722–4	1752–4	1772–4
	£	£	£	£	£	£
Americas	3,000	71,000	85,000	152,000	97,000	167,000
Mediterranean	91,000	90,000	92,000	124,000	149,000	267,000
East India	16,000	8,000	8,000	3,000	1,000	3,000

N.B. The area covered under 'Americas' includes North, Central, and South America, and the West Indies.

The Mediterranean comprised Spain, Portugal, and their islands, Italy, and the Levant.

East India signified the lands bordering on the Indian and Pacific Oceans.

The mid-seventeenth century figures for the import of dyestuffs from East India, principally indigo, considerably exceeded those from the Americas, both indigo and cochineal and the Yucatán and Honduras dyewoods. However, the most significant figure would be that of the Mediterranean region. For, this included the re-export from Seville or, subsequently, Cádiz, of the dyes of the Spanish Indies. This is evident in the figures for 1699–1701. For, of the £90,000–£92,000 worth of dye-stuffs imported into England from that area, the total value of cochineal imports reached £67,000.[2] This re-export from the Andalusian ports represented approximately 75 per cent of England's dye import from the Mediterranean.

A symptom of the Spanish Crown's concern at the activities of foreign powers in the dye trade was the *Real Cédula* of 29 August 1751, sent by the Marqués de Ensenada to the Viceroy of New Spain, Conde de Revilla-gigedo the Elder. It explained that in the Crown's estimation the cochineal dye was one of the most valuable products of the Indies. For, it proceeded to factories throughout the world. Indeed, the major part of the cargo which left the Indies went to foreign ports as its ultimate destination. For that reason, the Crown was anxious to know the total amount of cochineal actually cultivated in the Bishopric of Oaxaca, in order that its exports

---

[1] R. Davis, 'English Foreign Trade, 1660–1700', *Economic History Review*, series II, vol. vii (1954–5), 150–66; and 'English Foreign Trade, 1700–1774', *Economic History Review*, series II, vol. xv (1962–3), 285–99.   [2] Davis, 'Trade, 1660–1700', 166.

should be rechanneled to the Peninsular factories. What there was in surplus could then be re-exported from Spain to the other European manufacturing countries. Naturally, one of the principal objectives of such a measure would be to ensure the correct observation of Royal taxation rights over the products of the trade.

This *Cédula* continued the Bourbon trend of replacing private or corporate supervision of the Royal revenues in favour of Royal bureaucratic appointees. It authorised Royal officials, rather than agents of the Consulado of Cádiz, to supervise the imported cargoes of dyes on arrival in Spain. The Crown specifically stated that its intention was not to impose any tax on the lucrative cochineal trade, but to increase its own revenues through the better organisation and management of it. In the meantime, the Crown regretted any inconvenience caused to the Cádiz merchants by depriving them of their former practice of inspection.[1]

The reality of the Metropolitan Government's fears was amply attested by the role of the English merchants behind the scenes in the Oaxaca trade. Illustrating this, the British chargé d'affaires in Mexico in 1827, H. G. Ward, referring to the middle of the eighteenth century, wrote, 'In the year, 1756, a government registry office was established in Oaxaca —as a result of the complaints of some English merchants who had received cargoes of adulterated cochineal—in which all cochineal produced in the province was ordered to be examined and registered.'[2]

Such a demand on the part of the English merchants, and its influence on the administration in Oaxaca, indicated the importance both parties attached to the pure quality of the export dye. The Royal authorities duly established the official supervisory agency in the city for the inspection of all dye cargoes entering it, and vested this function in the office of Corregidor. The regulations, entitled the 'Ordinance, Method, or Regulation, which are to be observed in order to ensure the closure of the door to the perpetration of frauds in the cochineal', was issued in 1756, reissued in 1760, and once more in 1773.[3] Nevertheless, reports of repeated adulteration of the dye plagued the Superior Government to the extent that the set of instructions was reissued finally in 1817, when the inspection procedure was entrusted to the Intendant of Oaxaca, whose office incorporated the functions of the former Corregidor.[4]

---

[1] AGN *Reales cédulas* (origs.), 71, exp. 161, ff. 578–81.

[2] H. G. Ward, *Mexico in 1827* (2 vols.; London 1828), i, 64.

[3] Barbro Dahlgren de Jordán, *Nocheztli, La grana cochinilla* (Mexico 1963), photostat reproduction of the ordinances, following the appendices.

[4] Archivo del Estado de Oaxaca, uncatalogued and unclassified legajo for 1817. See also

Struggle for control

Direct access to the source of bullion and precious dyes was secured by the British merchants through Parliament's passage of the Free Port Acts, the issue of which coincided with Charles III's commercial reforms in Spain and the Indies. The first of the British Free Port Acts, in 1766, opened certain ports in Jamaica and Dominica to foreign ships. Products in competition with those produced in the British West Indies were, of course, specifically excluded from the provisions of the Act, but the import of indigo from Guatemala, and the cochineal dye from New Spain, was to be encouraged. For their import through the British West Indian islands circumvented the delays and costs of the Cádiz monopoly trade system.[1] These commodities, together with other dye-stuffs, wool, cotton-wool, skins, and cacao, were in fact especially singled out for importance in the Second Free Port Act of 1787.[2] In that year, Thomas Irving, Inspector-General of the Customs in England, reported to the Privy Council that goods to a very considerable amount, suited to the Spanish American market, were annually exported from England to Jamaica, where they were generally shipped on board small armed vessels for transportation to different parts of the Spanish Main. There they would be sold or exchanged in a clandestine manner for Mexican dollars, cochineal, Guatemalan indigo, and other dye-stuffs, dye-woods, mahogany, and hides. He estimated the receipts earned by Britain from this trade with the Spanish colonies to be no less than one million dollars. This sum furnished not only the British islands in the West Indies and the British colonies on the mainland with a medium of circulation, but also afforded a considerable object of remittance in specie to England, besides the quantity of cocoa, cotton, wool, cochineal, indigo, other dye-stuffs, and hides secured.[3]

Christelow explains that one of the problems for European powers such as Great Britain was the fact that the Spanish Empire produced certain raw materials which were of vital importance for their economic activities. 'Spanish dollars, for example, were the one key which effectively opened the Asiatic market, for when England in the early years of the seventeenth century began to develop her sea trade with India, American silver was the one thing which made success a possibility. Spanish-

BSMGE, MSS J. M. Murguía y Galardi, *Estadística del estado de Oaxaca* (1826–8), Miahuatlán, f. 28 *et seq.*

[1] F. Armytage, *The Free Port System in the British West Indies. A Study in Commercial Policy. 1766–1822.* (London 1953), 41–2. [2] *Ibid.* 59–60.

[3] British Museum (BM), Add. MSS 38, 345, ff. 208–13 *v.* (Liverpool Papers), Thomas Irving to the Right Honourable the Lords of H.M.'s most Honourable Privy Council for considering the matters of Trade and Plantations.

American dyewoods were equally necessary for reducing production costs in the expanding English textile trades. ...'[1]

The balance of the Free Port trade generally favoured the British rather than the Spaniards. For the outward cargo from the West Indies to Spanish America was nearly always greater in value than the inward. The explanation for this was that the main purpose of the development of the West Indies' Free Port system by the British Government was the furthering of the interests of British manufacturers, and, in particular, the export of British manufactured goods. In consequence, the adverse balance of trade suffered by the Spanish territories concerned had to be covered by the export of bullion. Thomas Irving estimated that in 1792 the total value of British manufactured goods exported from the British West Indies in both British and foreign ships totalled between £400,000 and £500,000.[2]

As a result of the commercial penetration of the Spanish Indies by the foreigners, Spain throughout the course of the eighteenth century was attempting to restrain the flow of bullion out of her empire both by developing the Spanish metropolitan textile industry and by encouraging the export to Spain of the precious dyes and tropical products of America. The American market became one of the central objectives of the Royal woollen textile factories established firstly at Guadalajara in 1719, and subsequently at San Fernando and Brihuega. For, the new factories, financed by the State in an attempt to create industrialisation in Castile, suffered from perennial lack of consumer demand for their products. For example, between February 1719 and 1726, the factory produced over 160,000 *varas* of woollens, but sold only 10,000 *varas*. Moreover, expenditure considerably outpaced revenue. In 1735, the Guadalajara factory suffered a deficit of over 490,000 reales *de vellón*.[3] Nevertheless, it was upon the success of such a factory that the Ministry in Spain set its hopes for the ousting of the English woollen manufacturers and other northern Europeans from their predominant position in the Spanish Indies' market.[4]

---

[1] A. Christelow, 'Contraband Trade between Jamaica and the Spanish Main, and the Free Port Act of 1766', *HAHR*, xxii (1942), 309–43.

[2] Armytage, *The Free Port System*, 70, 72, 73, 92.

[3] La Force, *Development of the Spanish Textile Industry*, 19–22, 38–44. The factory expanded from 51 looms in 1731, to 142 in 1754, and 670 in 1784. The maximum size of the factory was attained between 1784 and 1791, when by the latter date, the entire labour force consisted of 24,000.

[4] Richard Herr, *The Eighteenth Century Revolution in Spain* (Princeton 1958), 123, 'the greatest efforts were devoted to the cloth manufacture at Guadalajara, for it was hoped that through its success would end the shameful dependence on England for cloths woven

However, unable to bear the cost of continual losses, the Crown handed over the administration of the Guadalajara factory to the *Cinco gremios mayores de Madrid*, in 1757. These five guilds, constituted as a sole commercial unit back in 1686, occupied the chief economic role in Castile, and enjoyed a privileged position at court through their activities as a source of credit. The guilds continued to run the factory until 1767.[1] During the time of their administration, and after, they gradually established a secure trading position within the Indies market. By 1778, the *Cinco gremios* had three commercial agents in the Mexican merchant town of Jalapa, and, under the *Real Orden* of 9 June 1784, they set up a trading factory in Mexico City.[2]

Intimately connected with the *Cinco gremios* was the Casa de Uztáriz, an eminent joint-stock trading company, described by Arcila Farías as the strongest that existed in Spain, at least as regards Spanish trade to the Indies.[3] Along with the *Cinco gremios* of Madrid, the Casa de Uztáriz, at the instance of the Ministry of Finance, formed what amounted to a society for the expulsion of the foreigner from the trade of the Spanish Indies, and for the dominance there of the products and interests of the Spanish metropolis.[4]

In March 1762, the Casa de Uztáriz took over the management of the Royal silk textile factory at Talavera. In return for this service, the Crown conceded the House the right to despatch three registered ships to the Indies, one to New Spain and one to Peru, and the other to Havana. The objective was, of course, to prevent the serious drain of Mexican and Peruvian bullion across the Pacific to purchase Chinese silk textiles proceeding through Canton on the Manila Galleon. In order to perfect the finishing processes of the Spanish silk textile, the Crown conceded the House, under the *Reales Cédulas* of 18 April 1765 and 23 December 1766, the right to import into Spain on return voyages from the Indies, cochineal to the value of the freight charges, a sum of 108,000 pesos. By 1770, the House had eight ships profitably employed in the Indies trade. As one of the partners, the Conde de Reparaz, Juan Bautista de Uztáriz, ex-

from Spanish wool'. See also La Force, *Development of the Spanish Textile Industry*, 43: 'English merchants dominated the Spanish American woollen textile market with their cheaper, lighter, and more colourful product, in contrast to the sombre, heavy, often defective Castilian garment.'

1 J. Carrera Pujal, *Historia de la economía española* (5 vols.; Barcelona, 1943–7), iii, 608.

2 AGN *General de parte* 60 (1778); E. Arcila Farías, *El siglo ilustrado en América. Reformas económicas del siglo XVIII en Nueva España* (Caracas 1955), 27–8; M. Capella and A. Matilla Tascón, *Los cinco gremios mayores de Madrid. Estudio crítico-histórico* (Madrid, 1957), 288–9, where the date of the Mexico City factory is given as April 1784.

3 Arcila Farías, *El siglo ilustrado*, 27–8, 29–31.   4 *Ibid*

plained, the use of the cochineal dye helped to keep the silk industry of Talavera in operation. The House's main concern was that its surplus silks should be shipped to the Indies, sometimes supplemented with a cargo of mercury for the New Spain silver mines, in order to return with quantities of bullion, cochineal from Oaxaca, and indigo from Guatemala.[1]

At this time, during the period 1769–78, the cochineal of Oaxaca was attaining the peak of its production. The highest level of production recorded in the Registry in the city of Oaxaca was reached in 1774 at 1,558,125 pounds. The peak price level of this phase of expansion was reached in 1771, at 32 reales per pound, resulting in a total value for that year's crop of 1,050,187½ pounds at 4,200,750 pesos.[2] This figure was really substantial, and it represented the peak value in a period of high yields. Some indication of the value of the cochineal in the 1770s can be seen by comparing the figures with the total value of silver and gold coined in the Casa de Moneda of Mexico City. In 1771, a total of 13,353,432 pesos were coined, and in 1773, a total of 20,237,325 pesos.[3]

As regards the high prices recorded in the later 1760s and earlier 1770s, we can compare these with some remarks on prices made by two Oaxacan parish priests, both writing to the Audiencia of Mexico in 1776. The first, Fray Vicente Magán, parish priest of Lachixio, reported that in 1722, when his father and others engaged in the cochineal trade returned from business in Spain, the price in Oaxaca was as high as 32 reales per pound. By 1740, however, the price had fallen to 16 reales. In 1762, during the Seven Years' War, the British captured the key Spanish port of Havana on the Fleets' route to Spain. The price of cochineal fell, in consequence, to only 12 reales per pound at the most. When peace returned in 1763, the price again moved upwards, to 19 reales at first, and by 1771, up to 32 reales. Even though production remained high, the demand for the dye was sufficiently great on the world market to prevent a substantial decline of prices. These maintained themselves at high levels, such as 30, 28, and 26 reales, though showing a gradual tendency downwards. The decline

---

[1] La Force, *Development of the Spanish Textile Industry*, 44. The *Cinco gremios* took over Talavera's management in 1785; AGI *Indiferente general* 2485 (Papers concerning Uztáriz Company).

[2] Dahlgren de Jordán, *Nocheztli*, app. II, no page number; BSMGE, Murguía, *Estadística*, tome VIII, Miahuatlán, f. 18.

[3] M. Lerdo de Tejada, *Comercio exterior de México* (Mexico 1853), número 54, Noticia de las cantidades de oro y plata extraídas de México, desde la conquista hasta fin de 1852: acuñaciones hechas en la casa de moneda de la ciudad de México. See also pp. 169–70 below.

accelerated, however, until by 1776 it had dropped from 20 to 18 and 16 reales.[1]

The basic trend of these prices is corroborated by the report of the parish priest of Ecatepec, in the Chontal region of the Alcaldía Mayor of Nejapa, an important cochineal-producing area. He stated he had been familar with the dye for thirty-five years. The price had fallen in 1740 to 12 reales in Chontales, and the crop had been regarded with total disdain. The reason was, he considered, the outbreak of war in Europe and the Atlantic in that year, which cut off communications between Spain and the Indies. A gradual recovery of prices was experienced in 1741 and 1742, up to 14 and 16 reales, respectively. The price then rose to 18 reales, at which it remained until the renewal of war in 1756. After the return of peace in 1763, a new height was reached at 24 and 28 reales. This rise continued, according to the priest, until 1776, when a notable decline set in, with the present price at a low level of 14 reales per pound. This drop, he speculated, could be due to the fall of cochineal prices in Spain.[2]

The cochineal trade was characterised by a series of periodic, but reasonably regular and not too drastic fluctuations. This was the case, according to the Oaxaca Registry figures, between 1758 and 1782. After that date, a substantial decline set in, which was never to be reversed.

The years 1758 and 1759, represented one group of low levels, rising to a climax in 1760. A further downward cycle began in 1761, dropping to its nadir in 1763, but rising up again to a new peak in 1765. The next downward cycle opened in 1766, with its base at 621,000 pounds in 1768, but rising again to a sustained and increasing climax between 1769 and 1771. A new cyclical drop began in 1772, with its base in 1773, and a new climax in 1774 with the total crop registered valued at 3,408,398 pesos. The next cycle opened in 1775, dropping to its base, exactly as the two priests had written, in 1776. However, in that year, the base level reached was the highest figure of all the previous bases recorded. In fact, the base levels throughout the period 1758 to 1778 tended to settle at increasingly higher figures, and the cycles moved at ever contracting paces. This meant that, given the overall characteristic of cyclical fluctuation, the cochineal trade was both fluctuating at a diminishing pace, and at an evident upward rate, evidence of the stabilization of the trade. These figures are presented in Appendix 1.[3]

Such cyclical trends were reflected in the amounts of dye exported on the fleets departing from Veracruz for Cádiz during the same period.

---

[1] Dahlgren de Jordán, *Nocheztli*, 25, 74.
[2] *Ibid.*   [3] See p. 30, note 2 below.

On the 1760 fleets, 24,089½ arrobas of prime quality cochineal (*grana fina*) was sent, at a value of 1,541,728 pesos. Two years later, the 1762 fleet took 29,569 arrobas 15½ pounds. The 1765 fleet carried 20,827 arrobas 14¾ pounds, representing the downward effects of the low phase of the cycle of 1761–5. The subsequent 1769 fleet, catching the effects of the downward phase of the 1766–8 cycle, took even less, 19,038 arrobas. In 1772, the fleet reaped the benefits of the sustained climax of 1769–71, exporting a maximum total of 32,261 arrobas 20 pounds at the peak price of 85 pesos per arroba, giving a cargo valued at 2,997,253 pesos. The last fleet under the old trading system, that of 1776, however, coincided with the base of the cochineal production cycle, and carried only 1,194 zurrones or 4,776 arrobas, despite the fact that the 1776 base was the highest of the cyclical production bases recorded in the period. Unless the growers found some other substantial outlet for their product, they must have sustained considerable losses in that year. These figures are presented in Appendix 3.[1]

The profits of the dye trade encouraged the Visitor-General of New Spain, José de Gálvez, to attempt a reform of the method of payment of the *alcabala* at the port of Veracruz. Gálvez considered Oaxaca to be the richest province in New Spain, due to the abundance there of the precious cochineal dye.[2] Anxious that the Crown should participate in the benefits of the trade through full assertion of Royal rights of taxation, Gálvez, under the *Bando* (Viceregal administrative order) of 16 March 1767, insisted that the *alcabala* should be paid on entry into Veracruz for all goods. The rate was to be reduced from 6 to 4 per cent.[3]

This apparent reduction, however, did not operate in practice. For traditionally all inland-bound goods had been falsely declared as destined for the domestic consumption of the town of Veracruz. In such a way, they had not, therefore, been subject to the payment of any *alcabala*. In practice, then, the supposed 2 per cent reduction meant an increase of 4 per cent on *alcabalas*.[4] The *Bando* of March 1767 ordered the Veracruz

---

1 Lerdo de Tejada, *Comercio exterior*, números 3, 4, 5, 7, 8, 11; AGI *Mexico* 1369, *Duplicados del virrey*, no. 673, Marqués de Croix–Julián de Arriaga, 2 May 1770, Carga que conducen a los reynos de Castilla los navíos capitana y almiranta de flota del mando del jefe de esquadra, marqués de Casa Tilly, y dos mercantes que quedaron de ella en este puerto de San Juan de Ulúa.
2 AGI *Indiferente general* 1713, and AGI *Mexico* 1973.
3 H. I. Priestley, *José de Gálvez. Visitor-General of New Spain. (1765–1771)* (Berkeley 1916), 190 *et seq.*
4 AGI *Mexico* 1368, *Duplicados del virrey* (1768), no. 194, Marqués de Croix–Julián de Arriaga, 10 April 1768.

merchants to present sworn statements of all the property in their possession at the present time, and up to the end of the month, in order that they could be properly assessed for taxation. As some measure of compromise, the Visitor reduced the rate of taxation from 4 to 3 per cent.[1]

The Veracruz merchants protested to their parent body, the Consulado of Mexico, on 30 March 1767, requesting that guild to put their case before the Viceroy. As a result, the Consulado requested the Viceroy to disavow Gálvez' principle that the *alcabala* should be paid on entry to Veracruz. They advocated that the nature of the tax was a sales-tax, and that, therefore, a distinction should be made between a tax on imports and a tax on sales. No tax should be paid just because of the mere fact of entry into Veracruz. Otherwise they would have to pay two taxes, one on entry and one on sales. Especially angered were the merchants dealing in cochineal. They saw a potential rise in the price of their product, which might deter the buyer. Domingo Ignacio de Lardizábal, in the name of the merchants of the Spanish trade, requested that cochineal be exempt from the reformed tax.[2]

An examination of the cases of protest shows the connexions of some of the cochineal merchants. One of the vigorous opponents of the Gálvez measure was Antonio Ibáñez de Corvera, an influential Oaxaca merchant, whose family were to occupy a predominant role throughout the later eighteenth century and early nineteenty century. The moves to establish the new form of taxation had been initiated just as he was acting under the terms of his commision to send 46 zurrones of cochineal to the merchant house of Gaspar Saenz Rico, Sons & Co. of Veracruz, for shipment to Spain, at the account of Ambrosio de Meave, one of the Veracruz merchants.[3] The cochineal was to be deposited in Veracruz with the wealthy merchant and Alcalde Ordinario of the Ayuntamiento, Bernardo Rodríguez del Toro.[4] A further 12 zurrones to the account of the Puebla merchant, Candido González Maldonado, were received by the same House of Gaspar Saenz Rico in September 1767. Ibáñez de Corvera also acted as commercial agent for two Mexico City merchants,

---

[1] *Ibid.*

[2] *Ibid.* The dispute was resolved against the interests of the merchants, whose position had, incidentally, been supported by the Minister of the Indies himself, Landázuri. The two Fiscales of the Council of Castile, Campomanes and the future Floridablanca, assured the victory of the Gálvez position. It is significant of the Bourbons' departure from the old Habsburg view that the Realms of the Indies were separate kingdoms in their own right, that the decision to support the Gálvez view should have come through the influence of the Council of Castile, rather than through the Council of the Indies. See Priestley, *Gálvez*, 190 *et seq.*

[3] AGI *Mexico* 1369. For Antonio Ibáñez de Corvera, see Glossary of Personnel.

[4] *Ibid.* Rodríguez del Toro was chosen 'por su notorio abono'; see also p. 34, note 3, below.

Juan de Soto Sánchez, for whom he purchased 14 zurrones, and Juan de Castañiza, with 25 zurrones. The former cargo was consigned for shipment to Seville on the warship, *Castilla*, for the Sevillano merchant, Juan Justo de Vera. The latter was to proceed to Cádiz, where the Gaditano merchant, Matheo Fernández Alejo, would receive it.[1]

A commercial agent in Tehuacan, Alberto Cantoya, dispatched 7 zurrones at the request of the Consul of the Consulado of Mexico, Eliseo de Vergara, charged to the account of two Oaxaca merchants, Mariano de Mimiaga and Juan López de Carvajal, and a further 12 zurrones for Domingo López de Carvajal, for shipment to Spain.[2]

Most of the above quantities of cochineal were to become part of the cargo of the *Aquilés*, a ship owned by the Casa de Uztáriz. This ship, which left in 1768, also carried cargoes of cochineal sent by such eminent Veracruz merchants as Francisco Gil, and Juan de Atenas, and of the influential *aviador* of Alcaldes Mayores, Pedro Alonso de Alles.[3]

Spain attached such importance to the cochineal from Oaxaca that Gálvez' associate in Cádiz, the *síndico* (attorney) of the Ayuntamiento, the Conde de Villamar, in 1778, recommended in a confidential letter to his mentor, that the Crown should set up a cochineal monopoly, in the manner of the tobacco monopoly. Under such a monopoly, the Royal financial officials in the Indies would purchase all the cochineal at a fixed price according to quality. A corresponding set price would be fixed in Spain for sale there. The object was to reduce the fluctuations of price on the European market, and guarantee a regular profit to the grower in New Spain.

The Conde explained that the Viceroyalty of New Spain produced about 400,000 arrobas annually, but could produce more if the cultivation of the *nopaleras* were pursued with greater determination. Moreover, the trade was also harmed by the practice in European textile industries of adulterating the dye in order to economise on quantity during times of high prices and shortage. The problem, of course, was that the dye did not enjoy sufficient channels of release on to the world market, confined as it was, in the legitimate trade, to the Cádiz monopoly trade system. In response to Gálvez' inquiries to clarify his points, the Conde took up this problem, and advocated a solution. He believed that Spain's

---

1 *Ibid.*
2 *Ibid.* Mimiaga, see Glossary of Personnel.
3 *Ibid.* Juan de Atenas and Bernardo Rodríguez del Toro were associates in covering the *fianzas* of the Alcalde Mayor of Zimatlán–Chichicapa, from July 1775 until November 1782: see Archivo Histórico de Hacienda (AHH) (AGN) legajo 277, exp. 22. For Alles, see Glossary of Personnel.

trade with the Indies would be stimulated by the extension of the experimental *comercio libre* to the Viceroyalty of New Spain.[1]

Villamar also pointed out to Gálvez, who undoubtedly was able to confirm the fact from his own personal experience as Visitor-General, that much of the Mexican cochineal trade was conducted with great detriment to the indigenous population of Oaxaca. For the Royal justices were accustomed to accumulate great profits. Given the connexions involved in the dye trade between the justices and the Mexico City merchants operating in context of the Cádiz monopoly trade system, Villamar warned that there was bound to be considerable opposition to his proposed reforms by the wealthy groups concerned.[2]

An examination of the details of some of the negotiations of the Spanish mercantile houses in the dye trade shows the connexion between them and the local Alcaldes Mayores.

In January 1779, the ship *Nuestra Señora del Rosario*, property of the *Cinco gremios mayores de Madrid*, requested Viceregal permission to exchange its cargo of mercury and wine from Cádiz for 500,000 pesos in silver and 250 zurrones of cochineal, purchased as a result of sales on the past two fleets.[3] In the following month, the *Concepción*, a ship of the Casa de Uztáriz, received permission to return to Spain with a cargo of cochineal, in company with the frigate *Nuestra Señora de la Victoria*, which was about to depart for Cádiz with a cargo of 117 zurrones of cochineal, pertaining to the Alcalde Mayor of Villa Alta.[4] The Alcalde Mayor of Miahuatlán, Fausto de Corres, in October 1778, requested permission for the embarcation of 114 zurrones of cochineal to Cádiz. Viceroy Mayorga granted the petition in view of its urgency. For already the cochineal had been held up in Veracruz, because of the outbreak of war between Spain and England. At that time there was a shortage of maize in Miahuatlán. The Alcalde Mayor could not purchase relief supplies until he had received the proceeds from the sale of his cochineal.[5] Corres traded in both 1777 and 1778 with the Veracruz merchant house, the Casa de Cosío.[6]

The Minister of the Royal Treasury at Veracruz, Pedro Antonio de Cosío, a Gálvez appointee, reported that approximately 1,000 zurrones of cochineal left the port annually. The crop was so highly valued that, in

---

1 AGI *Indiferente general* 2409, *Cartas reservadas del conde de Villamar sobre el comercio libre a Indias*, Villamar–Galvez, Cádiz, 12 May 1778 (res.). 2 *Ibid.*
3 AGN *Industria* 9, exp. 8, f. 59. 4 AGN *Industria* 9, exp. 7, f. 55.
5 AGN *Industria* 9, exp. 9, f. 75. For Corres, see Glossary.
6 AGI *Mexico* 2374, *Expedientes de real Hacienda (1807–10)*, primer cuaderno, 2 January 1784, no. 437; and AGI *Mexico* 1400, *Duplicados del Virrey* (1782).

accordance with the Royal *Proyecto* on trade of 1720, warships were either to transport it or to escort it, in the same way as gold or silver. In the present year, 1780, he said, the Customs House in Veracruz had registered 3,632 zurrones of cochineal, an extremely high figure. The bulk had sailed on Ulloa's fleet in 1776, and various merchant ships afterwards. Since, however, some remained, in view of the lack of sufficient warships available to transport it, the minister secured a Crown order for the despatch of 250 zurrones for the *Cinco gremios mayores de Madrid* in merchant ships.[1]

The Veracruz Casa de Cosío, exporters of cochineal, Guatemalan indigo, and Mexican vanilla, requested permission in October 1780 to export the considerable amount of 3,400 zurrones of cochineal, at that time detained in Orizaba, Córdoba, and Tehuacan. A total export, including the quantities in Oaxaca, of between 6,500 and 7,000 zurrones was expected.[2] In the following month, the Consulado of Mexico petitioned the Viceroy to listen to a request from the Deputies of Commerce in Oaxaca for immediate shipment of their cochineal to Cádiz on three warships now in Veracruz, for the Laws of the Indies regarded cochineal as similar in priority to gold and silver.[3]

The Casa de Muñoz, also engaged in the dye trade, was another link in Veracruz between the Oaxaca and Mexico merchants, on the one hand, and their Cádiz patrons, on the other. Franciso Antonio de la Mora, Oaxaca cochineal merchant, for example, sent his patron's 29 zurrones of cochineal to Veracruz for deposit in the warehouses of the Casa de Muñoz, before shipment to Cádiz on a ship, the *S. Juan Nepomuceno*, property of the Cádiz merchant, Francisco Guerra de la Vega. The cargo of cochineal was to be insured for as much as 6,000 pesos. Its destination was the Cádiz market, where cochineal prices ranged from 60 to 70 pesos per arroba for pure dye (*grana fina*). This ship sailed under the Superior Order of 20 August 1792.[4]

The profits of the Oaxaca trades offered the prospect of wealth to holders of public office there. There was considerable demand for appointment to the most lucrative Alcaldías Mayores. Jicayan, on the Pacific Coast and Villa Alta, in the northern sierra, were the two most desired. When, for example, the Marqués de Guardiola wished to restore the family finances after his father's accumulation of debt, he petitioned Minister

---

[1] AGN *Industria* 9, exp. 3, f. 31, and exp. 4.
[2] AGN *Industria* 9, exp. 12, f. 103, and exp. 15, f. 123.
[3] AGN *Industria* 9, exp. 16, f. 132.   [4] AGN *Industria* 9, exp. 22, f. 185.

of the Indies, José de Gálvez, in June 1777, for either one of the Alcaldías Mayores of Jicayan, Villa Alta, or Teotitlán del Camino.[1]

Shortly afterwards, in July 1777, the incumbent Alcalde Mayor of Teotitlán del Camino, apparently dissatisfied with the poor yield of the province during his term of office, requested Gálvez for a more lucrative post. He had in mind one of the Alcaldías Mayores of Jicayan, Villa Alta, Nejapa, or Miahuatlán. Since he made his request, however, he heard of the projects for the establishment of the Intendancies in New Spain. Therefore, he requested the post of Intendant-Corregidor of Oaxaca, but added that, should such an appointment be impossible, he would be satisfied with an office in Mexico City, such as that of Accountant-General of the Royal Tributes.[2]

The practice of regarding public offices as if they were private property assumed great importance in such jurisdictions as Jicayan and Villa Alta on account of their products: cotton, mantles, cochineal, and others. Generally, outside financial backers entered the field by furnishing the Alcalde Mayor with capital (*avío*) and securing the appointment of one of their agents as the administrator's lieutenant.

A very considerable amount of cochineal in 1778 from Jicayan reached the Oaxaca merchants, Alonso Magro,[3] Lorenzo Murguía,[4] and Feliciano Larrazábal, from the Alcalde Mayor they had financed.[5] The following Alcalde Mayor, Joseph González de la Mesa, received his *avío*, or *habilitación*, from the widely connected and active Mexico City merchant, Pedro Alonso de Alles, after 1782. This *aviador's* chief interests were cochineal for delivery to the Veracruz Casa de Cosío, and cotton for delivery to the Puebla *obrajero*, Joseph Bringas, for employment in the Puebla cotton textile industry. Alles and the Alcalde Mayor agreed to a *compro-*

1 AGI *Mexico* 1861, *Expedientes é instancias de partes, 1775–1776*. The Marqués de Santa Fé de Guardiola, Joseph de Cervantes y Padilla, was a creole. There had been a tradition of Royal service in the family since the reign of Philip II, and the family had acquired an entailed estate (*mayorazgo*) in Granada and Motril. The father of the first Marqués had risen to the rank of Oidor of the Chancery of Granada in 1657–9. The first Marqués had gone to Santo Domingo as Oidor of the Audiencia there, in 1669, and had risen to the rank of President, Governor, and Captain-General of the island. In 1680, he was promoted to the Governorship and Captaincy-General of Cumaná. The present Marqués' grandfather, a native of Santo Domingo, had married a native of Mexico City. His father had become creole Corregidor of Mexico City, between 1729 and 1734, and his mother belonged to one of the eminent Mexican creole families. He himself in 1764 became an infantry captain in the Second Battalion of Grenadiers of Mexico City, and in 1773, became Alcalde Ordinario de Primer Voto on the Cabildo of Mexico City.   2 *Ibid.*
3 See Glossary of Personnel.   4 See Glossary of Personnel.
5 AGI *Mexico* 1868, *Expedientes é instancias de partes, 1782*, Fiscal Merino–Galvez, 10 March 1779.

37

miso, or *convenio*, under the terms of which the *aviador* was to secure a monopoly of supplies of the two products in Jicayan. The management of the issue of cash in the *repartimiento* to the Indians and *mulatos* of the area would be organised by an agent of Alles, acting as the administrator's lieutenant, Salvador Dolz, who had himself been Alcalde Mayor of Nochistlán-Peñoles between 1774 and 1777.[1]

Another prominent Mexico City merchant, Manuel Ramón de Goya, dealt in the cotton mantles produced in Villa Alta. In the 1770s, in order better to secure control of the trade, he became what was described as the *compañero aviador* of the Alcalde Mayor of Villa Alta.[2] Goya was also interested in the cochineal dye, and from his position in the Consulado of Mexico, he became the *aviador* of the Alcalde Mayor of Zimatlán-Chichicapa, in the Valley of Oaxaca. The agreement between Goya and the administrator, Ildefonso Sánchez Solache, was called a *compañía* for the issue of cash to the Indian producers. In this *repartimiento*, the total sum of 60,000–70,000 pesos in cash was to provide for the complete *habilitación* of the area. Apparently this was to be only a first instalment. For, if further necessity should arise, the administrator would receive an added 20,000–25,000 pesos. Principally, such sums were for investment in the cochineal dye. After the *repartidores* received the final product, the contract specified that the final destination was Veracruz, where the dye would be sold to merchants in the Cádiz trade. Out of the sums issued, the Alcalde Mayor would be able to supplement his living with a salary of 1,500 pesos, out of which he was also expected to pay his lieutenant. In return, Goya undertook to pay into the Royal Treasury in Mexico City the sum due to the Crown from the Indian tribute revenue the three times a year when it was due.[3]

In the same way, acting as both *fiador* and *aviador* of the Alcalde Mayor of Ixtepeji was the Mexico City merchant and warehouse-owner, Joaquín de Colla. The agreement between Colla and the Alcalde Mayor made the same reference to a *compañía*.[4] The trade in cotton, through a *repartimiento* to the Indians, was the object of another such company formed between the Alcalde Mayor of Huajuapan, and his *aviador* in 1785.[5] In the adjacent jurisdiction of Teposcolula, the Alcalde Mayor, Francisco Rojas, received as *aviador* his brother-in-law, the Conde de Sierragorda,

---

[1] AGI *Mexico* 1400, *Duplicados del virrey, 1782*, and AGI *Mexico* 2374, *Expedientes de Real Hacienda, 1807–1810*, Cuaderno Tercero.
[2] *Ibid.*, and AGI *Mexico* 2374, Cuaderno Cuarto. For Goya, see Glossary.
[3] Biblioteca Nacional, Mexico City, MSS 58, ff. 147–9.
[4] AGN *General de parte* 60 (1778), and AHH (AGN), leg. 276, exp. 28.
[5] AGN *General de parte* 69 (1785–6), ff. 284 v–286.

who had secured the first 1,000 pesos of the total *avío* from none other than Pedro Alonso de Alles, the *aviador* of Jicayan.[1]

In this way were conducted the cochineal and cotton and cotton-mantle trades of Oaxaca. At the same time, Royal revenues from the Indian tribute were guaranteed. They would, in fact, often be paid by a private individual, usually a merchant of the politically powerful Consulado of Mexico. This private person covered the Royal revenues due for collection by the administrator he patronised, in return for the issue of *repartimiento* by the Alcalde Mayor. The *aviador* played no formal part in the administration of the jurisdiction concerned. His authority was exercised by the lieutenant, who often enjoyed more power than his chief, the Alcalde Mayor. None of these private individuals, either the Mexico City or the Oaxaca merchants, enjoyed any official function within the Royal bureaucracy in the localities concerned. Their activities, nevertheless, converted impartial bureaucratic office into the property of private persons. Their contracting with the Alcalde Mayor to secure a trade monopoly was often highly prejudicial to the Indians. In any case, the legality of such operations was highly suspect.

Naturally the news of the impending establishment of Intendancies in New Spain frightened several investors into withdrawing their capital—at least momentarily. In the case of Tehuantepec, the Alcalde Mayor, Tomás de Mollinedo, on taking possession of his post in March 1783, celebrated a contract with Colonel Manuel Fernández Vallejo, who had been the previous Alcalde Mayor, for the *habilitación* of the region. The *aviador*, however, died in September of the same year. The instalments were, nevertheless, continued by his widow and her second husband, Andrés Fernández de Castañeda, who was Administrator of the *Alcabalas* in Tehuantepec. These sums stopped in August 1786. The *aviadores* explained that no further payments would follow, because of the prohibition of *repartimientos* contained in Gálvez's Plan for the Intendancies in New Spain.[2]

The same threat preoccupied Juan Baptista de Echarri,[3] *aviador* of the Alcalde Mayor of Teotitlán del Camino, Manuel Josef López.[4] The news of the forthcoming establishment of an Intendancy in Oaxaca under the Gálvez plan motivated the withdrawal of investments from the *repartimiento* in that sierra jurisdiction. Echarri went in person to Teotitlán, and at the same time requested the Superior Government in Mexico City to

---

[1] AGN *Vínculos* 56.   [2] AGN *General de parte* 67, ff. 129–30.
[3] See Glossary of Personnel.
[4] See Glossary of Personnel.

send an order to the Alcalde Mayor of Teposcolula to help in the recall of his investments. This despatch was sent on 23 June 1787.[1]

The insolvency of the Spanish régime in the Indies lead to its inability to enforce the plenitude of power claimed by the Absolute Monarchy. The key, of course, was the inadequate payment of its local bureaucracy. This ensured that administrators would either indulge in peculation and oppression, or would fall into the financial power of private parties, whose commercial agents they would become.

José de Gálvez considered Oaxaca one of New Spain's richest provinces. For that reason he was determined to eliminate both the malversation of Royal revenues and the contracting for trade with the Indians. A firm believer in the Absolutist political theory of the Spanish Bourbons, he was anxious to employ their power effectively for the reform of the abuses. He was incensed at the capture of control of Royal offices by private interests. At the same time, by the prohibition of *repartimientos*, he hoped to release local trade from the Mexico and Oaxaca merchants' agreements with the Alcaldes Mayores, and, thereby, enable the Indians to benefit from competitive commercial exchange, increase production, and stimulate consumption. All these factors would contribute to the increase of the Royal revenues. Gálvez's long-term aspiration, then, was to replace the Spanish Peninsular merchants' political dominance of the province of Oaxaca with the effective authority of an efficient, honest, sufficiently salaried Royal bureaucracy that had a vested interest in securing the continuation of the reform. Their enforcement of the law would ensure the ending of the abuses stemming from uncontrolled private enterprise.

[1] AGN *General de parte* 67 (1785–9), ff. 113 *v*–114 *v*., and ff. 152–52 *v*.

CHAPTER 3

THE PROBLEM OF REFORM, 1768-1786

Visitor-General Gálvez's *Plan de intendencias* of 15 January 1768, described the government of New Spain as having reached a similar nadir to that of Old Spain at the time of the death of Charles II in 1700. The means of recuperation would be the establishment of Intendancies. In this way Gálvez aspired to make the government in New Spain uniform with that of the Peninsula.

Centering his attack on the Alcaldes Mayores, Gálvez explained that they doubled the Viceroy's work rather than lightening it. The real problem was that there had been no adequate authority between the Viceroy and Audiencia at the peak of the administration, and the Alcaldes Mayores in the locality. This intermediary role would be played by the Intendants, whose seats would be in the provincial capitals, such as Puebla, Oaxaca, Valladolid de Michoacan.

The problem required more than this. For, Gálvez considered, as long as the Alcaldes Mayores remained in office, no subject was safe from their oppression. Gálvez's radical solution—one that was to be much criticised—called for the total abolition of the offices of Alcalde Mayor and Corregidor, and the extirpation of their very name. One of the worst practices of all, the Visitor believed, was their custom of appointing lieutenants. Such men tended to be of low extraction, devoid of a sense of social responsibility, and unversed in the law, which it was their duty to uphold.

Gálvez recommended the replacement of the old corrupt and compromised justices by a fresh administrative corps, the Subdelegates. These officials were designed to act as subordinates of the Intendants in the Indian towns and the immediate locality. The Crown was expected to pay them a proper salary.

The deplorable conditions subsisting in such a province as Oaxaca dictated the urgency of such an administrative departure. For, both the precious cochineal dye and the fate of the Indian populations were at stake. There Gálvez grieved to report that the Indian tribute revenue and the *alcabala* languished in decay because of the peculation of the Alcaldes Mayores. In the case of the Alcaldía Mayor of Nejapa, for instance, the *alcabala* yielded only 500 pesos, while its Alcalde Mayor enriched himself with an income of between 10,000 and 15,000 pesos without any more

41

effort than the operation of the *repartimiento* to the Indians. Moreover, the Crown continually suffered loss of revenue from such *repartimientos*, because *alcabalas* were not paid by the administrators concerned.[1]

Gálvez's *Plan de intendencias* initiated two decades of discussion on the question of the outside financing of the Alcaldes Mayores. The central core of dispute was whether the Intendancies and Subdelegations would be any improvement in solving the endemic problem of violence and corruption in the locality.

Viceroy Bucareli, an equally dedicated reformer in the tradition of the Spanish Enlightenment of Charles III's reign, did not, however, favour the extreme abolitionist position of Gálvez. A more cautious and discreet man than the intemperate and often violent Gálvez, he took his stand on two principles. Firstly, the fault lay not inherently in the administrative system, but in the present administrators, and, likewise, the Laws of the Indies were not at fault, but were vitiated by the men who administered them. Secondly, the way to eliminate the abuses was not by creating an expensive administrative confusion through abolishing the old offices and setting up new ones in their place, but by strengthening the organs of government already in existence. Such a reform would, of course, centre on the Audiencia at the core of the bureaucracy. This reply was sent to the Crown on 27 March 1774.

The essence of Bucareli's view was that it would be unwise to jeopardise the present excellent state of Viceregal finances by attempting to pay for a costly and probably unnecessary administrative reform. The Superior Government would have obvious difficulty in finding funds to cover the new scales of salaries for Intendants and Subdelegates. Moreover, the Crown would find immense problems in securing men fit to employ as Subdelegates. If they should not receive a proper salary, they would be even worse than the Alcaldes Mayores, who at least had enjoyed the fruits of the *repartimiento* as a means of livelihood. Bucareli warned against throwing the Viceroyalty into unnecessary confusion.[2]

Viceroy Bucareli's views received support from the Oidor of the Audiencia of Mexico, the Conde de Tepa.[3] In his *Dictamen dado reserva-*

---

[1] AGI *Indiferente general* 1713, and AGI *Mexico* 1973; Priestley, *Galvez*, 289–92; L. E. Fischer, *The Intendant System in New Spain* (Berkeley 1929), 11–15.

[2] AGI *Mexico* 1973, reply of Bucareli to the *Real Orden* of 15 April 1772 enclosing documentation for the plan for the establishment of the Intendancies now before the Council of the Indies; R. Velasco Ceballos, *La Administración de D. Frey Antonio María de Bucareli y Ursúa* (2 vols.; Publicaciones del AGN de México 1936), i, 186–204.

[3] The Conde de Tepa had had considerable experience in imperial administration. He was Francisco Leandro de Viana, who, after graduating in law at the University of Salamanca,

damente al virrey de Nueva España, written on 1 July 1775, the Count criticised Visitor Gálvez's apparent belief in the desirability of making the governments of Old and New Spain uniform in character. For, the two countries differed entirely. Hence, the Ordinance of Intendants for Spain issued in 1718 and again in 1749 could not be adapted to conditions in New Spain. While attacking Gálvez's first propositions, Tepa, nevertheless, recognised the necessity of reform in the governmental system of New Spain. This reform, however, should not take the form of needless innovations, but of strengthening its traditional system. To replace 150 Alcaldías Mayores with Subdelegations would be merely to change a name.

On the matter of the cochineal trade, Tepa followed Gálvez in emphasising its importance. For, in the province of Oaxaca, the lieutenants of the justices might enjoy a salary of as much as 2,000 pesos annually from their operation of the *repartimiento*. It was precisely that commerce which set the economy of Oaxaca in motion. Therefore, rather than prohibit them and abolish the Alcaldías Mayores, the Crown should attempt to staff the offices with men of proven conduct, who would trade under specific Royal regulations. In such a way, the Intendancies proposed by Gálvez would be unnecessary. The Gálvez Plan only served as a deterrent to private investors, whose often beneficial intervention could be observed in the formerly backward area of Jicayan, whose incumbent Alcalde Mayor was at that time being financed by one of the richest merchants of Mexico City. In his six years of office, Jicayan had never been more prosperous. In Villa Alta, where similar *repartimientos* were being practised, there was the same flourishing trade. In neither of the two areas had there been any complaints of abuses. Similar benefits from outside financing of the *repartimiento* could also be seen in Nejapa, previously prostrated in decay, and Teotitlán del Camino. Such economic advantages justified the retention of the existing system of government.

These *repartimentos* were to stay. For, the Count explained, they were the means by which the Indian population was incorporated into the

had been made Fiscal of the Audiencia of Manila, in 1756. There he condemned the negligence of the administration in his 'Miserable and Deplorable State of the Philippine Islands', in 1766. In 1767, he passed to New Spain as Alcalde del Crimen of the Audiencia of Mexico, where, in 1771, he reached the rank of Oidor, receiving his title of Count in 1775. On his return to Spain, he was appointed to the high rank of Minister of the Council of the Indies with special attention of Mexican and Philippine affairs. In 1782, he became the Council of the Indies' representative on the Junta administering the Banco Nacional de San Carlos, in which he himself held 150 shares, valued at 300,000 Spanish reales de vellón. See J. A. Calderón Quijano, *El banco de San Carlos y las comunidades de indios de Nueva España* (Seville 1963), 18.

economic life of the Viceroyalty. Moreover, 'the *repartimientos* are a type of partnership between the Alcaldes Mayores and the Indians, in which the former invest their capital, and the latter put their labour. Without this investment by the Alcaldes Mayores, the labour of the Indians would not be possible. Without that, America would sink to its total ruin'.

Nevertheless, the Alcaldes Mayores should pay the Royal alcabala on their commercial transactions, and their activities should be subject to closer scrutiny by the Audiencia. Tepa favoured a return to the policy of 1751. The just tariff of prices established by the Junta of Ministers should be implemented. This Junta might also consider a scheme of formal payment for the justices.

Like Bucareli, Tepa favoured a reform of the existing system of government. The main method conceived by both of them was the strengthening of the Audiencia. Tepa recommended the despatch of an Oidor to the Indian towns every three years to investigate conditions and to ascertain what grievances needed to be redressed, punishing excesses. He would especially supervise the conduct of the justices, but he himself would be subject to cross-examination by his fellow magistrates of the Audiencia. Two further magistrates, entrusted with criminal jurisdiction, would undertake *visitas de la tierra*. As a final gesture, the Laws of the Indies, those admirable laws which Bucareli had said were not being obeyed, were to be published in every Indian head-town and village.[1]

A further criticism of Gálvez's plan came from one of the Fiscales of the Audiencia, Merino, on 10 March 1779. Merino reminded Gálvez of the difficulty of altering the traditional practice of the *repartimiento*. For, both the provisions of the *Reales Cédulas* of 1751 and 1761 had been ignored in New Spain. The provisions for the limited *repartimiento* regulated according to a just tariff of prices had remained a dead letter, and the attempt to renew the measures under the *Real Cédula* of 1777 had been ineffective. Moreover, the Junta set up in Mexico City back in 1752 had been of the opinion that a regulated rate of prices was impracticable in New Spain. Therefore, though they had, he said, been successfully introduced in Peru, nothing had been done in New Spain.[2]

Merino defended the *repartimiento* on practical grounds. Like both Viceroy Bucareli and the Conde de Tepa, he regarded it as both useful and indispensable. Indeed, he claimed, the Crown itself adhered to the view, as the legislation of 1751 bore witness. However, like most official defenders of the *repartimiento*, Fiscal Merino required the elimination of

[1] AGI *Mexico* 1973.
[2] AGI *Mexico* 1868, *Expedientes é instancias de parte, 1782*.

coercion and violence. Such a policy the Audiencia had been traditionally attempting to uphold, but without any measurable success.

Merino reiterated the plight of the Alcaldes Mayores as a preliminary to his justification of their trading practices. They were poor and needy men, struggling against adversity to maintain themselves in backward provinces. Even in the lucrative province of Oaxaca there were many instances of their covering their administrative costs, even the very paper they wrote on, out of their own pockets. Only a few Alcaldías Mayores were profitable, and most of those were in Oaxaca. Villa Alta was the best of all, because of the diversity of its trades, which offered a profit in both peace and war. Jicayan, Miahuatlán, and Nejapa also rendered profits in peace-time, but their dye trade suffered in war-time. The other jurisdictions yielding fruitful returns were Teposcolula, the Corregimiento of Oaxaca, Teotitlán del Valle, Chichicapa, Tehuantepec, all dye areas, and the cotton garment and cochineal dye region of Teotitlán del Camino. Apart from those, only three others in New Spain rendered a profit, Tehuacan, Maravatío, and Tulancingo. Yet, even in those cases mentioned, many instances revealed how an Alcalde Mayor might be ruined through lack of *habilitación*. In short, most justices, according to Merino's description of them as virtually self-effacing martyrs, were unsuccessfully attempting to live off an office incapable of maintaining them, and without any immediate prospect of amelioration.

Turning to praise the efforts of the *aviadores*, the Fiscal cited cases of the development of Oaxaca's regional trades through their intervention. In Jicayan, the financiers of the cochineal crop had been the prominent city of Oaxaca merchants, Larrazábal, Magro, and Murguía, in 1778. In Tehuantepec, where between 1762 and 1769 the Alcalde Mayor had been Juan Bautista de Echarri, that administrator, who founded his position as one of Oaxaca's most prominent merchants during his term of office, introduced the cultivation of the cochineal dye to the isthmus region. During the eighteen years of Echarri's activities there, the success enjoyed in dye production had been considerable. For, the total crop had doubled from 2,000 zurrones to the present level of 4,000, with the result that the price had fallen in the city of Oaxaca, in the port of Veracruz, and in Spain over the last fifteen years from 24 to 16 reales per pound.[1]

Despite the interests of *aviadores*, other merchants enjoyed complete freedom to trade in the Indian regions. The explanation for their absence from those regions was not their deliberate exclusion by the Alcaldes

[1] *Ibid.*

Mayores, but their own unwillingness to venture sums of money they knew they would never recover from such unreliable debtors as the Indians.

To impress upon the Crown just how much the Royal interests benefited from the *repartimiento*, Merino attested that it was precisely the combination of the merchants' *avío* with the coercive faculties of the justices that ensured the repayment of debts by the Indians. Respect for the Alcalde Mayor kept the Indians in order. The justices took care of their provinces, because their own personal interests were involved in them. Naturally such administrators should receive a proper salary, but the burden on the Royal Treasury would undoubtedly be too great to bear. Therefore, the best way out of the dilemma was to allow the *repartimientos* of the justices to continue.

In view of the incipient establishment of both the Intendant system and *comercio libre*, Merino proposed a compromise between the Gálvez Plan and the position of Bucareli. The Intendant should be put in charge of the administration of the laws of 1751 and 1761. The authority of Intendants could overcome the disregard for the Crown's efforts to secure a regulated *repartimiento*, unsuccessful as they had been over the past twenty-eight years.[1]

The ministers of the Council of the Indies and *Contaduría General* in Madrid reported to Gálvez, Minister of the Indies since 1776, on 2 August 1782. Between the time of Merino's report in 1779 and the consideration of it by the Madrid ministers in 1782, it had become clear that the Gálvez view of the problems of the Indies would triumph in the Spanish counsels of policy. Bucareli had died in 1779, removing the main obstacle to the implementation of Gálvez's plan. The Crown had not wanted to override its distinguished Viceroy by imposing the Gálvez solution against his will. In the following years, the Intendant system was introduced into Peru and the new Viceroyalty of the Río de la Plata. The accession of Gálvez to the supreme office of policy marked the climax of the radical reformist position in Indies affairs.[2]

The ministers, in consequence, proceeded to disregard Merino's case. The reform had already been decided. As a result, they considered that Merino's argument contributed nothing to the discussion. Rather than attempt to answer Merino point by point, the ministers dismissed his

---

[1] *Ibid.*

[2] For the background to the establishment of the Intendant system in the Viceroyalty of the Río de la Plata, see John Lynch, *Spanish Colonial Administration, 1782–1810, the Intendant System in the Viceroyalty of the Río de la Plata* (London 1958).

whole case, accusing him of partiality. He had thrown disdain on the disinterestedness of the clergy of New Spain when they had denounced the *repartimiento*. They accused Merino of being the panegyrist of the Alcaldes Mayores. Moreover, they said his discourse was confused—it was not—and his argument inconsistent. Such a lack of cogent thought, they declared, revealed that Merino failed to demonstrate that circumspection and careful forethought required of Royal magistrates, especially in a matter as important as the present one. Such an ill-conceived report was, therefore, useless. In any case, the Crown had already decided to implement the Gálvez Plan. As the corollary of the establishment of Intendancies in New Spain, the Crown proposed the abolition of the Alcaldías Mayores and Corregimientos, and the extinction of the *repartimiento*, which had already been suppressed in Peru. Since Merino had, in the meantime, died, his letter did not merit any reply.[1] From such a response, it was evident that the Gálvez group in Madrid did not wish to strike a compromise with its critics.

In Oaxaca, the chief enemies of the Alcaldes Mayores were the clerics, whose position was championed by the Bishop, Ortigoza, in the 1770s and 1780s. This Bishop was described as the 'St. Paul of his times', by Viceroy Revillagigedo the Younger.[2]

Merino had pointed out this rivalry in a subsequent letter to Minister Gálvez, sent on 26 June 1779. He had singled out the clergy for attack because of its hatred for the justices, and their animosity towards the *repartimientos*.[3] The matter was serious. The mutual hostility between the two local representatives of Spanish civilisation was founded in the different attitudes adopted by each to the nature and functions of the indigenous population. The Alcalde Mayor emphasised their incorporation into the Viceregal economy, through the activities of the *repartidores*. The clergy emphasised their role as wards of the Crown, and, within the context of the protective legislation of the Laws of the Indies, which the justices very frequently violated, attempted to achieve the incorporation of the Indian into the culture of Catholic Europe. In doing that, the clergy—when they were not themselves corrupt—sought to protect the Indian from economic exploitation by the Alcalde Mayor. This divergence of views between the two great representatives of Spain's authority, the Church and the Royal magistrate, was never resolved throughout the Colonial period. It repre-

[1] AGI *Mexico* 1868, *Expedientes é instancias de parte.*
[2] Padre José Antonio Gay, *Historia de Oaxaca* (2 vols.; Mexico 1881), ii, 331.
[3] AGI *Mexico* 1868.

sented the perplexing dichotomy between economic necessity and religious mission.

Back in 1762, the parish priest of Mitla had protested to the Audiencia against the abuses and avarice of the Alcaldes Mayores. In response, that supreme body had issued the *Real Despacho* of 22 November 1765. The ineffectiveness of that provision, however, occasioned a further fresh demand for action from the parish priest of San Ildefonso Villa Alta. The Audiencia's *Real Provisión* of 1772, therefore, ordered the Alcalde Mayor, on pain of a 500 peso fine, to desist from his extortionate dealings with the Indians, and to refrain from his previous interference with ecclesiastical jurisdiction in the parishes.[1]

From such cases it appears that the disputes between the Alcaldes Mayores and the local clergy, vigorously supported by Ortigoza, were reaching a climax in the 1770s—precisely the time of the greatest expansion of the cochineal trade.[2] Obviously this situation had to be resolved. The only way would be through the intervention of the Superior Government under commission from Madrid. The situation was clearly worsening. A conflict over ecclesiastical jurisdiction arose between the parish priest of Justlahuaca and the local Alcalde Mayor over clerical rights of burial.[3] At the same time, the sacristan of the Cathedral of Oaxaca, Lic. Antonio Justo Mimiaga y Elorza,[4] complained once more to the Audiencia against the overbearing pressure of the civil power in the province. Another of the Cathedral authorities, the attorney of the ecclesiastical court (*fiscal de la curia eclesiástica*), reported: 'All the Alcaldes Mayores of the Bishopric of Oaxaca were in conflict with the parish priests. This not only demoralised and cruelly vexed the Indians, but also trampled upon ecclesiastical jurisdiction.' The courts of the Alcaldes Mayores infringed upon the *fuero eclesiástico*,[5] and the justices were requiring accounts from pious foundations, chantries, and confraternities. Their pretensions resembled those of monarchs, requesting special seats in church, and a place in the ritual of the ceremonies.[6]

A different view of the *repartimiento* from that held by Bucareli, Tepa, and Merino, was that held by Bishop Ortigoza of Oaxaca, in the light of his visitation of the diocese between 1776 and 1783. Passing to the Indian villages, Ortigoza did not share Tepa's view that the *repartimiento* was a

---

[1] Gay, *Historia de Oaxaca*, ii, 327.   [2] See Appendix 1.
[3] Gay, *Historia de Oaxaca*, ii, 328–9.   [4] See Glossary of Personnel.
[5] A discussion of the position of the clergy at the end of the Colonial Period is N. M. Farriss, *Crown and Clergy in Colonial Mexico. The Crisis of Ecclesiastical Privilege, 1759–1821* (London 1968).   [6] Gay, *Historia de Oaxaca*, ii, 329–30.

type of partnership between Indian and Alcalde Mayor, a kind of contract between capital and labour. On the contrary, he considered that the violence involved contributed to the dissolution of the bonds of society. For, at the time of the collection of debts by the Alcalde Mayor and his band of men, Indians unable to repay the finished product would flee into the hills, and hide for fear of arbitrary arrest, and deportation in chains to the nearest hacienda. As a result, the Indians would become fugitives like animals. They would be deprived of their religion, their homes, and their families. The Bishop described the Indians of Oaxaca as a lost and abandoned people.[1]

He described the *repartimiento* in the following way: "This pest, which each day spreads more, increases by degrees the harm it brings. For, each moment new abominable methods are devised by the Alcaldes Mayores, or by their pernicious financial backers and directors, to enrich themselves by the iniquitous *repartimientos*, from which follow the inevitable and complete destruction of the Indians.'[2]

Moreover, the Bishop charged, the various *Reales Cédulas* for the instruction of the Indians in Christian doctrine and the Castilian language were not being observed in the province. This state of affairs most previous Bishops denounced. In the late 1750s, Bishop Ventura Blanco had been preoccupied with the Indians' ignorance of Christianity and the Castilian language. The *Real Cédula* of 5 June 1754 had ordered the establishment of schools for language instruction. The Bishop had pointed out that there were twenty-one Indian languages in Oaxaca alone, which made the teaching of Castilian extremely complicated. He advised stronger measures, and the introduction of the sanction of punishments. In March 1758, he recommended that the Indians should be included with the *gente de razón* in the jurisdiction of the Inquisition for all cases of idolatry and witchcraft, which, he said, abounded in the province. If this were not agreeable, then the secular clergy were to employ stronger penalties for such aberrations.[3]

Over twenty-five years later, Bishop Ortigoza was reporting the same idolatry, and the same ignorance of the Christian faith. Instead of the adoration of the divine mysteries, the Indians were given to superstition, and in the case of the parish of Acatlán in 1781, the Mije-speaking Indians had even practised pagan sacrifices. Even after the Bishop had absolved the guilty, fresh sacrifices had been made. The distressed parish priest of

---

[1] AGI *Mexico* 2587, *Expediente sobre la visita hecha por el rdo. Obo. de Oaxaca, D. Joseph Gregorio de Ortigoza, de aquella diócesis* (leg. 2).
[2] AGI *Mexico* 2587. [3] AGI *Mexico* 2585, documents of Oaxaca Bishops.

Acatlán lamented that from the very moment the Indian left his mother's womb he came under the influence of superstition, idolatry, and witchcraft, following the evil example of his forefathers.[1]

From the reports of other clerics, and from the evidence of his own eyes, the Bishop saw that the haciendas had no chaplain to say Mass, and no schools of Castilian. The Indians who sowed the cotton and planted and tilled the *nopaleras* for the cochineal dye would often live as far as ten leagues or more from their place of work. In consequence, they too received no instruction. The schoolmasters established by some of the Alcaldes Mayores were 'vagrants, turbulent men of evil habits, uneducated, over-bearing and fearsome to the Indians, and not infrequently they would be dependents and debt-collectors of the justices in the Indian towns'.

The legitimacy of these contracts of the justices was discussed, the Bishop explained, in the Fourth Mexican Provincial Council (1771), where the Church Fathers it seemed had not dared to come to any decision, neither approving nor disapproving. The greatest scandal of all was that, while this discussion continued, the funds of chantries and pious foundations were being employed in the *repartimiento*.[2]

Enclosed with Ortigoza's reports were several letters from the parish priests of Oaxaca. Most of these denounced the *repartimiento* in the strongest terms. The priest at Santo Tomás Ixtlán reported that debt-collectors were arresting Indians as they came out of Mass. As a result, debtors did not dare to go to church any more, and failed to receive the Sacraments. The priests generally advocated the full employment of ecclesiastical sanctions against the violence of the *repartidores*. The parish priest of Ayoquesco denounced the abuses of the Corregidor of Oaxaca. For, Indians of the Corregimiento had fled to other towns, or had sought refuge in the mountains. The sums involved in the *repartimiento* there had risen from 14,000 pesos to 25,000 pesos. The increasing absenteeism of the indigenous inhabitants meant that their houses were empty, their wives in prison, and their children abandoned.[3]

An anonymous discourse—possibly written by a cleric of Oaxaca—was received by the Council of the Indies in August 1777. Entitled '*Usuras de los repartimientos, y desórdenes en el gobierno económico y político de Oaxaca*', the author took an attitude towards the Alcaldes Mayores like that of Bishop Ortigoza. The debtors were in prison; others had fled; family life

---

[1] AGI *Mexico* 2587.   [2] *Ibid.*   [3] AGI *Mexico* 2588.

had been destroyed. From his trades, the Alcalde Mayor might derive five-yearly profits of from 50,000 pesos to 200,000 pesos. In Jicayan, the Alcalde Mayor, Gaspar de Morales, secured a profit of 302,000 pesos. Even allowing for any pious exaggeration on the part of the author, these sums were substantial indeed.

Worse still, the Alcaldes Mayores were in the habit of seizing Indian lands, planting them, and using the rightful owners as the labour force, paying them at a miserable rate. They appropriated the water supply—sparse enough in any case—for their own irrigation needs, to the detriment of other cultivators.

Such abuses had been roundly denounced by the parish priest of Zimatlán, in the Valley of Oaxaca. In reply, the interested parties, who included the local Alcalde Mayor, and the adjacent Alcalde Mayor of the Cuatro Villas del Marquesado, the Corregidor of Oaxaca (Pedro de Pineda), Juan Baptista de Echarri, and two others, all '*usureros públicos*', put pressure on the Bishop, predecessor of Ortigoza, for the public retraction of the condemnation by the priest in his pulpit. After this humiliation, they insulted the Bishop to the extent that shortly afterwards he died of grief.

In this diocese, priests and other clerics had been arrested for drunkenness, vice, and illegal trading with the Indians. Of the regular clergy, only a few lived according to the rule. The rest lived in license. The clergy hardly knew the Indian languages, with the result that not one-third of the Indian men, and not one quarter of the Indian women knew the Spanish language.

In the city of Oaxaca itself, the situation was no better than in the countryside and the Indian towns. The capital was governed without any sense of responsibility. The prisons were full of persons who had been in them for the past ten or fifteen years. The public squares were monopolised by the lower elements for their gaming. The shops cheated their customers by using false weights and measures. In short, drunkenness, theft, and blasphemy prevailed. Nor was anyone safe while more than five-hundred men were at large who should have been sent to the presidios.[1]

Though the document was anonymous, the Council of the Indies sent a copy of it back across the Atlantic for the views of Bishop Ortigoza, who replied to Gálvez on 21 August 1778. He verified its contents, pointing out that the situation in Oaxaca was, in fact, even worse. Ortigoza explained, however, that it would be impracticable to apprehend and

[1] AGI *Mexico* 1872, *Expedientes é instancias de parte (1785)*. See also, AGN *Civil* 1866, exp. 10 (1777).

discipline the recalcitrant clerics. For, to remove them would leave the parishes entirely unmanned. This, in view of the shortage of clergy, would leave the Indians uncared for. They, while not seduced by idolatry as the anonymous writer claimed, were nevertheless rude and simple people, inclined, like most lower castes, to put the material before the spiritual.

As regards the abuses evident in the city, these were entirely true. For, under the present Corregidor, party strife between the Regidores and the various private parties had reduced the government of Oaxaca to a state of abandonment.

The Bishop added that the *Reales Cédulas* and Viceregal *Bandos* concerning the regulation of conditions of Indian labour on the haciendas and sugar plantations and mills remained entirely unobserved and ignored. The masters treated their labour like slaves, making them work in fetters and shackles, a sight he himself had witnessed during his visitation. Moreover, the Alcaldes Mayores and other creditors, working in league with the *hacendados*, would send their debtors to work in such conditions on the haciendas, as if they were mules, in violation of the Indians 'natural liberty'.[1]

The Council of the Indies returned to discuss the whole vexing question at the end of December 1778, calling for the fundamental reform of the 'present weak and disorderly government of Mexico'. The Council then proceeded to prepare a *Real Cédula* to remedy the abuses. Its task, however, was delayed by Spain's entry into the War for American Independence (1779–83). On the restoration of peace, the Council returned to the matter. The *Real Orden* of 25 December 1783 ordered Viceroy Martín de Mayorga to apply measures to remedy the situation in Oaxaca, to contain the usurious transactions of the justices, and prepare the ground for the prompt establishment of the Intendancies in New Spain, the final solution of the problem of lack of proper government. The Viceroy's commission was also to include the remedy of abuses in the ecclesiastical sphere. For, employing the funds derived from the sale of the confiscated properties of the Jesuit Order, he was to endow a seminary for the proper education of the clergy, as the Bishop of Oaxaca had advocated. At the same time, Mayorga was to publish a *Bando*, warning all offenders that the Crown was informed of their illicit activities in Oaxaca, and advising them that it had never been the Royal intention that, in conceding the tacit issue of *repartimientos*, violence and usury should follow. Moreover, such a concession to the Alcaldes Mayores did not give them the right to enclose their

---

[1] AGI *Mexico* 1872.

areas of authority in a trade monopoly, to the exclusion of private traders, and in violation of the Laws. The Crown expected its administrators to observe the regulations for the *repartimiento*—it did not say which. Trustworthy persons were to take secret evidence to see whether the administrators conformed or not. The Crown did not say who these trustworthy persons were to be. Lastly, two orders were to be sent out. The first should request the Bishop of Oaxaca for detailed information concerning the disorders in the ecclesiastical sphere in his diocese, and the second should go to the Ayuntamiento of Oaxaca ordering it to set the municipal government in order.[1]

The Viceregal *Bando* was issued on 7 October 1784, by Viceroy Matías de Gálvez, a relative of the Minister of the Indies. It denounced the scandalous gains of the Alcaldes Mayores, and the violence they applied, and condemned the pernicious idea that they had the right to exclusive operation of trade, forming a monopoly to the public detriment.[2]

In October 1784, the Superior Government in Mexico City received detailed reports from its Alcaldes Mayores under commission from the Viceroy. The Corregidor of Oaxaca, Mariano de Llano, reported that all *repartimientos* there were voluntary, and at equitable prices. It was false to say there had been 50 or 100 per cent profits. He himself had received only 20 per cent gains, without deducting costs. He had been lucky to get that, and suffered frequent losses in his trade in cattle, which he imported from the Hacienda de Olachea in Guatemala at 14 pesos per yoke, selling it at 18 pesos. At present, there was no profit in cochineal. The price had sunk to 12 reales per pound, the level of the *repartimiento*. The Corregidor considered himself lucky if he secured a 5 per cent profit.[3]

Sánchez Solache, in Zimatlán, also disclaimed the use of force, and pointed to the current depression of cochineal prices, which had dropped, he said, to 14 reales in the city of Oaxaca. Profits did not exceed 33 per cent. In that trade, there were frequent losses, especially in good years, when the Indian growers would ignore their obligations to their creditors, and take their crop into the city for sale to the highest bidder. In the case of the mule trade, the gain there was only 12 or 13 per cent, after deduction of costs, risks, and salaries. Merchants traded freely, and some had shops. Indian properties were not confiscated, and the inhabitants would only be subjected to imprisonment for short periods in order to impress upon them the need for work. In short, the *repartimiento* sustained the Indian sector of the economy.[4]

---

[1] AGN *Virreyes* (primera serie), 15, f. 222, no. 363 (reservada).
[2] AGI *Mexico* 1872, *Expedientes é instancias de parte, 1785.*   [3] *Ibid.*   [4] *Ibid.*

Pedro de Quevedo in Teposcolula-Yanhuitlán attested to the presence of merchant-residents there and in Tlaxiaco, and of the activities of traders who came up from the city of Oaxaca. Such operations kept the price of Indian-produced commodities high, with consequent lack of sufficient profit for the Alcalde Mayor.[1]

In Teutila, there had never been any *repartimiento* of cash, oxen, or foodstuffs, though a small quantity of mules had been imported only to meet the needs of the Indians rather than for profit. They had been bought and sold for the same price of 24 and 25 pesos a pack. No other trader would undertake such a fruitless trade. In the cotton trade, an Indian town might owe 3,000 or 4,000 pesos, but pay only 200 pesos of its debt for the whole year. When there were gains, they would be no more than 25 per cent. So far from the employment of coercion, the Indians had to be persuaded not to take cash, lest they should prejudice their capacity for repayment.[2]

In Jicayan, the Alcalde Mayor explained he had reaped only small profits from the 400,000 pesos invested there over the past four years, in *repartimientos* for cochineal to the Indians, and for cotton to the negroes and *mulatos*. In the case of cochineal, he had inherited an Indian debt of over 30,000 pesos from his predecessor, with little hope of recovery since the debtors had fled from their homes. The voluntary nature of the *repartimiento* was evident from the fact that the Indians were only given a third of what they requested. In the case of cotton, the Alcalde Mayor intervened to ensure that demand for cotton did not prejudice local attention to Indian maize subsistence sowings. Outside merchants, taking Jicayan's products to the cities of Oaxaca and Puebla, were in no way molested. In cotton and cochineal, they themselves operated '*unos cuantiosos repartimientos*'. For example, in 1783, a resident of Jamiltepec, Francisco Losada, operated a *repartimiento* valued at 52,000 pesos. Such merchants, the Alcalde Mayor said, made their contracts with the reliable Indians, leaving the rest to the administrator. Even despite his *habilitación*, the office was not such an advantage to the Alcalde Mayor after all. For, from his short gains of 20 per cent, he would have to cover his administrative costs and the salaries of his staff.[3]

Likewise, in Villa Alta, the *repartimiento* was not permitted for all those who requested it. There had been no violence, and no imprisonment for debt. Little profit had been secured in the cotton-mantle trade, and little in cotton and cochineal.[4]

---

[1] *Ibid.*   [2] *Ibid.*   [3] *Ibid.*   [4] *Ibid.*

The inhabitants of the Indian town of San Ildefonso Villa Alta did not, however, agree with the Alcalde Mayor's answer. They denounced, on 9 December 1784, his *repartimientos* using force, and the extortion employed by his agents, the Indians of the *barrio* of Analco, who were his debt-collectors.[1]

Despite these protestations of innocence from the Alcaldes Mayores, Bishop Ortigoza was not convinced that any abuses had disappeared. In view of the letter of the Indians of Villa Alta, he requested stronger action from the Audiencia.[2]

The Crown's final verdict on the question was the *Real Ordenanza de Intendentes* of 4 December 1786, which codified and legislated Gálvez's plans for reform. Article 12 abolished the Alcaldías Mayores and the Corregimientos, and outlawed the *repartimientos* that had been issued by Royal officials. Article 61 reaffirmed the Indians' right to trade directly with any merchants, and, conversely, the traders' right to penetrate into the Indian towns. Intendants were to be set up in all the provincial capitals of New Spain, including the city of Oaxaca. There were to be twelve in total. One of the functions of the Intendant of Oaxaca was to assume the role of Corregidor of the city, and act as president of its Ayuntamiento, with a fixed salary of 6,000 pesos annually. Under him, on the expiration of their terms of office, the present Alcaldes Mayores were to be replaced by Subdelegates, paid from the Indian tribute revenue.[3]

[1] *Ibid.*   [2] *Ibid.*
[3] *Real Ordenanza de intendentes*, 1786. Extracted from its legajo, this document may be found in the library of the AGI in Seville. A translation of it appears in Fisher, *Intendant System*, 98–331.

CHAPTER 4

REFORM AND REALITY—THE CRISIS OF THE SUBDELEGATIONS IN THE 1790s

After the climax period, 1769–78, the last years of the 1770s initiated the downward trend of cochineal prices which continued until 1796.[1] The price decline was accompanied by the fall of production levels from the previous peak of between 1 million and $1\frac{1}{2}$ million pounds to 464,625 pounds in 1781, and 537,750 pounds in 1785. These low levels were main-tained—at between 430,000 and 600,000 pounds—between 1783 and 1796. They were accompanied by a price level between 15 and 17 reales per pound, or half the peak price level of 1771.

Production began to decline in 1781, with the drop to 464,625 pounds from a peak of 1,385,437$\frac{1}{2}$ pounds for the previous year. Such a sharp drop was the result of the reopening of war between Spain and Great Britain between 1779 and 1783. Bishop Bergoza of Oaxaca, writing in 1810, and looking back over the troubled history of the cochineal trade since the 1770s, attributed the decline to the British blockade of trade during those war years. For exports had been trapped in Oaxaca, or Veracruz, and even in Cádiz itself. The price of cochineal had slumped, with the result that the profitability of cultivating such a risky and delicate crop had declined. In consequence, the *nopaleras* had not been planted.[2]

This interpretation was shared by the merchants of Oaxaca themselves, writing to Viceroy Azanza in December 1799. Complaining of the adverse effects of the war after 1797, they compared them with those of the war of 1779–83, when the price of cochineal had at times dropped to 10 reales in the city of Oaxaca, without any prospect of sale even at such a low price.[3]

These arguments, and the previously cited evidence of the two parish priests in the province of Oaxaca, show the adverse effect of the war policies of the Spanish Crown on the cochineal producers and merchants, whose prosperity depended on the pacific transportation of their product across the Atlantic. Moreover, with the depression of the price in Oaxaca

[1] Full figures are presented in Appendix I.
[2] *Ibid.* For Bishop Bergoza's letter of 1810, see AGN *Industria y comercio* 20, exp. 6.
[3] AGI *Mexico* 2509, *Papeles del consulado y del comercio* (1800) This formed part of a file drawn up because of the request of the *Diputación de la Universidad de Comerciantes* of the city of Oaxaca on 25 February 1800 that their cochineal be shipped to Spain in warships.

and Veracruz, there would be less profit for the Alcalde Mayor from the *repartimiento*. In 1782 and 1783, however, as the initial effects of war began to wear off, and in view of several Spanish successes, production figures in Oaxaca registered new upward levels of 1,035,675 and 990,000 pounds respectively, levels comparable to those of the 1770s. In both years, the value of the crop was over 2 million pesos.[1] Nevertheless, after 1783, in contrast to 1748 and 1763, neither the price level nor the production level recovered. This phenomenon indicated a departure from the cyclical features of the period, 1758 and 1778, into a period of long and slow decline; that is, not a temporary crisis motivated by war blockade, but a fundamental crisis at the local level.

This crisis was brought about by four major factors. Firstly, Spanish cochineal growers, a small group of enterprising men who had emerged in the course of the eighteenth century, feared the attempts of the Church to exact a cochineal tithe upon them. Secondly, the *aviadores* of the Alcaldes Mayores were faced with the Superior Government's attempt to extend Gálvez's Veracruz reform of the *alcabala* payments to the local level. Thirdly, just as these conflicts were being resolved, the whole Viceroyalty of New Spain suffered the devastating famine and price rise of 1785–7. Lastly, into this situation came the establishment of the Intendancy in Oaxaca, and the prohibition of the use of *repartimientos* by the Alcaldes Mayores, and their successors, the Subdelegates.

The issue of a cochineal tithe had always been a source of contention between the civil and the ecclesiastical authorities throughout the eighteenth century. The Bishop of Oaxaca, Fray Angel de Maldonado, had requested it in 1702, and the Cabildo Eclesiástico had taken the matter up in 1715.[2] After that the issue remained dormant until Bishop Tomás Montaño issued a pastoral letter, on 16 March 1740, indicating that once more the *contaduría de diezmos* (tithe accounting house) wished to exact a full 10 per cent tithe on cochineal. However, a long law suit followed with the growers. The Audiencia secured a compromise solution, reaffirming the Indian growers' exemption from such a tithe payment, but establishing that the Spanish growers should pay a tithe rate of 4 per cent, wherever custom had not established a different one.[3]

The matter did not rest there. For in 1773, the Cabildo Eclesiástico, anxious to participate in the climax period of cochineal prosperity, and to

---

[1] See Appendix 1.   [2] See Chapter 1, pp. 14–16 below.
[3] Woodrow W. Borah, 'Tithe Collection in the Bishopric of Oaxaca, 1601–1867', *HAHR*, xxix (Nov. 1949), 498–517.

redistribute the proceeds amongst its clerics in the form of increased stipends, renewed its recourse of 1715, and called for a full cochineal tithe. The clerics declared that they would have remained silent had not the earthquake of 1741 ruined their Cathedral, and made the work of reconstruction necessary. These they could not finance out of their meagre income from the ninth-and-a-half part of the total tithe revenue. That, in any case, was destined for spiritual needs. They asked the Audiencia for a levy of the *medio real de fábrica* (half-real for church construction), which they explained the Cathedrals of Mexico and Puebla enjoyed. It was urgent, for the Cathedral of Oaxaca was poor, and suffered from frequent earthquakes.[1]

In its *acuerdo* (judgement) of 20 December 1773, the Audiencia once more emphasised the total exemption of the Indian population from the payment of a cochineal tithe. Such an exaction would only serve to perpetuate the state of misery in which they lived. Reaffirming its verdict of 1775, the Audiencia also prevented the Cabildo Eclesiástico from adding a *medio real de fábrica* to the already burdensome tribute payment of the Indians. Such a position was upheld by the Fiscal of the Council of the Indies in 1775, when he affirmed that under no circumstances would the Council allow any infringement of the Indians' exemption from cochineal tithes. In this way, the Council reaffirmed its decision of 1718 and 1719. The Superior Government ratified the decision in 1776.[2]

However, the new Bishop of Oaxaca, Ortigoza, during the middle period of his visitation of the diocese, issued what came to be known as the *Edicto Sangriento*, on 7 April 1780. In it, he threatened pain of excommunication on all growers of cochineal who did not declare on oath what they cultivated, and who did not pay a full tithe on their product. Such a strong measure, especially in view of the decision of 1776, motivated the protest of the Spanish growers of cochineal in Oaxaca to the Audiencia. This body declared once more against any innovation. The Fiscal de Real Hacienda, the adept Ramón de Posada, countered the clerics by emphasising that no document ordered a 10 per cent tithe on cochineal —an '*imaginario diezmo*'. It was true that the Laws of the Indies had laid down that such a tithe should be exacted, but those provisions had not applied for over one and a half centuries. Since the Indians were exempt, and there were only very few Spanish growers, the tithe by the latter should be levied in proportion to capacity of payment, a 3 or 4 per cent tithe, but not the 5 or 10 per cent which the clerics were unreasonably

[1] AGI Mexico 2693, *Expedientes inventariados* (1807), Oaxaca, 22 de julio de 1806, no. 20, Diferentes cosecheros de grana de la Intendencia etc. . . .   [2] *Ibid.*

demanding. There were certain precedents. White sugar paid only a 5 per cent tithe, and refined sugar a 4 per cent. Moreover, the protesters against the Edict of 1780 were by no means guilty of the heresy of Wycliffe, as Bishop Ortigoza claimed, for their resistance to the payment of a tithe to the Church.[1]

Posada went on to counter the entire arguments of the Oaxaca clerics. For, contrary to what the Cabildo Eclesiástico stated in 1773, the Cathedral of Oaxaca was not poor. Its clerics enjoyed more than a sufficient stipend for their positions and services to the Church. Back in 1759, for example, the dean received a salary of 1,945½ pesos, and the various dignitaries beneath him, archdeacon, precentor, and treasurer, received 1,687 pesos each. The canons each received 1,297 pesos. These salaries were in extreme contrast to the meagre incomes of the clerics of the Cathedral of Guatemala, for instance, who received only 150 pesos, 130, and 100 pesos each respectively. The Oaxaca salaries were increasing. In 1779, the same clerics were receiving 2,625, 2,334, and 1,757 pesos respectively. Such increases were to be seen against the background of rising tithe receipts—from 53,329 pesos in 1759, to 75,278 in 1768, and 65,870 pesos in 1779. All this was evidence that the clergy of Oaxaca really intended to use their supposed poverty as an excuse for cutting in on the profits of the cochineal trade. To enforce a 10 per cent tithe on the Indian growers would be to see the abandonment of cultivation by them. Posada was determined that such a development should not take place, for cochineal was a special commodity, being New Spain's only export crop. Its growth stimulated other products, and was contributing well enough already to the rising revenues of the Church. The Bishop and Cabildo's request for the 'restoration' of the tithe was utterly without foundation. Posada concluded that the Audiencia should hear the case of the Spanish cochineal growers of Jicayan, who had actually been compelled to pay the full 10 per cent tithe.[2]

The Audiencia's concern for the growers seems to have fallen victim to the Oaxaca tithe administration's determination to include the Spanish growers into its scope of jurisdiction. For, on 22 July 1806, various cochineal growers of the Intendancy of Oaxaca protested to the Crown against the imposition of a full 10 per cent tithe upon them, and complained that as a result of the tithe their industry was in a state of decline. They requested the entire removal of a tithe, in order to compete equally with the Indian producers, but they specified, that if the Crown did not agree

---

[1] *Ibid.*   [2] *Ibid.*

with its entire removal, then they would be prepared to accept a return to the situation of 1780, before the *Edicto Sangriento*. Each grower would then, as before, contribute in proportion to the impulse of his piety and the size of his crops, namely a tithe of 2, 3, or 4 percent.[1] At the same time, they explained that the *Jueces Hacedores*,[2] who had taken charge of the tithe revenue administration since the establishment of the Intendancy thought of nothing less than the full exaction of the 10 per cent tithe.[3]

A few months after Ortigoza's *Edicto Sangriento*, Viceroy Martín de Mayorga issued the *Bando* of 20 October 1780. Mayorga required the payment of *alcabala* on all merchandise when a sale had taken place. In the case of commodities involved in the *repartimiento*, payment was to be made on exit from the jurisdiction concerned, on the presupposition that a sale had already taken place. At the same time the *Bando* reestablished, for the duration of the war, the 2 per cent *alcabala de reventa*,[4] which had been repealed in 1754.

The Superior Government's attention to the problem of the *alcabala* in the locality formed part of a whole series of measures involving firstly the transference of the adminstration of the revenue to Royal bureaucratic control, and secondly the assurance that no one eligible would avoid payment. Both these aspects of the bureaucracy's policy severely aggravated the Spanish Peninsular merchants of the Consulado of Mexico, and their associates in Oaxaca. From 1 January 1754, Viceroy Revillagigedo the Elder authorised the establishment of bureaucratic control over the

---

[1] *Ibid.* An indication of the revenue secured from the 4 per cent cochineal tithe is given in Appendix 1–4 of Dahlgren, *Nocheztli*, Plan que manifiesta las cantidades satisfechas de diezmo de granas arreglado al 4 per ciento en esta Santa Iglesia de Antequera de Oaxaca en los seis años, 1784–1789,

	pesos
1784	63
1785	277
1786	578
1787	408
1788	503
1789	1,003
	2,832

[2] The *Jueces Hacedores* were the two canons of the Cathedral of Oaxaca to whom had been delegated the supervision of tithe collection. They headed a staff of secretaries and clerks in the *Contaduría de diezmos*, the tithe accounts department. See Borah, 'Tithe Collection'.
[3] AGI *Mexico* 2693, *Expedientes inventariados*.
[4] Maniau, Joaquín de, *Historia de la Real Hacienda* (Mexico 1914), 18–19, paras. 47–54. The 6 per cent *alcabala* had been raised to 8 per cent in 1644 to help pay for the Spanish war effort. This increase was known as the *alcabala de reventa*.

Reform and reality

alcabala revenues of the Mexico City region (including, among others, Coyoacan, Chalco, Cuautitlán, Zumpango, Tepozotlán), which had traditionally been administered by the Consulado of Mexico.[1] Viceroy Bucareli followed this on 3 October 1776 by ending all leases of the *alcabala* revenue, reuniting them to the central control of the Royal bureaucracy.[2]

The Bando of 1780 gave rise to vigorous protest from the main *aviadores* and Alcaldes Mayores of Oaxaca. Francisco Corres, Alcalde Mayor of Miahuatlán, thought that it surely could not imply the payment of *alcabala* if a sale had not taken place. For, the dye had not been sold at the time when it left Miahuatlán. All of it was sent, in 1777, 1778, 1779, and 1780, to Veracruz for sale there to the Casa de Cosío. The *alcabala* had then duly been paid into the Royal Treasury of Veracruz. Corres' position was upheld by the Fiscal of the Audiencia, Merino, who, nevertheless warned the Superior Government that the case in question might lead to dangerous precedents as a result of which Royal finances might suffer.[3]

Pedro Alonso de Alles, *aviador* of Jicayan, maintained that no sale had been made at the time of extraction from the locality. His cotton went directly to the Puebla cotton textile industry, where it would duly pay the *alcabala* on sale there. His cochineal went directly to the Casa de Cosío in Veracruz in the same way as that of Corres. Nevertheless, the Royal Administrator of *Alcabalas* in Jicayan was trying to exact payment of *alcabala* on departure from the region where the original *repartimiento* had been made. Fiscal Posada, who had applied his mind so acutely in the case of the cochineal tithe, discussed Alles' case before the Superior Government on 9 April 1782. Alles had formed a '*compañía*' with the Alcalde Mayor, who had taken office in January of that year. Posada explained that Alle's position rested on a clause in his contract with the Alcalde Mayor that there was to be no sale of the products of the *repartimiento* in the area of production. The Viceroy should order Alles to produce this '*compromiso*', that is, he should produce a certified copy of the *escritura de convenio*.[4]

Manuel Ramón de Goya, who was a merchant of Mexico City, like Alles, and *aviador* of Villa Alta, complained that there the Administrator

---

1 British Museum (BM) 9770 k. 3, exp. no. 10, Revillagigedo, 26 September 1753.
2 R. Velasco Ceballos, *La administración*, ii, 103–5. See also AGI *Mexico* 2347, *Expedientes de Real Hacienda*, (1740–79).
3 AGI *Mexico* 1400, *Duplicados del virrey* (1782), documents originally sent with letter no. 1683 of Viceroy Mayorga to Minister Gálvez, 29 May 1782, Consultas de la Dirección de Alcabalas sobre exacción del 2 per ciento más del 6 per ciento, Cinco testimonios de expedientes despachados por la Junta Superior de Real Hacienda. See also, AGI *Mexico* 2374, *Expedientes de Real Hacienda* (1807–10), cuaderno 1.   4 *Ibid.* cuaderno 3.

of *Alcabalas* was interpreting the *Bando* of 1780 to the letter, and was preventing the extraction of commodities under the *repartimiento* until the *alcabala* was first paid on them. His goods, however, were not sold in the locality, but were bound for Mexico City and other parts of the Realm, where they would then be sold. Hence, *alcabala* was being paid twice, once on departure from the locality, and secondly on final sale elsewhere. Such an abuse raised the price of the product, and prejudiced the interests of every agent involved in production and distribution. Posada explained that before the issue of the *Bando*, the practice had been to levy *alcabala* on goods leaving the locality only if a sale had actually taken place, and to levy it subsequently at the place of sale, if it had not. As a result, the Viceroy should publish another *Bando* to clarify matters. This Mayorga did, on 27 September 1781, ordering that there was to be no innovation on the question of *alcabalas*, and that the situation prior to 1780 was to be restored. This *Bando* applied in all cases, including those of Villa Alta, Jicayan, Miahuatlán, and others.[1]

On 24 May 1781, several of the Oaxaca merchants and deputies of commerce, including Juan Baptista de Echarri and Joaquín Jiménez de Morraz, advised the Viceroy of the fatal situation in which they said they now found themselves. For their interests were suffering because of the present war against Great Britain, and the recent question of the *alcabala*, which had given rise to certain 'disorders' practised by the subordinate officials of that branch of revenue. In view of the risks of war, they had been able to embark no more than half their cochineal sold. Current prices in the city of Oaxaca had fallen from between 19 and 23 reales in 1779 to 16 to 19 reales per pound in 1780. Into such a situation, the Viceroy had launched his *Bando* of 1780, which, besides the matter discussed above, increased the *alcabala* by 2 per cent.[2]

The recourse of the Oaxaca merchants was considered by the *Dirección General de Alcabalas* to fall into the same category as the requests of the Veracruz merchants for relief from the 2 per cent increase. This request also came under the provisions of the Viceregal *Bando* of 27 September 1781.[3] As a result, then, of their protests, the merchants and Alcaldes Mayores of Oaxaca gained the province's exemption from the changes legislated in the *Bando* of October 1780, but not before its initial effects had been felt.

The principal crop for the sustenance of the mass of the indigenous

---

[1] *Ibid.* cuaderno 4.   [2] *Ibid.*   [3] *Ibid.*

population in Oaxaca was maize. Its supply was a serious concern, for in the cochineal regions its cultivation had often been neglected, because of the pressure of the debt-collectors of the *repartimiento*. The availability of food was severely tested by the famine years of 1779 and 1780, and, especially, by the great famine of 1785–7.[1]

In 1779, shortage of rainfall produced a crop failure, and the death of livestock. This, in turn, was followed by the outbreak of smallpox, which swept from Miahuatlán through the Valley of Oaxaca, in the early months of 1780. In response to the population losses, the inhabitants of Miahuatlán, Teposcolula, Tamazulapan, Tejupa, Yanhuitlán, and Ixtepeji requested and received relief from tribute payment. In the cochineal areas, cultivation of the dye had been neglected, and the surviving inhabitants had been reduced to the most extreme straits.[2]

A far worse catastrophe followed in 1785. Severe and unseasonal frosts in August and September produced the great maize crisis of 1785–7. Once more the Indian towns petitioned the Superior Government for relief from tribute payments they could not meet in view of the population decline in their regions. This time, however, the requests came in just as the Government was planning the establishment of the Intendancies, in which the subordinate administrators, the local Subdelegates, were expected to maintain themselves from a 5 per cent levy from the Indian tribute income.[3]

On 25 October 1785, the Ayuntamiento of Oaxaca warned that there was a danger of food shortage in the city. For the city depended for its nourishment on the surplus produced in the four surrounding jurisdictions of Zimatlán, Huitzo, Teotitlán del Valle, and the Cuatro Villas del Marquesado, all in the fertile Valley of Oaxaca. However, these regions also supplied the jurisdictions of Villa Alta, Ixtepeji, Miahuatlán, Peñoles, and Teojomulco, and indeed the bulk of the Mixteca. For those territories did not cultivate maize. Their chief occupation was the production of the cochineal dye. The demand for that dye was so great that the indigenous population there even neglected their own subsistence maize crops, in order to produce it. As a result, in times of food shortage, there would generally be competition between them and the public granary of Oaxaca city.[4]

---

[1] A full discussion of maize agriculture may be found in Charles Gibson, *The Aztecs under Spanish Rule*, 310–16. [2] AGN *Tributos* 14.
[3] Gibson, *Aztecs under Spanish Rule*, 316. See also AGI *Mexico* 1141, 'Consejo de Indias en pleno de 2 salas', no. 30, 3 September 1804, for the whole discussion of the payment of the Subdelegates from the tribute revenue. [4] AGN *Intendentes* 33.

In Zimatlán, the local Alcalde Mayor reported that the maize price had risen to a peak of 48 reales per fanega from the moderate level of 16 reales. As a result there was a shortage of food among the indigenous population, who were incapable of paying such an inflated price with their low wage level of 1½ reales per day.[1] In Nochistlán, there was a perennial deficiency of maize owing to the dry and craggy nature of the soil. In most years the Indians would travel down as far as the Valley of Ocotlán to purchase maize.[2] In Tehuantepec, the Indians' crop had been ruined by northerly winds and rains. In view of the fact that there were no cereal-producing estates, only cattle-raising haciendas and ranches, in the vicinity, which sowed hardly more grains than were necessary to maintain their workers, the Indians expected a shortage in the harvest of 1785.[3]

In times of famine such as 1785 the correlation between the rise of price of maize and the fall of cochineal production was frequently observed. Both the parish priests, writing in 1776, whose views concerning cochineal prices have already been discussed,[4] noted precisely such a phenomenon. The depression of the cochineal price moreover would, conversely, be the cause of great shortages of foodstuffs in Oaxaca. A crisis of export, such as the outbreak of war, or of production, such as unseasonal weather, would help to turn the price levels of maize upwards. For, the Indian cochineal grower could not earn his livelihood, or cover his debt obligations, through the sale of his product. In consequence, he would be forced to cut back his production and consumption of maize. If, on the other hand, a crisis in maize production occurred, production of cochineal would suffer. For labour and capital would have to be employed combating the onslaught of famine. Such a crisis faced the newly established Intendancy of Oaxaca.

The failure of the Crown to award a formal salary to the Subdelegates under the Intendant system ensured that the burden of maintaining those officials would fall on the Indian tribute revenue.[5]

Towards the end of the eighteenth century, before the issue of the Ordinance of Intendants of 1786, the Indians and castes paid the following tribute levies. A full tributary was an Indian between the ages of eighteen and fifty, except a married man, who paid full tribute even if he were under eighteen. In this category also fell the *mulatos* married to *mulatos*, and all free negroes. Half tributaries were the unmarried and widowers, and Indians or *mulatos* who married persons of another caste. Certain

---

[1] *Ibid.*   [2] *Ibid.*   [3] *Ibid.*
[4] See Chapter 2, pp. 30–1.   [5] See AGI *Mexico* 1141.

groups were exempt, such as spinsters and widows, relieved from tribute payment in the 1720s and in 1758 respectively. The quantities for payment were small. Indians were expected to pay between 4 and 24 reales, while *mulatos* and free negroes ranged between 20 and 24 reales. There were different rates for those married to persons of another caste. An Indian married to a *parda*, for instance, paid $14\frac{1}{2}$ reales, while a *pardo* married to an Indian woman paid $18\frac{1}{2}$ reales, a *pardo* to a *parda* paid 20 reales, and an Indian to an Indian woman 21 reales. An Indian bachelor paid $6\frac{1}{2}$ reales, in contrast to a *pardo* bachelor, who was required to pay 20 reales.[1]

Great efforts were made to evade these tribute obligations, indicating the Indians' incapacity to pay the sums. Despite the complicated scales of caste difference, and the various modifications and reservations for old age, illness, and dire poverty, tributaries often were forced to pay twice. They would pay their normal levy in their villages, but would be apprehended by the tribute commissioners on the road to the provincial capitals, or to Mexico City, where they would be going in order to sell their wares. The commissioners would demand from them a letter of payment. If this could not be produced, the Indians would be required to pay again, and would be sent to prison until they did. In this way, many extortions were made. For, in many Indian towns, it was not the custom to issue certificates that payment had been made. The Audiencia attempted to deal with the abuses, but the Alcaldes Mayores declined to pay much attention.[2]

In the years 1778 and 1779, the collection of tribute had almost completely ceased. One-third of the revenue had in fact been consumed in expenses alone. Such a problem had motivated Viceroy Mayorga's appointment of the Oidor, Guevara, in January 1780 to discover why the tribute revenue was in a state of decay, and to draw up reformed regulations. Guevara considered that the first priority was the collection of past debts, and that while this was going on, the old system should continue. Over 200,000 pesos were collected, with the result that the Superior Government decided to remit the rest in the formation of the assessment for 1784, on condition that all tributaries presented themselves to be counted. By the time the Ordinance of Intendants had been legislated in Madrid in 1786, Guevara had brought the tribute accounts up to date.[3] He then proceeded to draw up new regulations, which guaranteed finally

---

1 Fonseca, Fabián, y Urrutia, Carlos de, *Historia general de la Real Hacienda* (6 vols.; Mexico 1845–53), i, 447, para. 88. See also Gibson, *Aztecs under Spanish Rule*, 202–18, for fuller background on the tribute assessments.
2 Fonseca y Urrutia, *Historia*, i, 447, para. 81.   3 *Ibid.* paras. 81–8.

the exemption of all women. These were put into force, but after a time were allowed to slide, and the former administrative ineffectiveness crept back.[1]

Under pressure of the famine period, 1785–7, however, the tribute figures once more dropped. From the 1779 figure, the year of confusion in the revenue which had necessitated the intervention of Oidor Guevara, when the total tribute revenue of New Spain had totalled 880,885 pesos, the famine years saw a drop to 742,536 pesos in 1785. This figure sank to a disastrously low level of only 435,569 pesos in 1786, and continued low, at 524,728 pesos in 1787.[2]

The Royal Ordinance of Intendants introduced a different plan of reform from that of Guevara. The Superior Government, in consequence, was faced with a choice between the plan formed in Mexico, and that conceived in Madrid. Article 137 of the Ordinance became a source of contention. For it abolished the status of half tributary, and upgraded those in that category to the status of full tributary, at the annual rate of 16 reales without distinction of bachelor, married man, or widower.[3]

The whole tribute problem was referred by Viceroy Flores to the Council of the Indies after January 1788. The Viceroy decided that the complicated matter of the Subdelegates' 5 per cent levy as a salary should be resolved by Madrid, which could also deal with the issue of just what Article 137 of the Ordinance of Intendants actually meant. Meanwhile, the Junta Superior de Real Hacienda, the supreme administrative body for finance set up under the Ordinance, ordered that no innovation was to be made concerning the tribute assessments until the Crown's decision should be known. In this way the implementation of the tribute reform, on the basis on which the new Subdelegates were to be maintained, was delayed until Madrid could take the final decisions.[4]

A series of letters and files on the question followed, sent by Viceroy Flores to the Council of the Indies. Flores wrote on 28 October 1788 that nine files of documents had been formed on the tribute issue arising out of Articles 127–40 of the Ordinance of Intendants. In general, Flores supported the suspension of the reform by the Junta Superior de Real Hacienda on the grounds that the Indians would be incapable of paying the new rates, with the result that they would desert their homes, and wander as vagrants. The Viceroy declared that, in face of such a problem, he would not allow the changes to be effected. Given the Indians' frequent

---

[1] AGI *Mexico* 1141. [2] Fonseca y Urrutia, *Historia*, i, 441–50.
[3] *Real Ordenanza de intendentes* (1786) articles 127–40. See also Fonseca y Urrutia, *Historia*, i, 441. [4] AGI *Mexico* 1141.

inability to pay even their present rates, he feared disturbances in the Realm, especially the interior—'*donde había algunas provincias conmovidas*'.

These despatches passed from the Council of the Indies to the *Contaduría General*, which gave its verdict on 24 September 1795, seven years after the initiation of the discussion. That office wanted to know why none of the reforms contained under Articles 127–40 had ever been put into practice in New Spain. This strong tone was supported by the Fiscal of the Council of the Indies, the same Ramón de Posada who had been Fiscal de Real Hacienda in the Audiencia of Mexico, and by the Council itself on 4 November 1795. After this decision, the Council informed the King of its views in January of the following year, but he returned the file of documents asking the councillors to explain to him what connexion it had with Viceroy Flores' letter of 28 October 1788. The Council then sent the whole pile of documents back to the *Contaduría General*, which passed them to the Fiscal, who passed them back to the Council (*en sala primera*), which, on 5 December 1797, ordered them to be transferred to the full Council (*en pleno de dos salas*).[1]

There the whole matter remained, forming part of the general discussion of the reform or abolition of the Intendancies. On 3 September 1804, sixteen years after the question had first been opened, a decision was reached. The Crown decided that the issue of tributes should be regarded as part of the clauses of the New Ordinance of Intendants of 1803 dealing with Royal finance. For those were the only clauses that had not been declared suspended before the full Ordinance itself ever came into force. The Crown ordered, however, that no innovation was to be made that might give rise to confusion.[2]

Conscious of the inadequacy of the 5 per cent levy from the tribute revenue, the Royal Order of 14 December 1790 ordered the compilation of a file on salaries for the Subdelegates. These administrators replied as shown in Table 3, and their replies clearly indicated the impossibility of maintaining the purity of the new system in the locality if a proper salary were not awarded to them by the Crown.

These answers were sent by the Intendant of Oaxaca to the Viceroy on 30 October 1792. Throughout that year and the previous one the Superior Government was discussing the impossibility for many Subdelegates of finding *fiadores* to offer the necessary guarantees for the revenues to be collected by them. The new information from Oaxaca showed that,

1 *Ibid.*   2 *Ibid.*

Table 3   *Salaries of Subdelegates from tributes and other incomes*[1]

Partido	Subdelegates and Date of Taking Office	Incomes (in pesos)		
		5% levy	Other	Totals
Villa Alta	Bernardino Bonavia, 26 July 1790	2,383	600	2,983
Teposcolula	Pedro de Quevedo, 23 October 1790	826	375	1,201
Tehuantepec	Pedro Fesar, 26 January 1791	497	500	997
Huajuapan	Francisco Gutiérrez de Madrid, 18 June 1788	682	504	1,186
Teutila	Vacant, under an *encargado* (deputy)	470	50	520
Zitmatlán	Former Alcalde Mayor I. Sánchez Solache	391	100	491
Jicayan	Vacant, through failure to present a *fianza*	382	45	427
Miahuatlán	José María Cevallos y Franco, 16 September 1790	289	50	339
Cuatro Villas	Under old system of Alcaldes Mayores	300	—	300
Teotitlán del Valle	Former Alcalde Mayor, Esteban Melgar, 6 July 1790	259	40	299
Nejapa	Pascual de Fagoaga, 22 November 1790	240	150	390
Nochistlán	Antonio Gándara, 27 February 1791	159	150	309
Justlahuaca	Antonio Figueroa, not yet taken office	294	142	436
Teococuilco	Francisco Urquiza, but still no *fiadores*	213	45	258
Ixtepeji	Under old system of Alcaldes Mayores	135	42	177
Chontales	Fernando Marqués, 6 March 1792	138	—	138
Huitzo	....	120	—	120
Huamelula	José Fernández, 28 April 1791	54	15	69
Teotitlán del Camino	Old Alcalde Mayor, Manuel José López, 14 January 1787	400	—	400
Jalapa del Estado	Under the old system			....

Notes:
1   In the case of Villa Alta, the sum of 1,145 pesos was received from tributes in the form of the cotton mantles produced by that *partido*.
2   The category, 'other', represents fees from the administration of justice.
3   The *partidos*, Cuatro Villas and Jalapa del Estado, remained under the old Alcaldías Mayores, because they belonged to the Marquesado del Valle de Oaxaca, the old inheritance of the Cortés family. Similarly, the old system continued in Ixtepeji, which pertained to the Ducado de Atlixco.
4   Though López continued in office under the new system in Teotitlán del Camino, he was unable to find *fiadores*, with the result that the Superior Government declared the *partido* vacant, and put the administration under a deputy.

[1] AGN *Subdelegados* 51.

except perhaps in the three sole cases of Villa Alta, Teposcolula, and Huajuapan, no administrator could survive on the income he received. The prohibition of the *repartimiento* by the Ordinance of Intendants, moreover, ensured that in several important cases, where previously cochineal and other major products of Oaxaca had been strong, the ingoing Subdelegates could not find anyone to guarantee the revenues they were supposed to collect for the Crown. Without the commercial incentives of the old system, outsiders from Mexico or Oaxaca city were reluctant to cover incomes they might have to pay out of their own pockets. For such reasons, the Subdelegates of Jicayan, Teotitlán del Camino, and Teococuilco could not take office, and in Zimatlán and Teotitlán del Valle the former Alcaldes Mayores, on the expiration of their terms of office, continued as Subdelegates.

Reports of the inability of various Subdelegates to find suitable *fiadores* plagued the Superior Government throughout the 1790s and 1800s. In July 1794, Viceroy Branciforte pointed out to the Intendant of Oaxaca that, according to the Oaxaca Ministers of the Royal Treasury, the Subdelegates of Teutila, Huitzo, Tehuantepec, Huatulco, Nochistlán, Ixtepeji, and Zimatlán had failed to offer their required *fianzas*. For that reason, they could not be allowed to take office, nor could those Subdelegates whose *fiadores* had lapsed or become insolvent. Branciforte, therefore, requested that the Intendant should supply him with a fresh list of nominees for the offices concerned, in the hope that new men could find satisfactory *fiadores*. Of those suggested by Branciforte himself only one was able to offer the *fianza*. He was none other than Ildefonso Sánchez Solache, who had been Alcalde Mayor of Zimatlán–Chichicapa since 1782, and had been financed for the cochineal trade *repartimiento* by Manuel Ramón de Goya of the Consulado of Mexico. Yet the fact that for seven years he himself had been unable to secure *fiadores*, and that the Superior Government had not found anyone else to take office in Zimatlán after Sánchez Solache's five-year term of office had expired in 1787, indicated the lack of interest in the trades of the *partido* after the prohibition of the *repartimiento*.[1]

The Fiscal de lo Civil, Alva, pointed out on 19 February 1795 that the situation in Zimatlán was not unique: that also in Teotitlán del Camino the former Alcalde Mayor had not yet officially been replaced by a proper Subdelegate, and that López should be removed. Such an action, however, threatened to leave the *partido* entirely unmanned. Therefore, just as

[1] AGN *Civil* 1641, exp. 7.

Bishop Ortigoza had done in the case of immoral clergy, the *Asesor General* of the Viceroyalty, Bachiller, disagreed with Alva, and favoured the continuation in office of both Sánchez Solache and López, on the grounds that they were better than vacant posts. He justified his view further by explaining that the Crown had found nothing wrong with the conduct of either. As a result, Branciforte ordered that no change should be made in the case of Zimatlán. However, the Crown disagreed, and from Madrid wrote back on 16 July 1795 ordering that the Subdelegation of Zimatlán should be declared vacant.[1] The order was obeyed. On 18 February 1796 the new Subdelegate took office, Antonio Moreda, the first new administrator in Zimatlán since 1782.[2] In Teotitlán del Camino meanwhile, López had been removed in March 1795, and there also, in May 1795, the first new administrator since 1782 took office, as Subdelegate. This Subdelegate, Marcos Antonio de Verasalusen, remained in the *partido* only three months, after which he returned to Mexico City, where he still was when the inhabitants of his *partido* complained of his absence late in 1797.[3]

The problem remained, and on 16 August 1799, the Intendant informed the Viceroy that his Royal Treasury Ministers had told him that the Subdelegates of Villa Alta, Teposcolula, Teotitlán del Camino, and Ixtepeji still had been unable to find *fiadores*, and that a deputy had been put in charge of Justlahuaca.[4] Such situations apparently found no end. For the certificates of the same Ministers for the beginning of the year, 1802, pointed out yet again that the Subdelegates of Teposcolula, Nejapa, Jicayan, Huajuapan, Teutila, and Villa Alta, and the deputy in charge of Ixtepeji had not secured *fianzas*.[5]

The financial problems of the Subdelegates were such that *fiadores* were guaranteed to be discouraged. On the death, in 1808, of the deputy for Nejapa, who had been administering the *partido* for the Subdelegate, the Marqués de Uluapa, a Creole member of the Ayuntamiento of Mexico City, 1,000 pesos were owing to the Royal tribute revenue, and there was a total deficit of 4,000 pesos.[6] In Teposcolula, in the same year, the Sub-

---

[1] *Ibid.*   [2] *Ibid.* exp. 18.

[3] AGN Subdelegados 65, Licencia de D. Marcos Verasalusen, subdelegado de Teotitlán del Camino, para pasar a México (1799–1800).

[4] AGN *Tributos* 6, Mora y Peysal–Viceroy, no. 173, 16 August 1799.

[5] AGN *Subdelegados* 47, Mora–Viceroy, no. 9, 12 January 1802.

[6] AGN *Subdelegados* 21, Izquierdo–Viceroy, no. 62, 18 March 1808. The Marques de Uluapa was one of the members of the Mexico Ayuntamiento who took part in the events of July to September 1808 as a leading supporter of the Creole lawyers, Verdad and Azcárate. See Niceto de Zamacois, *Historia de Méjico desde sus tiempos más remotos hasta nuestros días* (21 vols.; Barcelona 1888–1901), vi, 33–51.

delegate owed 46,000 pesos to the tribute revenue.[1] Even worse was the case of Huajuapan, where the Subdelegate, Domingo Lasqueti, became so physically and mentally distressed by his burdens that he suddenly fled from his post, leaving only a note behind, in which he said that, 'only God knows where I go; for without an object, and without money, I do not know what will become of me. My soul rends itself within me while I write.' His debt was the sum of 17,534 pesos. The result of his flight was that the Superior Government in April 1809 ordered his *fiadores* to pay the debt.[2]

Since tribute revenue was proving so inadequate for the maintenance of the Subdelegates, and the difficulty of finding *fiadores* was so great, pressure was put on the Superior Government to rescind the prohibition of the *repartimiento*. Along with this argument of the impotence of the new system at the *partido* level came its corollary, which attributed the decline of the trades of Oaxaca to the prohibition. The decline had brought about the collapse of all branches of Royal revenue, and had contributed to the dissolution of social bonds in the Intendancy. For, the argument continued, the maintenance of social order in Oaxaca depended upon the coercion employed by the Alcaldes Mayores in ensuring that the Indians, naturally inclined to drunkenness and sloth, were usefully put to work. The restoration of the old system, that is, the abrogation of a very fundamental part of Gálvez's reform, would guarantee the recovery of the cochineal, cotton, and cotton-mantle trades, and secure the collection of the Royal revenues. What this argument meant was that under the Gálvez plan, dominant at Court in the 1770s and 1780s, the Crown had been attempting to administer New Spain without the intervention and co-operation of the old vested interest groups in the Consulado of Mexico, the *repartimiento* and *avío* system, and in the provincial cities like Oaxaca. In its attempt to bring into Oaxaca a fresh body of impartial administrators, the Crown and the Superior Government had shown the impossibility of government without the local power groups. The lesson of the 1790s was that a compromise would have to be worked out between the Gálvez reform plan and the old interest groups.

1 AGN *Subdelegados* 21, Izquierdo–Viceroy, no. 165, 19 July 1808.
2 Archivo del Tribunal de la Federación (Oaxaca), leg. 1, exp. 10; AGN *Subdelegados* 20, Sobre descubierto del subdelegado de Huajuapan. The *fiadores* requested Fiscal de Real Hacienda, Sagarzurrieta, to release them from this compulsion on 18 April 1812.

CHAPTER 5

THE GÁLVEZ PLAN UNDER FIRE, 1786-1804

The attitude of the first Viceroy who administered the new Intendant system was one of scepticism. Viceroy Flores, previously Viceroy of New Granada, where the system was never tried, questioned the practicability and usefulness of the reform. We have already seen his caution over Articles 127-40 of the Ordinance of Intendants, and his reluctance to attempt any of the changes prescribed by them. His fear of disturbing the traditional routine of affairs led him to veto a plan for the assignation of salaries to the Subdelegates. His reason was that the Royal Treasury was already sufficiently burdened with the salaries of the Intendants.[1] Summarising his experience in the government of New Spain, Flores informed his successor, Revillagigedo the Younger, that, 'so far from seeing up to now these beneficial effects (as a result of the establishment of the Intendancies), complaints are heard foretelling the final ruin of the Kingdom, and the forthcoming collapse of the Royal revenues, unless it is brought back to its previous system of government by its ancient laws, collections of regulations, and municipal statutes'.[2]

Revillagigedo, however, tended to think that the reform should be allowed time to recover from its early difficulties. For, he believed that the Intendancies would eventually become one of the main instruments in resolving New Spain's most pressing administrative and economic problems. In that spirit, he issued two Superior Orders of 24 November 1790, requiring strict compliance with the prohibition of the *repartimiento* contained in article 12.[3]

For Revillagigedo, the Intendancies were to be the means of a far-reaching investigation and remedy of usurpations of Royal rights and violations of the law. Taking Articles 61, 62, and 63 of the Ordinance of Intendants seriously, he recommended that the Intendants should examine the validity of the land titles of the *hacendados*, with the object of restoring usurped lands to their rightful owners, and ensuring that land capable of

[1] AGI *Mexico* 1675, *Sección de gobierno y fomento, negociado político, instrucción é industria* (1800 -21), Testimonio del expediente rotulado sobre el Real Orden del 14 de diciembre de 1790 ... sobre sueldos a los subdelegados.
[2] *Instrucciones que los virreyes de Nueva España dejaron a sus sucesores* (2 vols.; Mexico, 1867-73), ii, 46.
[3] AGI *Mexico* 1675, *Expediente sobre permiso de repartimientos a los subdelegados.*

cultivation was actually farmed. The Intendants represented the strong arm of justice, issuing forth from Mexico City to reach to all parts of the Realm.[1]

The chief centres of attack in the formative years of the Intendancies were Articles 9, 10, 11, and 12 of the Ordinance of 1786. These prescribed the abolition of the Alcaldías Mayores and the prohibition of the administrators' *repartimientos*, and attempted to install a Subdelegate wherever there had been either Alcaldes Mayores or their lieutenants. On these issues, Revillagigedo sent ten letters in strict secrecy which the Council of the Indies began to discuss on 1 August 1791. They were, in effect, summaries of the Intendants' replies to the Superior Government's circular order of 16 December 1789, requesting them to report back on the stages reached in their efforts to implement the reform.[2]

The Intendant of Oaxaca, Antonio de Mora y Peysal, reported that since he had arrived in the province, he had noted that the principal opponents and detractors of the new system were precisely those who had enjoyed considerable interests in the issue of *repartimientos* under the old. For, apparently, the final implementation of the Gálvez reform plan of the late 1760s really had deterred investors from their traditional operations in Oaxaca. The Indians had been severely pressed in 1787 to repay the debts they owed to the *repartimiento*, before the new system could be properly established. Nevertheless, the Intendant said, despite both this debt-collection and the shortage of *aviadores* at the present time, the Indians in 1788 had actually sown the *nopaleras*, and enough maize on their plots (*milpas*) for the maintenance of the public granary of the city.

---

1 AGI *Mexico* 1300, *Cartas y expedientes del virrey* (1791), 10 cartas reservadas, passed on 1 August 1791 by Pedro Lerena, Minister of Finance, to the Council of the Indies, no. 113, Revillagigedo–Lerena, Mexico, 2 Oct. 1790, paras. 258–65. Revillagigedo's views on the land question were advanced, following the tradition of the ideologists of the Spanish Enlightenment, such as Campomanes and Jovellanos: 'The Royal lands suffer well-known usurpations. Those in private ownership are distributed among great haciendas, which embrace hundreds of leagues, and belong to religious houses, clerics, *mayorozgos* (entailed estates), and private individuals. These latter are very small in number compared to the former groups. There are both Spanish and Indian towns, which, after permission to constitute themselves as such within the territories of the great haciendas, have no other lands than the gutters of their own houses. In short, agriculture is a sector monopolised in mortmain, and in few hands.'

2 *Ibid.* The full interpretation of Article 12 meant that even private persons were forbidden to operate *repartimientos*. The general discussion on the question of credit to Indians and castes dealt with this point, concluding that permission should be given to private merchants. This was granted by the Royal Official Letter of 13 May 1797 to Viceroy Branciforte, and confirmed by the Real Orden 13 June 1799. However, both were repealed by the *Real Cédula* of 7 April 1800, which commanded the full force of Article 12. See Fisher, *The Intendant System*, 109.

73

As a result of their enterprise, an abundant crop of cochineal had been collected in 1790. This success would have continued into 1791, had not rain damaged the *nopaleras*.

Mora clearly stated that to his knowledge none of the administrators near to the capital had been engaging in *repartimientos*, though further out into the province, the prohibition of 1786 still had not taken effect. The Intendant had rebuked the recalcitrant administrators, and was under the impression that only a few private individuals now issued them. In consequence, the trade of Oaxaca enjoyed freedom for the first time, and the trade with the Indians was at current prices. For example, whereas the Indians had been compelled to pay between 26 and 28 pesos for a yoke of cattle under the old *repartimiento*, they now were able to purchase at between 14 and 15 pesos, directly from the haciendas. Moreover, the fact of the prohibition of the *repartimiento*, by no means implied that goods formerly introduced into the Indian areas had now ceased to enter. On the contrary, the province had not become economically stagnant, whereas it was the Indians who received the profits of the trade. Such activity, and the incentives now offered to the Indians, fully justified the remission of capital despatched to the province by several of the merchants of Mexico City, Puebla, and Veracruz, in 1789 and 1790, for investment in the cochineal crop.

Not only did the Intendant emphasise the continued commercial activity in Oaxaca after the 1786 measures, but he also chose to praise the character of its indigenous population. 'I affirm that the Indians of Oaxaca are not as uncivilised and idle as the particular interest of a few persons would have us believe. It is not necessary to put the hoe into their hands, and apply lashes to them in order to make them work. For, some are industrious and inclined towards trading activities, and are sufficiently rational.'

With such views as these, the Intendant set himself firmly against the opinions of such powerful local interest groups as the Echarris and others involved in the cochineal, cotton, and cotton-mantle industries in the city of Oaxaca, who generally favoured coercion and the strong line of policy when Indian problems were involved. Exhibiting this considerable desire to understand and sympathise with the situation of the indigenous population, Mora y Peysal believed that the Indians would benefit a great deal from the extirpation of the *repartimiento*. He cited as evidence for his position the provincial Customs Books and the large numbers of Indians who frequented the weekly markets (*tianguis*).

Nevertheless, the Intendant was not unaware of the financial difficulties involved in setting the reformed administrative system on its feet. On the vexing question of the 5 per cent levy for the payment of the Subdelegates he pointed out to the Viceroy the difficulty of finding suitable persons to take office, especially in those *partidos* where the tribute income was small. However, in his anxiety to preserve the reform, the Intendant himself overestimated the yield of the Oaxaca partidos for a resident Subdelegate. For, before he had received the report from the localities concerning the amount of the tribute levies, Mora reported to the Viceroy that there were few *partidos* in Oaxaca where the tribute revenue was small. Judging the province by its predominant indigenous character, he omitted to consider the complex scales of exemption, reservation, and reduction involved in tribute payment, and did not take into consideration the effects of the famine years, 1785–7, which would inevitably lead to a scaling-down of the tribute quotas. Mora advised the Viceroy that in a province as predominantly Indian as Oaxaca, a Subdelegate would be able to live comfortably. He would even be able to employ a deputy administrator in some branch of Royal finance.[1]

The success of the new system, Mora believed, depended on a willingness of the part of the Subdelegates to depart from the profit incentives offered to the former Alcaldes Mayores in the *repartimientos*. As a result, he advised Revillagigedo to maintain the full force of Article 12. The Intendant's political position, however, was bound to bring him into conflict with those who suffered from a nostalgia for the old system, from both former investors or operators of profitable *repartimientos*, and from new administrators with a tendency to compare their 5 per cent levy with the previous Alcalde Mayor's income.

For these reasons a bitter dispute opened between the Intendant of Oaxaca and the new Subdelegate of one of the most lucrative *partidos* under the *repartimiento*, Villa Alta.[2] An anonymous document, undated, but obviously written at the end of the eighteenth century, placed Villa Alta at the head of its list of Alcaldías Mayores of the first class. For, the Alcalde Mayor there would receive 200,000 pesos in profits during his five-year term of office.[3] Such a sum would give him an annual salary

---

[1] AGN *Subdelegados* 35, ff. 23–36.
[2] According to the Revillagigedo Population Census of 1793 the *partido* of Villa Alta contained a total of 58,280 persons, making it the largest single political unit within the Intendancy of Oaxaca, even including the combined population of the city and Corregimiento of Oaxaca (56,772). Of Villa Alta's total, 58,088 were Indians, and only 120 mestizos, and 38 Spaniards: AGN *Historia* 523, Estado que manifiesta el número de poblaciones que comprende la provincia de Oaxaca, 18 December 1793.
[3] BN MSS 1385, ff. 208–9.

of 40,000 pesos a year. Even allowing for the payment of deputies and administrative expenses, it was considerably greater than the 2,983 pesos he was expected to receive as his 5 per cent levy and adjacent revenue. The anonymous writer, however, gave no source for his statements. If he himself was not, or had not been, an *aviador*, administrator, or deputy, his estimate of profits must surely have been largely based on hearsay. Nevertheless, assuming the actual income of the Alcalde Mayor was only half the sum quoted, even then he would have received as his gross salary nearly ten times that of a Subdelegate.

The central issue in Villa Alta was whether the prohibition of the *repartimiento* had deterred investment in the region's products, and had, thereby, contributed to a depression of its trades. The case for such a decline was set forward by Subdelegate Bernardino Bonavia in 1790, and was adopted by two such influential persons as Murguía y Galardi and Bishop Bergoza y Jordán. In such a way, there is considerable evidence presented to indicate that the prohibition resulted in economic crisis and decline. This argument served to reinforce the position of the critics of the reform, such as Juan Baptista de Echarri. Murguía, in his statistical survey of the State of Oaxaca composed between 1826 and 1828, stated that, before 1787, Villa Alta had produced between 50,000 and 60,000 cotton mantles, of 4½–5 yards, per year. These had been sold not only throughout the province of Oaxaca, but, more principally, had been sent to Mexico City, and the various mining communities of the interior, as far as Zacatecas, for sale. However, this trade had shrunk to barely between 10,000 and 12,000 pieces by 1828, inferior in both size and quality.[1] It was implied by the date of decline, 1787, that the cause of the decay was the prohibition of the *repartimiento* under Article 12 of the Ordinance of Intendants of 1786. This same interpretation was offered by Bishop Bergoza y Jordán of Oaxaca in 1810, with the sole difference that Bergoza placed the annual rate of production before 1787 at 200,000 cotton mantles per year, with a decline to between 60,000 and 70,000 by 1810.[2] If both writers disagreed on the actual figures, they agreed that there had been a decline, and that it was due to the detrimental economic consequences of the reform of 1786. Moreover, both writers approximately coincided on the extent of the decline, to between 20 per cent and 33⅓ per cent of former production levels.

Immediately after taking office in Oaxaca, Intendant Mora y Peysal had attempted to improve the condition of the indigenous population in

[1] BSMGE, MSS Murguia, *Estadística*, i, Appendix to 2nd Part, f. 29 *v*.
[2] AGN *Industria y comercio* 20 (1788–1821), exp. 6.

Villa Alta, believing it had suffered considerable exploitation under the *repartimiento*. Mora was especially anxious to stop the practice whereby the Indians were made to produce cotton mantles as part-payment of their tribute quotas for the Alcalde Mayor, who would then arrange for the distribution of the product to the market. Several Indian *repúblicas* within the jurisdiction of Villa Alta had already petitioned the Intendant for an end to the practice. In consequence, Mora had ordered the Alcalde Mayor, Pablo de Ortega,[1] to desist, but no notice had been taken. The Intendant's position rested on his interpretation of Article 129 of the Ordinance of 1786, which provided for the complete freedom of the Indians to sell their cotton mantles at current prices to any traders who dealt in them in free competition.[2]

The new system of Subdelegations came into operation in Villa Alta on 26 July 1790, with the entry to office of Bernardino Bonavia.[3] He immediately wrote to Viceroy Revillagigedo, on 17 September, arguing against the position of Mora, his political superior. Almost testifying to the truth of Mora's case that the new system was benefiting the Indians, Bonavia complained that, under the Subdelegations, the Indians were securing the profits rather than the administrator. For, the value of a cotton mantle was 8 reales. The cost of the cotton needed to produce it was $2\frac{1}{2}$ reales. Hence the Indian weaver now secured a profit of $5\frac{1}{2}$ reales on his original investment. For, the Indian would now acquire the raw material he used himself by travelling down to the areas of cotton production. Under the old system, 80,000 pesos had been invested in the production of such textiles, of which 25,000 pesos was the value of mantles offered for payment of tribute quotas. Since this latter was the only aspect of the old system still left in existence, the remaining 55,000 pesos would go to the Indians in profits.[4]

Under the *repartimiento*, the Alcaldes Mayores had procured the cotton employed in the manufacture of textiles by investing in it between 7,000 and 8,000 pesos annually, at the rate of 7 pesos per *carga* of cotton. Two *cargas* of cotton would produce between fourteen and sixteen mantles, valued at 8 pesos each, resulting in a profit for the administrator of between 90 and 100 pesos from an original investment of 14.[5]

In a similar manner, the cochineal dye had traditionally been secured,

---

1 Pablo de Ortega, see Glossary of Personnel.
2 AGN *Subdelegados* 35, Mora–Revillagigedo, 31 August 1790 (*reservada*), f. 203.
3 Bernardino Bonavia, see Glossary of Personnel.
4 AGN *Subdelegados* 35, Bonavia–Revillagigedo, 17 September 1790, ff. 208–11 and 31 July 1790, f. 211 *et seq.*   5 *Ibid.* 1 *carga* consisted of 8 *arrobas*.

at the rate of 12 pesos per pound for a crop of between 5,000 and 6,000 pounds per year. At the same time, the Alcalde Mayor also derived considerable advantages from his trade in oxen and mules, of which around three-hundred yokes of each would be issued annually, purchased at between 20 and 22 pesos per yoke. To supply the Indians with tools, the administrator under the old system had operated his own shop. Bonavia explained that the total amount of investment necessary to sustain these trades had been not less than 100,000 pesos per year, or between 500,000 and 600,000 pesos over the full five-year term. Of this, however, the Alcalde Mayor's profit would reach only 130,000 or 140,000 pesos over the whole period, with losses of about 13,000 pesos regularly suffered. Even an income such as approximately 27,000 pesos per year was still ten times the amount likely to be earned by a Subdelegate under the Intendant system.[1]

Presenting an argument guaranteed to impress the Superior Government, Bonavia emphasised that the commercial activities of Villa Alta produced benefits for the Royal revenues in the form of *alcabalas* paid on sales, which from the trade in livestock alone brought in an income of between 6,000 and 7,000 pesos. The entry of cotton mantles into Mexico City, moreover, produced a further 9,400 pesos, from a total introduction of between 90,000 and 100,000. Added to that would be the 1,152 pesos, which was the least amount usually paid on the cochineal entering the port of Veracruz. As a result, the Crown derived a sure income of at least 17,552 pesos annually in taxes on the products of Villa Alta.[2]

However, after the establishment of the Intendancy in Oaxaca in 1787, not one-eighth of this revenue was now collected. Bonavia claimed that there had been a drop of over 3,000 pesos in the consumption of tobacco alone due to the decline of the Indians' purchasing power. In view of the depressed state of the local economy, many Indian families had begun to migrate to the city of Oaxaca. Instead of the previous annual investment of 100,000 pesos in Villa Alta, there was now an exodus of funds to the extent of 80,000 pesos a year, and the region was well on the road to its ruin. Moreover, much of this Bonavia attributed to the new system of free competition. For, the private merchants who were now replacing the old trade system of the Alcalde Mayor lacked the judicial authority to enforce payment of debts. As a result their investments had not been as high as under the *repartimiento*. They knew that for every 1,000 pesos they invested, they would lose 700. Bonavia concluded his attack on the changes

---

[1] *Ibid.*   [2] *Ibid.*

issuing from the 1786 Ordinance by pointing out that in view of the 3,000 pesos of costs facing the Subdelegate, he was incapable of living off the 5 per cent levy from the tributes, which brought him in a meagre 1,205 pesos, even though Villa Alta was one of the most populous Indian *partidos*.[1]

Bonavia's grim picture of Villa Alta under the new system was not the only view of the Intendancy. In total contrast, the Subdelegate of Huajuapan, on 19 September 1790, reported an intensification of trading activity among the Indians. In the eleven years he had known the *partido*, as its Alcalde Mayor under the old system, never had he seen greater activity than at present. The fact that he chose as an example the lively commerce between the Indians of Villa Alta and those of Huajuapan threw a considerable amount of suspicion on the remarks of Bonavia. For the Villa Alta Indians would come down to Huajuapan to exchange their cotton mantles for yokes of oxen. Documentary evidence of such trade was presented by the chief customs officer of the city of Oaxaca, Lorenzo Murguía,[2] who testified to the same commercial activity of the Villa Alta Indians in Oaxaca itself, where to the Saturday *tianguis* they would bring as much as 1,543 cotton mantles for sale in the main square.[3]

Confronted with considerable diversity of views on the subject of the new system, Intendant Mora y Peysal put the whole case before Viceroy Revillagigedo, on 9 November 1790. He explained outright that he regarded the entire body of information presented by Bonavia as false. The object of this distortion of the evidence was to persuade the Intendant to return to the old practice of *repartimientos* managed by the Royal administrators, receiving part of the profits for themselves. Countering Bonavia's case, Mora presented the Viceroy with a description of some of the abuses under the old system. Indian women were expected to weave a cotton mantle (of five yards by one) within ten days. This, however, had been an impossible requirement, for the cotton had arrived in a raw state, unseeded and unspun. If an Indian woman had been unable to produce her work in time, she had been fined 8 or 9 reales, the value of a mantle. Anyone who had been incapable of paying, had been taken from her home, and placed in special houses owned by the *repartidores*. Under the new system, on the other hand, the Indian producers received a better price for the mantles. Free competition on the open market would bring them 10 reales, instead of the 8 previously offered by the Alcalde Mayor.[4]

---

1 *Ibid.*   2 Lorenzo Murguía, see Glossary of Personnel.
3 AGN *Subdelegados* 35, Mora–Revillagigedo, Oaxaca, 9 November 1790, ff. 217–27 *v*.
4 *Ibid.*

79

Elaborating further his refutation of Subdelegate Bonavia, Mora charged that under the former practices, the cotton used in the production of these mantles had been issued among the Indians with the utmost violence in Choapam, Latani, and Puxmetacan. Only 7 pesos would be paid to the cotton growers for a crop of 8 arrobas, the market value of which was really 17 pesos. What had been bought by the *repartidores* at 7 pesos would then be issued to the Indian textile weavers in a further *repartimiento* at 19 or 20 pesos. Mora went so far as to accuse Bonavia of falsifying his figures. For, though the Subdelegate had stated that oxen had been issued at 22 pesos under the *repartimiento*, Mora countered that the correct figure quoted should have been the extortionate prices of 26 and 28 pesos. In contrast to such abuses, the Indians at present were purchasing their oxen directly in the Mixteca for 14 and 15 pesos, eliminating the large profits that had gone to the Alcalde Mayor. Moreover, in contrast to Bonavia's claims that the Villa Alta economy was languishing in decadence, the Intendant himself, while on official visitation in Ixtlán, had seen with his own eyes Indians from Villa Alta on their way down to Huajuapan for the oxen trade.[1]

The worst abuse of all, Mora said, had been the Alcalde Mayor's shop. This scandal still existed under the present Subdelegate's administration. From the shop, the Indians were filled with hard liquor, with the result that the administrator kept them further bound down in debt. Combined with the degradation and enserfment of the indigenous population, the terror of the régime operated by the Alcalde Mayor and his armed men had deterred private merchants from remaining in the towns of Villa Alta. The present Subdelegate was guilty of similar behaviour. Fifteen private traders, all of them investors of considerable sums in cotton, textiles, and cochineal, who had ventured to Villa Alta had quickly returned to Oaxaca, and would not dare to return as long as the present Subdelegate held sway in that *partido*.[2]

In all respects Bonavia's régime represented a continuation of that of the Alcaldes Mayores. The last of them, Pablo de Ortega,[3] had employed a notorious lieutenant, Juan Carlos de Barberena.[4] Barberena was an intimate associate of Juan Baptista de Echarri, in whose house he had dwelt as a dependant.[5] It was Barberena who influenced Bonavia. Barberena, with other *repartidores*, was constantly prophesying the final

[1] *Ibid.* [2] *Ibid.* [3] Pablo de Ortega, see Glossary of Personnel.
[4] Juan Carlos de Barberena, *ibid.*
[5] AGI *Mexico* 2591, *Padrones de Oaxaca* (1777), Quadro 8, Casa de D. Juan Baptista Echarri. For Echarri, see Glossary of Personnel.

end of the Intendancies in New Spain, and the return of the *repartimientos*. Such views had pertinently been made known to any private merchant thinking of hazarding the journey to the *partidos*. For, prevented themselves from trading in their former manner, such interested parties in the old system were determined that no one else should trade. Against the background of such conditions, Subdelegate Bonavia contrasted his present income of 1,205 pesos with the profit of 27,840 pesos made by the Alcalde Mayor in 1784, and 74,645 pesos in 1785.[1]

While the Superior Government was attempting to decide whether it was the Subdelegate of Villa Alta or of Huajuapan who was telling the truth, Mora reported the open violation of Article 12 of the Ordinance of Intendants by the Subdelegate of Miahuatlán, José María de Ceballos, and his commercial associate, the Oaxaca merchant, Simón Gutiérrez de Villegas.[2] He had ordered both of them to appear before him in person in order to rebuke them. For they had tried to form a contract to set up a 'company' for the financing of their joint trade in the *partido*. Terms of the contract had already been drawn up. Under it, for the duration of the Subdelegate's term of office, the merchant would supply the three shops the Subdelegate was proposing to open in the *partido*, and also provide the Indians with whatever cattle and horses they might need. He was to ensure the cultivation of the cochineal crop by supplying the necessary cash for a *repartimiento*. The merchant's power was to extend to the political plane. For he was to nominate persons in his confidence to manage the above transactions. Only at his command were such agents to be removed from office, in the same way as the lieutenants under the old system. The Subdelegate, then, was to be strictly circumscribed by the merchant's men. As regards the profits from the trade, the Subdelegate could not extract his share until the termination of the contract, though the merchant could take out his either in whole or part at the end of each year. Both parties were to receive a third of the final profits each, and, in the meantime, the merchant undertook to pay the Subdelegate the nominal salary of 500 pesos a year, hardly more than he received under the 5 per cent levy, which, of course, he continued to exact, at 339 pesos a year. Out of the 500 pesos, the Subdelegate was expected to pay his Lieutenant-General 150 pesos a year. Nevertheless, it was not so much these nominal sums that attracted the Subdelegate, but the prospect of larger profits under the returned *repartimiento*.[3]

1 AGN *Subdelegados* 35, Mora–Revillagigedo.
2 Simón Gutiérrez de Villegas, see Glossary of Personnel.
3 AGN *Subdelegados* 35, Mora–Revillagigedo, Oaxaca, 8 March 1792, ff. 178–82.

When informed of such a contract, the Indendant of Oaxaca decided to take a course of strong remedial action, and ordered the immediate arrest of the merchant in his house in Oaxaca. However, when confronted with the charge of violating Articles 11 and 12 of the 1787 Ordinance, Gutiérrez protested that he did not know that such a contract was illegal. He requested his prompt release in order that he might take measures to dissolve it.[1]

What the Superior Government in Mexico City had to decide, in consequence, was the feasibility and political practicality of maintaining Articles 11 and 12 in full force. This was an especially complicated matter in view of Viceroy Revillagigedo's two Superior Orders of 24 November 1790, ordering strict compliance with the prohibition of *repartimientos* issued by Royal justices.[2]

The Fiscal Protector de Indios, Borbón, once more reminded his fellow ministers of the difficulty of finding Subdelegates. The interpretation of the articles of the Ordinance at issue, moreover, was complex. For, the prohibition of lieutenantships under Article 12 seemed to imply that Subdelegates were to be established in every Indian town where there had previously been lieutenants. For, they were to act as the parallel to the Alcaldes Ordinarios, who administered the Spanish towns, under Article 11.[3] The whole question of what exactly the Ministers in Spain meant by their wording of those articles fell on the Superior Government in Mexico to decide. The many ambiguities and the many poorly defined clauses of the Ordinance of Intendants prevented clear decisions from the Superior Government. Many of the ministers in Mexico were divided over interpretation, emphasis, and feasibility of various changes proposed by the Ordinance. Moreover, the reform had been legislated in Madrid, by Ministers most of whom had never visited Mexico, and who possessed no direct knowledge of conditions there. At the same time, while the ministers of the Viceroyalty of New Spain were attempting to implement the Ordinance, they were subjected to severe political pressures to dilute the force of the new system on the grounds that difficulty of interpretation of the Ordinance precluded its enactment.

Back in August 1788, the Junta Superior de Real Hacienda, faced with the insuperably difficult task of replacing the Alcaldes Mayores with Subdelegates, calculated that the average salary of the new administrators would come to only 390 pesos a year. The Junta had, as a result, requested the Crown to suspend Articles 11, 12, and 129. Fiscal Borbón took this

1 *Ibid.*   2 AGI *Mexico* 1675.
3 AGN *Subdelegados* 51, expediente sobre repartimientos.

request as his precedent. Advocating the return of lieutenantships as an administrative necessity, he joined the Junta in requesting the withdrawal of the unworkable parts of the same articles, but, in the spirit of Revilla-gigedo's two Superior Orders, on condition that no administrator should take part in a *repartimiento*.[1]

The issue of the administrative practicability of Gálvez's reform plans was complicated by another, that of the economic and financial advantages or disadvantages of maintaining the prohibition of *repartimientos*. While the Superior Government was hovering between full enforcement or suspension of various controversial articles, the Minister of the Royal Treasury in Oaxaca, Francisco Antonio Villarrasa Rivera, sent, on 22 April 1793, a detailed report entitled, 'The Decadence of the Royal Interests in the Populations of America, their Causes and Remedies', to Minister Gardoquí in Madrid.[2]

This report was a defence of the old *repartimientos*, made not by one who had enjoyed profits from the old system, but by a Royal Treasury official with a reputation for impartiality.[3] Essentially his argument rested on his view of the character of the Indians, given to idleness and drunkenness. Admittedly there had been abuses in the *repartimientos*, but now that the coercive factor had disappeared under the Subdelegations, ignorance, vice, and crime dominated the province. In contrast to the Alcalde Mayor, the Subdelegate, without his financial interests to protect, would rarely visit the Indian towns. Similarly, once the cochineal *repartimiento* had ceased, the Indians were unable to pay their tributes, and no longer received basic subsistence commodities such as seeds for the planting of maize and wheat, and meat after the slaughter.[4]

In the cotton textile town of Villa Alta, the arrival of cotton had depended on its *repartimiento* by the Alcalde Mayor, at current prices, repaid in the finished product. However, the present prohibition was bringing the industry to a standstill. Export of Indian cotton-mantles from Villa Alta, and *huipiles*, the women's cotton garment, from Teutila and Teozacualco to other provinces, such as Mexico, was in decay through lack of *avío* and the mule transportation provided under the old system.

The removal of the authority by fear exercised by the Alcaldes Mayores was resulting in serious insubordination among the indigenous population. Villarrasa's implication was that the aspirations of the reformers had dashed all proper respect for authority, and was jeopardising the successful

---

[1] *Ibid.*   [2] AGI *Mexico* 1780, *Expedientes diarios* (1796-7).
[3] Villarrasa Rivera, see Glossary of Personnel.   [4] AGI *Mexico* 1780.

operation of a system which had secured both commercial activity and the Royal revenues. Not only was the reform not working, it was expensive, and the experiments involved in trying to implement it were disastrous in view of the precarious loyalty of the indigenous population to the constituted authorities.

The cultivators of the land could sow hardly one-third of their haciendas through the Indians' refusal to offer their services as labour. As a result, the raising of cattle was being abandoned, and the incomes of the landowners lost.[1] All these disasters were breaking at a time when the Intendant system was supposed to bring good government to the Indies, ensure the full collection of Royal revenues, and stimulate greater commercial activity. No such thing had happened in Oaxaca. Instead, the province was characterised by increasing anarchy. The deputy in Teutila, for instance, had nearly been killed in a riot of the inhabitants, who had tried to burn down the Royal residence there. As a result, the deputy had remained five months in the city of Oaxaca. Similar insults had occurred in Teotitlán del Camino, Zimatlán, and Chontales. In Sola, the justice had fled in the night for fear of being killed at dawn by the Indians. In Huehuetlán, insults against the parish priests were still unpunished.[2]

The essential weakness of the new system, as all previous commentators have pointed out, was the fact that they were destitute of the means to maintain themselves. For such reasons, the temptation to supplement their incomes by abuses in the administration always lay before them. The result of the slack régime of the Subdelegates could be seen in the public squares of the Indian towns, which were monopolised by drunken idlers, who frequently resorted to violent robbery of the local inhabitants. Some towns had been totally ruined, and their population had fled into the mountains.[3]

While Villarrasa was attacking what he believed to be the consequences of the reform, Viceroy Revillagigedo was writing to the Crown defending its goals. The Viceroy's Report on Trade, sent in 1793, dealt with the whole complex of reforms initiated in the 1780s. Primarily, he was concerned to defend the 1789 incorporation of New Spain into the régime of *comercio libre* from attack by the Spanish Peninsular merchants of the Consulado of Mexico, principal beneficiaries of the old régime. Revillagigedo pointed out the obstacles to reform before their proper results

---

[1] The Alcalde Mayor of Zimatlán, adopting the *hacendados'* point of view, complained of the same problem to the Viceroy on 19 October 1785, attributing the cause to the Viceregal *Bando* of 23 March 1785, which had reiterated the Indians' freedom of labour: AGN *Intendentes* 33.   [2] AGI *Mexico* 1780.   [3] *Ibid.*

could be observed. One of the impediments was the lack of *avío* in the indigenous regions. The main reason had been the prohibition of the *repartimientos*, which the former Alcaldes Mayores had accustomed the Indians to receive. Without such an advance of basic necessities, both tools and work animals, their fields were not being cultivated. The Viceroy believed that one of the explanations why no alternative practice had arisen was the erroneous idea that all cash advanced to the Indians constituted the prohibited *repartimiento*, and that all sales had to be cash down.[1]

Moreover, the Subdelegates themselves had prevented the emergence of other practices, because they considered that the long discussions in Mexico City on the subject of the Intendant system would lead to the suspension of the prohibition. As a result, they viewed any gains made by private traders as prejudicial to their own interests. For their part, the private merchants feared that any day they would be informed of the withdrawal of the prohibition, and that, therefore, they would lose everything they had invested. In any case, the Indians rarely honoured debts they contracted, with the result that coercion was necessary to persuade them. On that point, at any rate, Viceroy Revillagigedo agreed with the most virulent opponents of the Intendancies, and implied that his view of the nature and role of the Indians was no different from that of Villarrasa Rivera.

The Viceroy explained to the Spanish Ministry that the departments of government in Mexico City had been considering a large file of documents on the Intendancies and *repartimientos* for some time. As yet, no decisions had been taken. Meanwhile, the abuses continued in the locality. Revillagigedo believed that the new system should be allowed to take root and conceded sufficient time to recover from its initial difficulties. Under no circumstances, therefore, should the new administrators indulge in *repartimientos*. They should confine their activities solely to the administration of justice. In the same spirit as his letter of 1 June 1791, Revillagigedo advocated the maintenance of the Intendancies.[2]

Within the Superior Government itself, a similar position to that of Revillagigedo was held by Borbón, the Fiscal de lo Civil. His verdict of 14 November 1793 denounced the *repartimiento* as a type of monopoly, restricting within itself the trade of the territory concerned. The argument that it had stimulated agriculture and industry was immaterial, because

---

1 Revillagigedo, 'Informe sobre el estado del comercio. de Nueva España' (31 August 1793), in AGN *Correspondencia de virreyes* (reservada) 26, f. 42 et seq.; reprinted in *Boletín del Archivo General de la Nación*, i (Nov.–Dec. 1930), and ii (Jan.–Feb. 1931).
2 *Ibid.*

according to the law, it was prohibited. So far from benefiting the Indians, as its defenders claimed, the Alcaldes Mayores derived large profits from an intrinsically evil usury, and their practices resulted in the desolation and ruin of the Indian towns.[1]

However, Borbón was succeeded in office by Alva, who took the opposite point of view in his reply of 8 September 1794. He declared that new reasons for the restoration of the former practices had arisen from the replies of the various Intendants, and from the nature of the discussions now before the Superior Government. Only two Intendants remained opposed to the suspension of the prohibition, those of Puebla and Oaxaca, which were, significantly, two principal indigenous regions. Alva centered his argument on the continued failure to provide the Subdelegates with a satisfactory income. If that could not be given, then the government should restore the *repartimiento*. Seven years of experience of the new system should have been enough to disillusion even the most determined opponent of the *repartimiento*, in proving that the Indians were not, and never would be, capable of paying cash down for anything worth more than 2 reales. Alva concluded that the Superior Government should suspend the prohibition.[2]

During these discussions, Viceroy Revillagigedo was recalled to Spain, and replaced by a Sicilian, Branciforte, brother-in-law of Spain's new chief minister, the young favourite Godoy. It was to Viceroy Branciforte that Juan Baptista de Echarri addressed his defence of the old system on 21 November 1794. Echarri described to the Viceroy how seven years of the Intendant system had produced decay in all the means of subsistence for the Realm and its indigenous population, and in trade and Royal revenues also. Much had been written on the causes. Some attributed it to the consequences of *comercio libre*, which had produced a great outflow of circulating medium from the Casa de Moneda in Mexico City. Others believed the cause to be the establishment of the Intendancies, and its prohibition of the *repartimiento*. Yet others attributed the decay to the abuses of the Alcaldes Mayores under the old system. He himself favoured the second reason, and advised Branciforte that the Fiscal de Real Hacienda and all the Intendants, except those of Oaxaca and Puebla, were in favour of the suspension of Article 12. For, instead of Indian labour sustaining the economy as it should, natural laziness and drunkenness was only encouraged by the system of Subdelegations. As a result, the cochineal

---

[1] AGI *Mexico* 1974, *Creación y expedientes de las intendencias* (1792–1804), Testimonio del expediente sobre permiso de repartimientos a los subdelegados.
[2] *Ibid.*

crop, one of Echarri's major interests under the old system, had fallen to one-third of its former level of production.[1]

Branciforte passed the whole file to the Consulado of Mexico, because of the 'connexion that the question of *repartimiento* has with commerce'. The merchant guild, heavily involved in the old system, for which its members provided the *avío*, produced its report on 24 November 1794, pointing to the obvious decline of all parts of the economy due to the prohibition, and the abolition of the Alcaldías Mayores. Added to that, there was no guarantee that justice was better administered by the Sub-delegates, who, in fact, were frequently absent from their *partidos*. The Consulado stated that the reason why no proper salaries could be given to the Subdelegates was that, 'in the present circumstances, it is impossible to attend to the remedy of these abuses, and others, that as a natural con-sequence originate from them, by the payment of a fixed salary at the cost of the Royal Treasury. The needs of war demand the allotment of as many sums as may be conceived for an object of greater importance'.

The Consulado's point was clear, the cost of war precluded the financing of reform measures. In any case, the *repartimiento* was not intrinsically evil. Moreover, the advantages of the restoration of the old system would far outweigh the abuses that might recur, if it were managed with justice and equity. The Consulado, therefore, advocated the removal of Article 12, and the permission for the administrators to organise *repartimientos*. They wanted the Subdelegates to be everything the Alcaldes Mayores had been, except in name. Since the new régime could not be paid for, the logic of the situation was to return to the old. All it required was for the Superior Government tacitly to recognise realities.[2]

The final decisions were taken by the Junta Superior de Real Hacienda. In its *acuerdo* of 28 November 1794, the Junta pointed to the permission previously given by the Crown for *repartimientos* of garments in the provinces of Puebla and Tlaxcala under equitable rules. In contrast to the present decay reported by the Intendants all over the Viceroyalty, that system had enabled the Indians both to provide for their basic needs and to honour their debts. The Junta believed that under the present circum-stances, the suspension of the prohibition to issue *repartimiento*, advocated by the Fiscal de lo Civil, should be enacted by the government. Neverthe-less, even though the full right of *repartimientos* should be awarded to the Subdelegates, the Intendants were to supervise their conduct, in their role as intermediary authorities between Viceroy and locality. In this way, the

---

[1] AGN *Subdelegados* 51.   [2] AGI *Mexico* 1974.

Junta sought a compromise between the old system and the new. It sought to maintain the authority of the Intendants, while at the same time providing the Subdelegates, whom the Royal Treasury could not afford to pay a salary, with an additional means of livelihood. Under no circumstances was the decision of the Junta a capitulation to the parties involved in the old system. For, the government in Mexico City was determined that no *repartimientos* organised by the Royal Subdelegates should become an excuse for maintaining a commercial monopoly in the *partidos*. The Junta specifically stated that rigorous prohibition was to continue on forced and illicit *repartimientos*. Only the voluntary reception of it by the Indians was permitted, and then on condition that the full trading rights of private merchants were not interfered with.[1]

The Junta recommended the Viceroy to issue a *Bando* declaring the end of the 5 per cent levy from the tributes and an end to the file on the payment of the Subdelegates. Those officials should henceforth be allowed to appoint lieutenants in the same way as the Alcaldes Mayores. Finally, the Junta advised the Viceroy that Article 306 of the Ordinance of Intendants conceded him the faculty of dispensing with any clauses of the Ordinance that should prove 'unworkable' or 'detrimental', and that this was the case in respect to Articles 11 and 12. The faculty, therefore, should be exercised. He was reminded also of the *Real Orden* of 13 May 1791, which conceded him the right to resolve issues in dispute in New Spain on his own authority.[2]

The decision of the Junta Superior de Real Hacienda led some of the Subdelegates to believe that they had been entirely absolved from the spirit of Articles 12 and 61, and that they had been given full authorisation to return to the old practices of commercial monopolies. Several administrators interfered with both the right of private merchants to enter the Indian towns, and with the right of the Indians to trade freely with them.

Under the Superior Order of 5 August 1794, the new Alcalde Mayor of the Cuatro Villas del Marquesado, Adrián de Cerain, a former Corregidor of Toluca, was arraigned by the Superior Government for his violations of Article 12.[3] In 1796, proceedings were begun against the Subdelegate of Villa Alta, Ruiz de Conejares.[4] On 19 September 1797, one of the parish priests of the Valley of Oaxaca, Paz y Mendoza, denounced the illicit character of the *repartimientos* of the Subdelegates of

---

[1] *Ibid.*   [2] *Ibid.*
[3] AGN *Subdelegados* 51. For Adrián de Cerain, see Glossary of Personnel.
[4] *Ibid.*

Oaxaca, and warned the Superior Government of the violence done against the Indians. Especially, he singled out the Subdelegate of Teutila for condemnation.[1]

The Intendant of Oaxaca himself reported to the Superior Government in Mexico on 24 April 1798 that, 'all the Subdelegates of the Intendancy of Oaxaca were behaving with a licence and abandon that perhaps could not even be compared with former abuses, when the Alcaldes Mayores, without restraints to contain their cupidity, attempted to enrich themselves by the most reprehensible means'.

Mora lamented that the most beneficent intentions of the Crown were greeted with disdain in Oaxaca. Illicit *repartimientos* were conducted openly, as if permitted by law. Indian towns were molested, and merchants hindered. All principal authorities, Administrators of *Alcabalas*, parish priests, and loyal vassals would testify to the beating of Indian debtors, and even their sale to the haciendas in the areas where the Subdelegates conducted *repartimientos* of oxen, mules, cotton, and cash for the cochineal dye. The flight of Indians to the hills was jeopardising Royal revenues, and spreading misery among Indian families.[2]

Mora's legal deputy, the *teniente letrado*, Izquierdo,[3] was at that time dealing with a complaint from the Indian village of Osolotepec, in Miahuatlán, that their Subdelegate, Fausto de Corres,[4] a principal beneficiary of the old régime, was oppressing them with his *repartimientos*. The Intendant summoned Corres to the city of Oaxaca to appear before him, on one of those occasions when he would be there for his business transactions. Mora admonished him, and told him not to violate the law again. There was little else the Intendant could do. For, if he had ordered the arrest of Corres, someone else would have to be found to be Subdelegate of Miahuatlán. All these proceedings were then forwarded to Mexico City, where they were attached to those concerning the Cuatro Villas and Villa Alta.[5]

At the same time the Council of the Indies was discussing the report from the parish priest of the Valley of Oaxaca. The Spanish Ministry opposed the unilateral suspension of the prohibition of the *repartimiento* by the Junta Superior de Real Hacienda in 1794, and sought to convince Mexico City to return to the purity of Article 12. A note of the Council

---

1 AGI *Mexico* 1890, *Expedientes é instancias de parte* (1800–01), Expediente sobre quejas dadas por el cura de la parroquia del Valle de Oaxaca, D. Josef Vicente María de Paz y Mendoza, acerca de los injustos repartimientos que hacen a los indios los subdelegados de aquella parroquia.   2 AGN *Subdelegados* 51.
3 Izquierdo, see Glossary of Personnel.   4 Fausto de Corres, *ibid.*
5 AGN *Subdelegados* 51.

on 5 June 1798 stated that one of the principal reasons for the introduction of Intendancies in New Spain had been precisely to root out the Alcaldes Mayores' *repartimientos*. Therefore, the Council decided to send the parish priest's letter to Viceroy Azanza of New Spain for his comments.[1]

Azanza replied on 27 July 1799 that he lacked the authority to pronounce on the question until the Crown had received Viceroy Branciforte's statement after his return to Spain, and could then instruct him what to do. He explained that he based his conduct on the *Real Cédula* (*reservada*) of 13 May 1791, which had ordered the Viceroy to proceed with prudence and a certain tolerance. As a result, he had taken no new measures in general cases, because already there existed enough files of documents on the subject. In particular cases, however, Azanza stated he would ensure that the abuses were remedied. For its part, the Council of the Indies in Feburary 1800 reiterated its desire to extirpate the *repartimiento*, and discussed Azanza's reply in detail in March. Most seriously, the Council complained that it was still awaiting the decision of the Crown. Until that verdict arrived, the Council declared it could have no use for Azanza's letter. The Ministers, therefore, returned it to him in Mexico.[2]

In Mexico City, the Fiscal Protector de Indios, Sagarzurrieta, announced on 21 June 1800, that, despite all the discussion on the question, nothing at all could be decided on the *repartimiento* until former Viceroy Branciforte had returned to Spain, and reported to the Crown and Council. In the meantime, the Fiscal pointed to the administrative confusion within the Superior Government. For, neither the case of Villa Alta nor that of Miahuatlán had been included, when they should have been, in the general file on the *repartimientos*. Moreover, the case of the Cuatro Villas had been included, though in such a confused manner that the order of the files had been mixed up. In addition, the two important Superior Orders of Revillagigedo, issued on 24 November 1790, had been but scantily distributed. Despite all the misunderstandings, the Superior Government had not changed its policies since the Revillagigedo period, not even under Branciforte, notwithstanding the decision of the Junta Superior de Real Hacienda in 1794. The Fiscal demanded that this decision should be revoked. In short, he maintained that Article 12 still stood in its full force. Therefore, the three recalcitrant Subdelegates of Cuatro Villas, Miahuatlán, and Villa Alta should be punished for the pernicious example they had set.[3]

---

[1] AGI *Mexico* 1890, *Expedientes é instancias de parte.*
[2] *Ibid.*   [3] AGN *Subdelegados* 51.

In the midst of its discussions, the Superior Government received complaints from private merchants who had been attempting to take advantage of the provisions of the 1786 Ordinance to pursue their commercial activities in the *partidos*. These were exactly the men Gálvez had hoped to benefit by his reforms, and Revillagigedo by his defence of the Intendancies. One Mexico City merchant, Manuel Urquijo, complained that the Subdelegate of Miahuatlán and his agents were hindering the freedom of commerce he had previously enjoyed. His dye trade with the Indians was in danger, because the Subdelegate, who was his trading competitor in the *partido*, had threatened Indians who traded with him.[1]

Similar complaints came from Tehuantepec. Captain Cantolla of the Oaxaca Provincial Militia denounced the activities of the Subdelegate and his dependents, who for the last two years were impeding his trade with the cochineal-producing towns. Cantolla's trading interests extended through Tehuantepec to Chontales, Nejapa, Villa Alta, and Teotitlán del Valle, but the Subdelegate of Tehuantepec was determined to block him out, and set up a monopoly there. Azanza responded with the Superior Order of 2 October 1798, ordering the Subdelegate to conform to the law and allow the free trading activities of private merchants.[2] Another Superior Order, issued on 9 March 1801, repeated the prohibition of *repartimientos* in the case of Villa Alta, where the Subdelegate had sent debt-collecting missions to the Indian towns, and had issued a cochineal *repartimiento* at the low rate of 10 reales per pound.[3] The Fiscal de lo Civil once more pointed out that the prohibition of *repartimientos* had not been derogated. The Viceroy responded with yet another Superior Order, on 16 August 1800, ordering all previous ones to be obeyed. However, this apparent strictness was followed by a compromise in the interests of the Subdelegate. Fiscal Borbón stated that the maintenance of the prohibition by no means implied that debt obligations had in any way been removed.[4]

The Fiscal Protector also received similar complaints from the mer-

---

1 AGN *General de parte* 76, and AGN *Tierras* 1264, exp. 11.
2 AGN *General de parte* 77 (1798–1800).
3 AGN *General de parte* 78 (1801–4). The current price of cochineal in the city of Oaxaca was 18 reales per pound. Cash for the cotton mantles had been issued at the rate of 8 reales each, when the market price was currently at between 12 and 13 reales.
4 *Ibid*. The product of the *repartimiento* had, in any case, already been guaranteed by the Mexico City merchant, Pedro González Noriega (see Glossary of Personnel), regarded as trustworthy in financial transactions by Fiscal Borbón. The Fiscal also emphasised the Subdelegate's good character and worthy conduct in his present post, justifying the confidence shown in him by his *fiadores* and by the Pious Works that acted as his creditors for the *repartimiento*.

chants trading in Jicayan against the Subdelegate, who had offered them a contract for the joint exploitation of the resources of the region. They had declined to accept, with the result that he had threatened them, and had attempted to persuade the Governors of the Indian towns to exclude them from the cochineal trade. As a result of the Subdelegate's *repartimientos*, the Indians had been unable to pay their debts to the merchants. In 1797, they calculated they had lost 11,000 pesos, and they feared the same for the following year, because, as a preliminary to his trading operations, the Subdelegate had already leased the chief lieutenantships. The merchants explained that there was no shortage of persons anxious to participate in the lucrative trades of Jicayan, but their activity depended entirely upon the full enforcement of Article 12 of the Ordinance of 1786.[1]

Alva, the Fiscal de Real Hacienda, on 18 February 1801, was reluctant to advocate any course of action concerning the removal of recalcitrant Subdelegates, even though the issue of the *repartimiento* was most serious of all in Oaxaca, where the policies of the Superior Government were still openly being defied. He favoured Azanza's position. Nothing should be done until Branciforte had reported to the Council of the Indies. Viceroy Marquina agreed with that view.[2]

While the Superior Government in Mexico was arguing itself into a policy of no action, Branciforte gave his report to the Council of the Indies, on 18 May 1800. He took the position of the opponents of the reform. He attacked the prohibition of the *repartimiento* as the cause of the decline of livestock, and the loss of Royal revenues. The decay of agricultural production was resulting in rising food prices and shortage. Mine-operators faced a crisis of labour and animals, and it was proving impossible to transport maize to the mining settlements to feed the workers. Some owners had even been forced to suspend operations, with the result that the Crown was losing its income from the Royal Quint. The shortage of mule transport was hindering the despatch of exports to Veracruz and Acapulco. In such a situation of declining revenues, the Subdelegates were expected to live off the 5 per cent levy. Branciforte concluded that they should be allowed the right to *repartimiento* as an immediate priority, and that the 5 per cent provision should be derogated along with the entire provisions of Article 12. Nor would such a derogation be very exceptional, he inferred. For, already many clauses of the Ordinance had been suspended, because they had proved to be what he called 'prejudicial'.

[1] AGN *Subdelegados* 51.   [2] *Ibid.*

With the removal of Article 12, the Crown would no longer have any difficulty finding men to be Subdelegates.[1]

The Council of the Indies, however, did not agree with Branciforte's interpretation of the situation. That body had begun its final discussion of the reform of the Intendancies under the *Real Orden* of 27 March 1802. A committee of reform had been set up under the presidency of Jorge Escobedo, recent Visitor-General of Peru, a firm protagonist of the Intendancies, and a product of the school of Gálvez.[2]

Escobedo singled out for condemnation the self-interest of those who attacked the Intendant system and its reform programme. Under his influence, the Council and the *Contaduría General* declared that the work of Gálvez should continue, and that his reforms should be extended, starting firstly with the proper payment of the Subdelegates.[3]

The result of the Council's committee was the New Ordinance of Intendants, made public on 23 September 1803. Under this revised ordinance the suppression of the Alcaldías Mayores and Corregimientos was reaffirmed, and Article 54 severely prohibited the *repartimiento*. No Subdelegate, legal deputy, Intendant, Royal official of any kind, minister of religion, hacendado, mine-owner, or *obraje*-owner, was permitted to trade in any commodity whatsoever. Instead, the Subdelegates would receive salaries varying between 2,200 pesos and 1,500 pesos per year, depending upon the importance of their area.[4]

This new measure, however, never came into effect. For, on 11 January 1804, the Crown suddenly ordered its suspension. The motive was criticism of it by the military chiefs of the Royal Artillery and Engineers' Corps, who believed that the cost of the enactment of the reformed Ordinance would prejudice recent legislation in their favour. The Council of the Indies protested against this suspension, on 4 May and 13 July, emphasising the urgency of the reform. As a concession to the Council, the Crown evolved a compromise by which the financial clauses of the

---

1 AGI *Mexico* 1675.
2 Escobedo had been born in Jaén, descended from the Condes de Cazalla. In 1752, he had entered the Colegio Mayor of Cuenca to study civil and canonical jurisprudence, history, and fine arts. From there he went to the University of Salamanca. In 1776, he became Oidor of the Audiencia of Charcas, and then Political and Military Governor of Potosí, and Superintendent of its Casa de Moneda, Banco de Minas, and Cajas Reales. After the Tupac Amaru rebellion, he rose to the rank of Oidor of the Audiencia of Lima. In 1782, he was appointed to complete Areche's general visitation of the tribunals of justice and Royal finance of the Viceroyalties of Peru and Río de la Plata. See C. Deustua Pimental, *Las intendencias en el Perú, 1790–1796* (Seville 1965), 4.
3 Luis Navarro García, *Intendencias en Indias* (Seville 1959), 129–31.
4 AGI *Indiferente general* 666.

new ordinance were to be effected, while everything else remained suspended.[1]

That was all the Council could salvage. In consequence, in the Indies the issue of the maintenance of Articles 11 and 12 still remained equivocal. The Council's struggle for reform had been dashed by the Crown's need to compromise with a small group of military chiefs in Spain. The conduct of Charles IV, throughout the discussions, indicated an ignorance of the issues involved, and a clear failure to back up the reform strongly enough with the full force of the Royal authority. Given the weak personality of the King, a programme of reform could not be adopted and enforced, no matter how much the Council of the Indies wanted it and considered it vital for the interests of the Crown.

[1] AGI *Indiferente general* 1713.

CHAPTER 6

FINANCE, TRADE, AND THE MERCHANTS, 1789-1808

One of the principal objectives of the *comercio libre* legislation of 1789 had been to release Spain's trade with New Spain from the traditional control of the Consulados of Cádiz and Mexico.[1] The generation of Gálvez believed such monopolies to be a hindrance to the expansion of trade. Into that context fall the efforts of the Metropolitan Government, Viceroy Revillagigedo, and Intendants Flon of Puebla and Mora of Oaxaca to secure the full prohibition of the *repartimientos* issued by the Alcaldes Mayores. For they had been financed by Mexico City merchants or their local associates. That system had, thus, enabled the Mexico merchants to maintain trade monopolies within several of the jurisdictions containing large indigenous elements.

The aim of the 1786 Ordinance had been to prevent the offering of *avío* by the Mexico merchants to the local justices. As this measure coincided with the issue of the 1789 *comercio libre* reform, the Spanish Government hoped that a new generation of smaller-scale, but more enterprising and efficient merchants would compete alongside, and eventually replace, the old merchants of the Consulado of Mexico.

We have seen how, realising the imminent end of the Alcaldías Mayores, several investors, in particular, Juan Baptista de Echarri, attempted to cut their losses by withdrawing their investments from the *repartimiento*. Nevertheless, the whole complexity of the discussion on the interpretation of Article 12 of the Ordinance of 1786 enabled elements of the old system to creep back during the middle of the 1790s in Oaxaca. However, despite the opposition to the reforms of 1786 and 1789 by the Mexico merchants and their local associates in Oaxaca, those enactments were never, in their entirety, reversed by the Crown. In consequence, several effects of the new system could be detected in formation alongside the old. Catalonia, for example, was experiencing the zenith of her industrial expansion in the period, 1786–96, and, now that the Principality

[1] For details of the whole body of legislation concerning *comercio libre*, see R. Antúñez y Acevedo, *Memorias históricas sobre la legislación y gobierno del comercio de los españoles con sus colonias en las Indias occidentales* (Madrid 1797), article 1, 36–8, and article 4, 111.

had at last been allowed to trade directly with the Indies, the Barcelona merchants were interested in both the dyes of Oaxaca and Guatemala and the cotton produced in the Gulf coast regions of Veracruz and north Oaxaca.[1]

The benefits of the new commercial legislation were slow to come. Like the Subdelegate of Villa Alta, the Intendant of Veracruz, Pedro Corbalán, in February 1790, lamented to Viceroy Revillagigedo the passing of the old 'indispensable system' of *repartimientos*. He complained of the irreparable harm and disruption of local production that was resulting from the 1786 legislation. As a consequence, he explained his incapacity to fulfil his proper functions as Intendant under Articles 62, 63, and 64 for the stimulation of the economy. He requested the reconstitution of the Subdelegates on the lines of the former Alcaldes Mayores.[2]

Corbalán's view, however, was very superficial. For the problem was not so much the unworkability of the new system, but the endemic and unsolved problem within the localities themselves. For the administrators and their *aviadores* would attempt to eliminate their competitors. Back in 1783, for instance, the Alcalde Mayor of Teutila had arrested two merchants from Tlacotalpan, in the Veracruz coastal region, not of the Mexico Consulado, and had confiscated their crops, despite their protests of exemption from his jurisdiction on grounds of their enjoyment of the *fuero militar*.[3] The Crown's response to that action had been the *Reales Órdenes* of 25 December 1783 and of 19 April 1785, reaffirming full observation of liberty of trade within the Alcaldías Mayores.[4]

Obviously another series of *Reales Órdenes* was inadequate, and out of this frustration of policy failure came the reforms of 1786 and 1789. What Corbalán failed to observe was that even as early as 1790 changes were already taking place. For, while the remaining Alcaldes Mayores might still illegally attempt to impede the free access of other merchants, several freelancers, some of whom were Catalans looking for materials for Barcelona's textile factories, would travel in canoes up the Alvarado River, in order to sell their wares directly to the Indian cultivators. From

---

[1] For the industrial development of Catalonia in the eighteenth century see Pierre Vilar, *La Catalogne dans l'Espagne moderne* (Paris 1962). Reference to the interest of Catalan traders in Mexican products is made in tome II, 123, 128–9, 137–8, 447–51, 532–3, 554–5.

[2] AGI *Mexico* 1974, *Creación y expedientes de las intendencias* (1792–1804), Testimonio del expediente formado en virtud del orden Circular del 16 de dic. de 1789 para que los intendentes informen sobre los repartimientos que prohibe el art. 12 de la R.O. del 4 de dic. de 1786.

[3] AGN *General de parte* 68, f. 40, Lyle N. Mc Alister, *The 'Fuero Militar' in New Spain, 1764–1800* (Univ. of Florida, Gainesville 1957) discusses the full implications of this privilege. [4] AGN *General de parte* 68, f. 40.

the cotton-growers of Huaspaltepec, in the Intendancy of Veracruz, who were, in fact, Indians from Latani and Choapan in the *partido* of Villa Alta, they secured what supplies were available without the intervention of the local administrator.[1]

Such developments were only tentative as yet. In the meantime, the citizens and merchants of the chief cotton-growing town of the Gulf region, San Martín Cosamaluapan, pathetically regretted the passing of the old system. They explained to Viceroy Revillagigedo, in July 1791, that the former traders had provided the capital and supplies necessary for the cultivation of cotton by the local mulatto populace. These used to pay their *avidores* in the final crop, at an interest rate of 25 per cent, it was true, but, at least they had secured a sale for their unique product, upon which their livelihood totally depended. Now that the *avío* was no longer forth-coming, they were faced with the grim prospect of having to leave their families and their lands, in order to earn their living as day-labourers. Such an occupation would only pay them a sum of 3 reales per day, and, in any case, none of the misery which faced them on their return would be alleviated. The petitioners did not see why the local populace was now no longer permitted to receive *avío*, when the *hacendados* who grew tobacco for the Royal Tobacco Monopoly received it from the Royal Treasury.[2]

The changes were becoming more evident as the decade progressed. For, in 1793, in his *Report on the State of the Trade of New Spain*, Viceroy Revillagigedo explained to the Metropolitan Government that the merchants of the Consulado of Mexico felt themselves seriously threatened by the legislation including New Spain under the régime of *comercio libre*. In fact, he reported, there were only two merchants of the Consulado who were in favour of the new system. The Viceroy said: 'The old style merchants who had been wise, as soon as they saw the change in system of trade coming, and that they could no longer derive from it a large interest from their capital, as they had done previously without risks, cares, or necessity for mutual co-operation, have pulled out their capital in time. They have reinvested it in agriculture, or revenues on lease, and, in part, also in mining. Trade was left to new speculators with less capital, but with greater ability in the new ways of mercantile conduct, and less used to excessive profits with a perfect security and calm.'

These newer merchants were, of course, anxious to earn an income beyond their mere subsistence, but did not, as the monopoly merchants

---

[1] AGN *Intendentes* 23.   [2] AGI *Mexico* 1974.

of the Consulado of Mexico had, aspire to found entailed estates (*mayorazgos*), and thereby enter the ranks of the titled Castilian nobility. The Viceroy considered that such a redeployment of capital into the Realm's backward agriculture, and into its all-important mining industry, was a wholly beneficial occurrence. Moreover, instead of Mexico City, the new commercial centre had now become Veracruz. At the same time, the increased competition resulting from the liberalization of the trade between the Peninsula and New Spain had brought about a fall in price of imports, and the lessening of freight, insurance, and commisssion costs. There was now a greater subdivision of capital ownership, with a larger group of persons owning capital to the moderate extent of between 20,000 and 30,000 pesos, instead of the great few, the old merchants of the Consulado of Mexico, who had enjoyed sufficient surplus capital to found convents and colleges.[1] In his desire for the fuller liberalization of the trade between the two Spains, Viceroy Revillagigedo went so far as to advocate the total suppression by the Crown of the Consulado of Mexico, or else the dispersal of its consular authority throughout the chief towns of the Viceroyalty.[2]

The institutional corollary of the reform of 1789 was the incorporation of the Consulado of Veracruz under the *Real Cédula* of 17 January 1795.[3] In this way, the Crown hoped to give the new merchants a permanent footing within the Viceroyalty, and to show the Mexico merchants that their services were not indispensible.

The first stages of the process of the constitution of the Veracruz Consulado had taken place in November 1789, when Revillagigedo sent to the Council of the Indies the petition of the Veracruz merchants for their incorporation as a Consulado.[4]

Throughout the 1790s and 1800s the Consulado of Mexico challenged the very existence of the Consulados of Veracruz and Guadalajara, beginning with its protest of 28 April 1794 at the impending establishment.[5]

---

[1] Viceroy Revillagigedo, 'Informe sobre el estado del comercio de Nueva España' (31 August 1793), in AGN *Correspondencia de virreyes* (reservada) 26, f. 42 *et seq.*; reprinted in *Boletín del Archivo General de la Nación*, i (Nov.–Dec. 1930), and ii (Jan.–Feb. 1931).
[2] Viceroy Revillagigedo, 'Instrucción reservada', in *Instrucciones que los virreyes de Nueva España dejaron a sus sucesores* (2 vols.; Mexico 1867–73) ii, 463.
[3] The *Real Cédula* is contained in AGI *Mexico* 2506, *Expedientes del consulado y comercio*.
[4] *Ibid.* Revillagigedo, carta reservada no. 10.
[5] *Ibid.* See also AGI *Mexico* 1818, *Expedientes inventariados* (1808): Expediente sobre la extinción de los consulados de Veracruz y Guadalajara, beginning with no. 336 (reservada), Branciforte–Godoy, 26 Sept. 1796, in which the Viceroy, in complete contrast to his

Finance, trade and merchants

The *Reales Órdenes* of 1795 explained that the protection and development of trade were the principal charges of the new institution. It was commissioned to attend to the advancement of agriculture, the improvement of methods of cultivation, the introduction of machinery and new implements, the greater extension of the area under cultivation, and the construction of good highways, namely that to Jalapa to connect Veracruz with Mexico City. In order to further the development of the Gulf coast cotton zone and its populace, the Crown placed under the Consulado's jurisdiction the five towns of Tlacotalpan, Alvarado, Medellín, Boca del Río, and Tlalixcoyan.[1]

The *Junta de Gobierno* of the new Consulado took its task seriously, and in its annual reports continually emphasised the importance of the mercantile profession and of the effective exploitation of agricultural lands as factors contributing to the prosperity of the Realm. In the first Junta, the new Consulado's Secretary, Vicente Basadre, denounced the elements in New Spain's society who poured disdain on physical labour and professional activity. 'Unfortunately for our nation, it consists of many men, who, basing the honour of nobility in birth, despise all manner of labour, no matter how useful and beneficial it may be. They consider incompatible with their pride and vanity anything that does not involve the girding on of a sword or dressing up in a robe.'[2]

In his *Discourse on the State of Commerce of Veracruz*, in January 1798, the subsequent Secretary, Juan Donato de Austria, complained of the detrimental effects of the war against Great Britain on the trade and interests of the Veracruz merchants. The paralysis of trade, he argued, was rendering impotent the attempts of the Consulado to bring the area under its jurisdiction on to a productive basis. The populace of the five towns, small in number as it was, still lived dispersed in miserable huts, abandoned to their lot, with only a bare subsistence from fishing and small plantations. Due to the war, the Consulado could still only speak of hopes rather than achievements.[3] Nevertheless, despite the lack of capital and an adequate labour force, the cultivation of the local cotton had increased over the last twenty years due to the inclusion of New Spain into the system of *comercio libre*.[4] Merchants of Veracruz were beginning to take

predecessor, states that there is need for only one Consulado in New Spain, that of Mexico City.
1 AGI *Mexico* 2506, articles 22–30; see also AGI *Mexico* 1144, *Consultas, decretos y reales órdenes* (1807–10), no. 9, consejo de Indias, pleno de 3 salas, 2 March 1808.
2 AGI *Mexico* 2507.   3 AGI *Mexico* 2508, 'Noticias político-económicas'.
4 *Ibid.* 'Noticias político-mercantiles (May 1798). In 1787, 1788, 1789, and 1790, the annual average export to Spain was 20,942 arrobas in contrast to the meagre 773 arrobas exported

99

an interest in the export of this cotton to Spain, where the ultimate destination would be the Catalan cotton textile industry. The merchants were beginning to make contracts with the producers, acting as their *aviadores*, in what must have been a freer, more congenial form of *repartimiento*, but without any intervention of the local administrator. The area of cultivation was being extended, but the chief reason was not so much the Spanish trade, but the increasing demand of the textile *obrajes* within New Spain itself, stimulated into a revival because of the war blockade.[1] Moreover, the main area of supply for the *obrajes* had traditionally been the region of the '*Mar del Sur*', the Pacific coastal territory of Oaxaca, namely Jicayan, which had under the old system of *repartimientos* received its *avío* from merchants of the Consulado of Mexico.[2]

On 26 November 1798, Viceroy Azanza reported to Francisco de Saavedra, Minister of Finance for the Indies, that New Spain's trade with the Metropolis had almost ceased. For only some small blockade runners had managed to slip the British fleet's effective vigilance. In consequence, textiles were in great shortage and at excessive prices. The merchants were complaining of the absolute inactivity. Over 8,000 zurrones of cochineal, and large amounts of Guatemalan indigo and Mexican sugar, were locked in Veracruz warehouses. The problem of contraband off the

on the last of the fleets in 1778: Baron Alexander von Humboldt, *Essai politique sur le royaume de la Nouvelle Espagne* (5 vols.; Paris 1811), iv, ch. 12, bk. 5, 439, Exportation de la Nouvelle-Espagne par la Vera-Cruz du temps des flottes et à l'époque du commerce libre. Humboldt gives the 1778 figure as 173 arrobas. M. Lerdo de Tejada, *Comercio exterior de México* (Mexico 1853), a more reliable source, gives 773, (Numero 10).

[1] Of the total estimated Gulf zone production in 1797, i.e. 896,000 arrobas, only the very small amount of 12,216 arrobas was exported to Spain, while 883,784 remained within New Spain to be consumed in the *obrajes*. See AGI *Mexico* 2508, where Gulf zone figures are given as:

	tercios
Acayucan & Paso de S. Juan	36,000
S. Andrés & Santiago Tuxtla	30,000
Cosamaluapan	20,000
Tlalixcoyan, Antigua, Río de Cotasta, & Medellín	20,000
Teutila (Oaxaca)	12,000
Tesechuacan & Huaspala	10,000

The total of 128,000 tercios of 7 arrobas represented a final figure of 896,000 arrobas. This, however, was the weight of unseeded cotton. As there were at this time no cotton gins at the areas of production, the whole bulk weight had to be transported at enormous cost and inconvenience to its place of manufacture to be unseeded. The total effective cotton was found to be 294,594½ arrobas.

These figures do not, of course, include the amount produced on the Pacific coast, for which the Consulado had no information.

[2] See Chapter 2.

Gulf coast was practically irremediable, because of its enormous profits.[1]

To escape such difficulties, the Crown conceded the Spanish merchants the right to sail from neutral ports and in neutral ships, and allowed friendly neutrals, principally the United States, to trade with the Spanish Indies. These concessions were issued under the *Real Orden* of 18 November 1797.[2]

In 1796, the Consulado of Veracruz began to record the export figures of the basic products leaving the port. In that year, the total amount of cochineal exported reached 152,800 arrobas, valued at 439,609 pesos, but, in the following year, due to the effects of the war, it had fallen to a disastrous level of only 20,950 arrobas, valued at 54,471 pesos. The effects of the neutral concessions were that for 1798 and 1799, the export figures spiralled to 305,500 arrobas, valued at 804,903 pesos, and 1,015,050 arrobas, valued at 2,703,471 pesos, respectively.[3] Most of the cochineal thus released would have proceeded by way of Havana, which through the neutral concessions was to become the prosperous entrepôt for British and North American cargoes *en route* for the Spanish Indies, replacing Jamaica's role enjoyed in the Free Port trade.[4] On 6 February 1799, the *Contaduría Principal de Ejército* in Havana produced a report after several merchants of the port had requested permission to export in neutral ships various quantities of cochineal and indigo that had come to Havana from Veracruz, Honduras, and Cartagena. They wished to export them to various foreign colonial ports.[5]

The importance to the cochineal trade of the concession to neutrals was emphasized by the Secretary of the Consulado of Veracruz in his report to the Viceroy on the state of trade of the port for the year 1799. The neutral trade, he claimed, had enabled the export of a large amount of the precious products previously confined to storage in the Veracruz warehouses, and their price had now risen to the height they now maintained. Cochineal enjoyed a higher price than during peace-time, and

---

1 AGI *Indiferente general* 2466. Viceroy Azanza's notice of English forces in Mexican waters, sent to Cayetano Soler in Madrid, no. 803, 27 February 1800, may be found in AGI *Indiferente General* 2467.
2 See Archivo Histórico de Hacienda (AHH) (AGN), *Colección de documentos publicados bajo la dirección de J. Silva Herzog*, i, 'La libertad del comercio en la segunda década del siglo XIX' (Mexico 1943), 6–8.
3 For these figures, see Lerdo de Tejada, *Comercio exterior de México*.
4 See Archivo Histórico de Hacienda, *Herzog*, 7–8, 17–18. Also Harry Bernstein, *The Origins of the Inter-American Interest, 1700–1812* (New York 1965), 15–51, and Armytage, *The Free Port System*.
5 BN MSS 1407, ff. 49–54.

now 40,602 arrobas had been exported to Spain, and a further 5,586 arrobas to other parts of Spanish America.[1]

The neutral concessions, however, brought into New Spain a large quantity of British manufactures, carried on United States' ships. The Consulado of Veracruz complained of the resulting drain of bullion, and, fearing the loss of its Indies trade to neutrals who were merely masks for British economic penetration, the Crown, under the *Real Orden* of 20 April 1799, repealed the concessions.[2]

Nevertheless, the British blockade continued. The problem of how to transport the precious dyes to their markets remained. In December 1799, the *Diputación del Comercio* of the city of Oaxaca wrote to Viceroy Azanza requesting that the dyes should be conducted to Spain on warships, which were also to transport 8 million pesos' worth of bullion. This request was granted. However, no one could ascertain when the warships would be able to leave Veracruz. Therefore, a further request was made on 25 February 1800 to the Minister, Cayetano Soler, in Madrid. The Oaxaca merchants emphasised the importance of the cochineal dye for the export trade of New Spain, stating that there was a great demand for it in the manufacturing industries of Europe. Because of the blockade, however, the product faced the danger of destruction through lack of export, which created a crisis that was reverberating downwards to the level of the Indian *nopaleras*. For, owing to its delicacy, the cochineal could not be left on the *nopales*, because of danger from other insects. Unless, then, extraction were guaranteed, production would yield diminishing returns on investment in what was traditionally a heavily capitalized industry, especially in its initial outlays. Moreover, the product could not be stored by the Indian producers, because their poverty precluded provision of adequate facilities. Therefore, if export ceased, a flight of capital could be expected from an unprofitable crop, and the producers would be forced to sell at the lowest prices. They would, in consequence, view with aversion a product in no way inferior to the richest products of Asia, which so much called the attention of the European nations. The only method of saving the crop was by its export on Royal warships.[3]

However, Tomás Murphí,[4] one of the most influential of the merchants of the Consulado of Veracruz, did not view this recourse of the

---

[1] AGI *Mexico* 2509, Juan Donato de Austria, 25 February 1800, Noticias y reflexiones político-mercantiles.
[2] AGI *Mexico* 2508, Consulado–Soler, 28 February 1799. Also AHH (AGN), *Herzog*, 7–8, 17–18.
[3] AGI *Mexico* 2509.   [4] Tomas Murphí, see Glossary of Personnel.

Oaxaca merchants with sympathy. For, he said, so far from the price of cochineal falling as the merchants feared, in the past year its price had been higher than ever, varying between 18 pesos per arroba for the lowest quality (*polvo de grana*), and 80 pesos for the highest (*grana fina*). The amount of cochineal exported in 1799 had been considerable, a fact that could not be denied. As a result, he could see no other motive for the request of the Oaxaca merchants than partisanship in the struggle in which the Consulado of Veracruz was engaged with that of Mexico, and he stated that 'the recourse of the Deputies of Commerce in Oaxaca should be attributed to the influence that the merchants of Mexico City enjoy among them, rivals of those of Veracruz'.[1]

Nevertheless, the Crown ordered compliance with the Oaxaca merchants' request in the *Real Orden* of 12 October 1801.[2]

The whole issue between the two Consulados, with that of Mexico still questioning the usefulness of that of Veracruz, dragged on through the 1800s. The Council of the Indies in 1808 traced the course of the dispute, and discussed the opposing arguments. The final decision to maintain the rights of the Consulado of Veracruz was made on 2 April 1808, two weeks after the Motín de Aranjuez had overthrown the régime of Godoy.[3]

The competition between the Mexico and the Veracruz merchants was evident in the Oaxaca trades. Under the traditional system of *repartimientos* the merchants in Mexico City would frequently supply their associates in Oaxaca with *avío*. The purpose was the financing of the *repartimiento* either by an Alcalde Mayor connected with the local merchant, or by the merchant himself, independently or in association with the administrator. The cash issued to the Indians would be repaid in the final product and in tributes such as the cotton mantles of Villa Alta. These commodities would then be sent by the Oaxaca merchants or the Alcalde Mayor, either to Mexico City, or to the port of Veracruz credited to the account of the *aviador*. The Mexico City merchant then would pay his associate in Oaxaca by paying into the Royal Treasury General in Mexico City the sums due to the Crown from the revenues of the locality in which the *repartimiento* had been issued. The local treasury in the city of Oaxaca would then reimburse the Oaxaca merchant to the same amount. It would be this reimbursement in cash from the Oaxaca Royal Treasury that would perform the function of *avío* nominally issued to the Oaxaca

[1] AGI *Mexico* 2509.   [2] *Ibid.*   [3] AGI *Mexico* 1144 and 1818.

merchant by his Mexico City *aviador*, but, in effect, merely debited to his account. In this way, money was not transported across country, where it would be exposed to numerous transportation delays and security hazards. The financial relations between the merchants of Mexico City and those of Oaxaca operated, then, on the basis of bills of payment, *libranzas*. The system functioned smoothly due to the intermediary role of the Royal Treasuries of Mexico City and Oaxaca. That is, the revenues of the Crown in New Spain were inextricably bound to revenues and profits of private merchants.[1]

When the Intendant system came into operation, this traditional system was naturally jeopardised. For, the old guarantees of local commercial monopolies and agreements with the Alcaldes Mayores were no longer as certain as before. The entry of New Spain into the régime of *comercio libre*, moreover, further threatened the old relationships by introducing a potential new group of competing merchants, generally based in Veracruz.

The evidence of the accounts of the Principal Treasury of the city of Oaxaca indicate that both the Intendant system and the legislation of *comercio libre* were taking root, and producing important changes. For, firstly, the sections recording revenue (*cargo*), indicate that throughout the period of the Intendancy up to the political changes beginning in 1808, the total Royal revenues collected maintained a substantial pace of growth, from 101,428 pesos in 1790, to a peak of 752,446 pesos in 1806.[2] Secondly, the sections recording expenditure (*data*) under the category *Otras Tesorerías* show that the merchants of Veracruz were taking over control of the Oaxaca trade from those of Mexico City. Such a development indicates that behind the constant attacks on the Consulado of Veracruz to that of Mexico City lay a consciousness of the declining political and economic importance of the Consulado of Mexico City.[3] The detailed evidence of the rise of the Veracruz merchants in the Oaxaca trade is presented in Appendix 8.

The early years of the Intendancy and the first years of the operation of *comercio libre* showed only tentative changes, and even by 1792 there was still only one Veracruz merchant, Pedro de Cos, involved in the financing

[1] See principally the section, 'Otras Tesorerías' of the data in AGI *Mexico* 2131, *Cuentas de la tesorería principal de Oaxaca, 1790–6*, and ibid. 2132, *Cuentas de Real Hacienda de Oaxaca, 1797–1800*.
[2] AGI *Mexico* 2131; and AGI *Mexico* 2034, *Estados, cortes y tanteos de las cajas reales de hacienda, 1770–1820*, Oaxaca: Estados, 1797–1806, no. 5. For full details of Oaxaca's provincial finances under the Intendancy see Appendix 7 below.
[3] See under note 1 above.

of the Oaxaca merchants, namely in the provision of *avío* for Alonso Magro, whose traditional connexions had generally been with Mexico City.[1] However, as the 1790s advanced, a greater number of Veracruz merchants participated. In 1794, Pedro de Cos again appeared: 20,000 pesos were paid out of the Oaxaca Treasury to Alonso Magro for what Cos had paid into the Principal Treasury of Veracruz on his behalf. Other merchants of Veracruz, Pedro Miguel de Echeverría, Francisco Guerra y Agreda, and Juan Manuel Muñoz, and Juan Esteban Elías of the merchants of Jalapa, acted as the financial commissioners of their associated merchants in Oaxaca, Francisco Antonio Goytia and Juan Ramón López de Sagredo, both traditional dealers with the merchants of Mexico City.[2]

The determining factor which effectively established the supremacy of the Veracruz merchants over those of Mexico City in the Oaxaca trade was the foundation of the Consulado of Veracruz in 1796. For, the records for 1798 indicate that for the first time the Veracruz merchants outpaced their Mexico City rivals, and not just marginally, but by a long lead. The names of Pedro de Echeverría, Juan Manuel Muñoz, and Juan de Unanué of the Casa de Unanué y García virtually dominated the financing of the Oaxaca trade.[3] Moreover, alongside the traditional Oaxaca merchants arose a series of newer merchants, names not previously familiar, like Antonio Sánchez, Juan de Siga, Antonio Rodríguez, Vicente Domínguez, Francisco de Maza, and others. These were men who emerged in response to the role played by the Veracruz merchants.[4] These newer merchants subsisted alongside the older Oaxaca merchants, Alonso Magro, Felipe Ordóñez, Francisco Antonio Goytia, the Echarri brothers, and the various other names frequently cited. José María Murguía y Galardi appeared on the lists for the first time in 1795, connected with Mexico City, rather than Veracruz. However, by 1798, the future rebel Intendant's interests were entirely oriented towards Veracruz.[5]

These financial relationships are further illustrated by the negotiations undertaken between the merchants to ensure they met what obligations they could to the *Ramo de Consolidación de Vales Reales*. This procedure also revealed their intimate financial connexions with the Church, in particular with the convents and the diocesan *Juzgados de Capellanías y Obras Pías*, the tribunals of chantries and pious foundations.[6]

---

1 AGI *Mexico* 2131. For Alonso Magro, see Glossary of Personnel. 2 *Ibid.*
3 AGI *Mexico* 2132, and see Appendix 8 below. 4 *Ibid.* 5 *Ibid.*
6 For background see Michael P. Costeloe, *Church Wealth in Mexico, A Study of the 'Juzgado*

Politics and trade in Southern Mexico

The *Consolidación de Vales Reales*, commissioned under the *Real Cédula* of 26 December 1804, involved the consolidation by the Metropolitan Government of the Royal bills of payment which had been issued against the guarantee of the Royal revenues. As these revenues were not forthcoming due to the war effort, the Crown, faced with the need to secure more loans from foreign bankers, authorised the calling into the Royal coffers of the financial resources of the pious foundations and chantries of the Spanish Indies and Philippines. The receipts from this procedure would then offer the necessary guarantees required by the bankers.[1]

The *Juzgado* and several of the convents played the role of banks of loan. A merchant, administrator, landowner, anyone of substance wishing to cover the purchase of property, would be accustomed to request a loan, at the usual rate of interest of 5 per cent per annum, from the funds of pious foundations, chantries, or convents.

The endowment of these religious functions was a traditional practice among lay persons in New Spain. Often a sum in cash might be prescribed in a legacy for the foundation of a pious work, dedicated to a particular saint or purpose, or of a chantry for a certain priest or religious to say Mass for the soul of the deceased or his relatives. These sums would be collectively deposited in the *Juzgados*. In the diocese of Oaxaca, between the 1780s and the 1810s, the crucial role of Treasurer of the Cathedral, Vicar-General of the diocese, and Visitor of Legacies, Chantries and Pious Works, was occupied by Dr. Antonio José Ibáñez de Corbera, who was also one of the *Jueces Hacedores de Diezmos*.[2] These offices gave him the central position in the administration of ecclesiastical finance. He scrutinised applications for loans from the pious foundations, including those which might be made by his brothers, relations or associates. It was he whom Bishop Bergoza y Jordán, in flight from the Morelos advance of 1812, placed in control of the diocese during the Insurgent occupation.[3]

de Capellanías' in the Archbishopric of Mexico 1800–1856 (Cambridge Latin American Studies, no. 2. Cambridge University Press 1967). Also Asunción Lavrín, 'The Role of the Nunneries in the Economy of New Spain in the 18th century', *HAHR* xlvi, no. 4 (Nov. 1966), 371–94.

[1] AGI *Indiferente general* 666. For further details of the Consolidation, see Brian R. Hamnett, 'The Appropriation of Mexican Church Wealth by the Spanish Bourbon Government— The "Consolidación de Vales Reales", 1805–1809', *Journal of Latin American Studies*, i, no. 2 (Nov. 1969), 85–113. Reference should also be made to Earl J. Hamilton, 'Monetary Problems in Spain and Spanish America 1751–1800', *Journal of Economic History*, iv, no. 1 (May 1944), 21–48, for the financial background. General remarks were made by Lucas Alamán, *Historia de Méjico* (5 vols.; Mexico 1883–5 ed.), i, 153–4.

[2] Archivo de Notarías (Oaxaca), *Protocolos* 19 (1786), f. 82; Archivo Municipal (Oaxaca), *Tesorería municipal*, tomo I (1746–1829). See Glossary of Personnel for Ibáñez de Corbera.

[3] Eutimio Pérez, *Recuerdos históricos del episcopado oaxaqueño* (Oaxaca 1888), 86.

Finance, trade and merchants

In Oaxaca, the venerated Portuguese philanthropist, Captain Fiallo, who arrived in 1665 and died there in 1708, made very rich endowments. Out of his fortune, he donated large quantities to the convents and hospitals of the city for the purpose of building, decoration, and equipment costs. For example, 80,000 pesos were bestowed upon the Jesuit College, to which he eventually left most of his belongings in his will. A further 70,000 pesos were given to the Brothers of the Merced, for the rebuilding and decoration of their convent church. 30,000 pesos were donated to the Hospital of San Juan de Dios, and 3,000 to the Hospital de Belem. The Carmelite Fathers received 14,000 pesos, the Franciscans 20,000, and the Augustinians 30,000 for the rebuilding of their churches. These were by no means all the charities he bestowed upon the city. For 110,000 pesos were set aside for Pious Works. Moreover, Fiallo was the benefactor of the Colegio de Niñas, to which he donated 11,000 pesos. This college was to lodge a certain number of poor girls who would then be able to receive education. So that these young ladies could offer a dowry upon contracting marriage or selecting the convent of their choice, Captain Fiallo set aside the generous sum of 500,000 pesos—the *Obra Pía de Dotar Huérfanas*.[1] Much of the capital borrowed from the pious foundations in Oaxaca came from the funds endowed by Fiallo, in particular from the last mentioned.

The dye and sugar merchants of Teposcolula and Tlaxiaco borrowed heavily and frequently from pious sources. The settlement of the estates of Alonso Ruiz Riquel, who died in 1778, a Creole native of the city of Oaxaca, but whose parents had originated from the diocese of Seville, revealed that the principal for the purchase of the sugar-mill he possessed in Tlaxiaco, had been secured from the Monastery of the Nuns of the Conception in Oaxaca.[2] The two sugar-refining haciendas of Captain Joseph Mariano de Ita y Salazar, who died in 1788, were burdened with debts to the pious foundations. The first, 'San Miguel', had a debt of 3,000 pesos to a chantry and a further 4,200 to two lay patronages founded in Yanhuitlán. The second, 'San Vicente', which he held in partnership with a merchant of Tlaxiaco, owed 2,309 pesos to a guardianship fund, 500 pesos to another, and 500 pesos to the cult of the Image of Saint Joseph.[3]

The *repartimientos* practised by the Alcaldes Mayores might also be financed from the pious foundations, as could be seen from the request

---

[1] Padre José Antonio Gay, *Historia de Oaxaca* (2 vols.; Mexico 1881), ii, 245, 253–4.
[2] Museo Nacional, *Microfilm Collection*, Oaxaca, Roll 24: Archivo del Juzgado de Teposcolula, Civil 12.   [3] *Ibid.*

of the Alcalde Mayor of Villa Alta, Pablo de Ortega, for the sum of 25,000 pesos—'*para el giro de mis comercios*'. Having heard that such a sum existed in the treasury of the late Jesuit Order, he asked for a loan of this amount for two years at 5 per cent. He offered as his two *fiadores* (guarantors), Alonso Magro, merchant and Regidor Honorario of the Ayuntamiento of Oaxaca, and Felipe Ordóñez Díaz, Oaxaca merchant.[1] The request was granted by the Administrator of the Temporal Properties in Oaxaca in consultation with the Bishop, in January 1786, and Ortega duly received the sum from the funds of the Colegio de Niñas Educandas.[2]

Ordóñez himself reported in the following month that he had received notice that there existed in the Treasury of the Jesuit Temporal Possessions enough cash to cover a sum of 25,000 pesos which he needed '*para el giro de mis comercios*'. He offered three *fiadores*, Pedro Alonso de Alles, and two merchants from Jamiltepec, one of whom was actually the Alcalde Mayor.[3] The sum was conceded for two years at 5 per cent from the funds of the same college in February 1786. On the following day, Ordóñez requested a further 6,345½ pesos from the funds of the Convent of Our Lady of the Conception, again for his commercial operations over a term of two years, offering the same guarantees. This request was also conceded after consultations with the Abbess and the Administrator of the convent's properties and incomes, José Antonio de Bustamante.[4]

On 14 January 1786, Captain Pedro de Quevedo, Alcalde Mayor of Teposcolula–Yanhuitlán, took 20,000 pesos in loan for four years from the Colegio de Niñas Educandas, under the *fianza* of the Marqués de Sierra Nevada, Governor and Administrator of the Marquesado del Valle.[5] On the 16th he took a further 20,000 pesos for the conduct of his commercial operations from the funds of the same college, under *fianza* of several Oaxaca merchants, one of whom was Juan María García, associate of the Alcalde Mayor of Miahuatlán—'*personas todas de notorio abono*'.[6]

The Oaxaca merchant and Regidor Honorario, José Francisco Ibáñez de Corbera, brother of Dr. Antonio José, and acting as agent for Gaspar de Elías, merchant of Veracruz engaged in the trade with Spain, requested a loan of 50,000 pesos from the treasury of the *Juzgado Eclesiástico* for the period of five years. He presented as his *fiadores* a group of Veracruz merchants, three of whom were of the dye-exporting House of

1 For Magro and Ordóñez, see Glossary of Personnel.
2 Archivo de Notarías (Oaxaca), *Protocolos*, leg. 19, f. 5.
3 For Alles, see Glossary of Personnel.   4 Archivo de Notarías, ff. 50–5.
5 AGN *General de parte 72*.   6 Archivo de Notarías, f. 21.

Muñoz. On 8 March 1786, Dr. Antonio José conceded the loan, but only up to the sum of 24,552 pesos.[1]

The Casa de Muñoz again appeared in the financial dealings of the Oaxaca *Juzgado* on 3 October 1786, when Juan María García pointed out the large sums pertaining to the fund for the repair of the Cathedral building, existing in the treasury of tithe revenues. He requested the sum of 30,000 pesos—'*para el giro de negociación de Miahuatlán*'—for the period of six to seven months, to be distributed as '*avilitación*' throughout the *partido*. He offered Alonso Magro as his *fiador*, and as an additional guarantee, he also offered to mortgage 160 zurrones of cochineal, which he possessed in Veracruz under the charge of the Casa de Muñoz. This request was also granted, but for 24,000 pesos.[2]

The Alcalde Mayor of the Cuatro Villas del Marquesado, Adrían de Cerain,[3] in 1794, took 60,000 pesos at 5 per cent from the *Juzgado*, presumably as a contribution to his *repartimientos*, for which he was arraigned before the Intendant of Oaxaca and the Superior Government, as we have seen.[4] In the same year, he became lessee of the Hacienda de Montoya, the property of the convent of the Soledad in Oaxaca. He drew the principal against his account with the trustees of the Obra Pía de Fiallo, a sum of 32,000 pesos.[5]

The Archicofradía de Aranzazú was one of the creditors of the Oaxaca merchant Joaquín Jiménez de Morraz, who owed it 18,000 pesos. In 1795, in default of ability to repay, and illustrating one of the rare cases in which the ecclesiastical creditors required repayment of the principal, one of his *fiadores*, the Regidor Perpetuo, Diego de Villasante, was required to cover the sum of 10,000 pesos. An examination of the properties and credit of Villasante showed that he himself owed 3,000 pesos to the convent of the Soledad, 2,000 to a chantry, 8,000 to the convent of the Conception, 4,000 to a patronage fund, and 1,000 to the convent of St. Augustine. All of these sums had been borrowed to cover the lease of the Mill of St. Augustine in the Villa de Etla.[6]

The Murguía family, also, borrowed substantially from the *Juzgado*. Lorenzo Murguía, father of José María, borrowed from two pious foundations, and from the Convent of San Juan de Dios for application to his town house. José María Murguía borrowed from the funds of Fiallo, and applied them to the purchase of three haciendas in the *partido* of

---

1 *Ibid.* f. 82.   2 *Ibid.* f. 224.   3 For Cerain, see Glossary of Personnel.
4 AGN *General de parte* 76.
5 Archivo del Tribunal de la Federación, (Oaxaca) leg. 1, exp. 3 (1800).
6 AGN *General de parte* 75. See also Costeloe, *Church Wealth*, ch. 3, pp. 66–85.

Nejapa in February 1803. His brother, Manuel, borrowed from the funds of the parish of Cuilapan in May 1800, and their sister, María Manuela, and her husband took a loan of 10,000 pesos from the revenues of the Colegio de Niñas Educandas.[1]

Even as late as April 1805, when news of the *Consolidación de Vales Reales* was becoming known throughout New Spain, one of the Oaxaca merchants, Francisco Antonio Goytia, took out the sum of 25,000 pesos at 5 per cent from the funds of the Colegio de Niñas Educandas and the Royal Hospital of Oaxaca, under commission from the Querétaro militia colonel, Manuel Espinosa Tello, for whom the Prior of the Consulado of Veracruz, Tomás Murphí, was acting as *fiador*.[2]

Under the consolidation procedure for the Indies, the Spanish Crown undertook to pay interest of 3 per cent of the capital consolidated from the pious foundations, implying that, in effect, it would only be taking the sum as a loan on interest from the Pious Work concerned. In the Bishopric of Oaxaca a Junta Subalterna, subordinate to the Mexico City Junta of Consolidation, operated under the presidency of the Intendant, and in the presence of the Bishop. This local junta's function required the calculation of the value of the diocesan pious foundations and chantries, and of the landed properties pertaining to them. Although the landed estates of churches and religious communities and the capital resources of convents were specifically excluded from the procedure, all persons whose term of loan from the pious foundations had now been completed were required to present themselves before the Royal agents of the consolidation for the purpose of paying back the principal. They were, however, allowed to pay by instalments rather than cash down immediately. This practice was known as '*composición*'. It accounts for the small amounts that were actually paid into the provincial treasuries during the years 1805–8 when the consolidation was operative in New Spain.[3]

All proceeds from sales of landed properties of pious foundations, and from the redemption of loans were to be collected in the Principal Treasury of the diocese, recorded in a special account book kept by the Ministers of Royal Finance, and then sent to Mexico City without delay for prompt shipment to Spain.[4]

The *Real Cédula* reached Bishop Bergoza y Jordán of Oaxaca in April 1805, and entries into the Oaxaca Royal Treasury began after 20 August of that year. However, by the autumn of 1805, normal maritime com-

---

[1] AGN *Consolidación* 5, ff. 182 v.–183, 211. [2] AGN *Civil* 26, exp. 6, ff. 1–43 v.
[3] AGI *Indiferente general* 666. Especially Article 15. [4] *Ibid.* Articles 35 and 38.

munications between Spain and New Spain had once more been interrupted by the British blockade of Spanish Atlantic sea-routes. In consequence, Spanish ships were often unable to carry the proceeds of the consolidation to Spain. Hence, these sums had to be transported in neutral ships under the neutrality concessions, re-legislated under the *Real Cédula* of 24 December 1804. It was against such a practice that the Consulado of Veracruz protested on 15 November 1805.[1]

The expropriation of the funds of pious works and chantries affected, in the Bishopric of Oaxaca, most of the principal merchants, several hacienda-owners (who might at the same time be merchants themselves), most of the members of the Ayuntamiento, whose members were generally both merchants and land-owners, and most of the leading officers of the provincial militia, almost all of whom fell into one or other or all of the previous categories. Clearly, the most powerful and the most wealthy, both Peninsular and Creole, were thus abruptly required by the Royal administration to settle their outstanding debt with the pious foundations. A select list of personnel involved, and the amounts they paid into the Royal Treasury in the city of Oaxaca is presented in Appendix 9, followed by a table of the amounts consolidated in the Bishopric, in Appendix 10.

Principal merchants involved were men of the category of Pedro de Estrella, who had purchased the office of Regidor Perpetuo of the Ayuntamiento of Oaxaca for 1,500 pesos at the auctions of 1798.[2] Others enjoyed wide contacts in Mexico City with the merchants of the Consulado there; among them were the Oaxaca merchants Francisco Antonio Goytia, recently deceased, and Juan Francisco de Echarri, both retired Lieutenant-Colonels of the Oaxaca Provincial Militia.[3] Hacienda-owners, such as the Murguías, Simón Camacho, or Lic. Mariano Castillejos, and others, were expected to pay back their loans, even if they had mortgaged all or part of their properties as guarantee of repayment of the principal.

The total cash that passed into the Oaxaca Provincial Treasury came to only 663,572 pesos, out of a possible total eligible under the *Real Cédula* of approximately 1,700,000 pesos.[4] The discrepancy between the two

1 AGI *Mexico* 2512, Consulado de Veracruz, no. 271. 15 Nov. 1805, 'Expone los perjuicios que padece el comercio por las gracias concedidas a la consolidación de Vales'.
2 AGN *General de parte* 74 (1793–9). See also Glossary of Personnel.
3 AGN *Consolidación* 5, and see also Appendices 8 and 9 and Glossary of Personnel.
4 The Oaxaca total comes from AGN *Consolidación* 5. The 1,700,000 pesos is calculated from José María Luis Mora, *Obras Sueltas* (Mexico 1963 ed.): Abad y Queipo, 'Escrito presentado a D. Manuel Sixto Espinosa', 231. Abad y Queipo, 231–41, estimated the total value of the capital pertaining to the pious foundations and chantries in New Spain at 44,500,000 pesos, though estimates of this value varied considerably, as is discussed in Hamnett, 'Appropriation of Church Wealth.' Arrangoiz, the Consolidation's chief administrator in Mexico City

figures, between aspiration and achievement, is accounted for by four factors: firstly because under the *Real Cédula* the principle of '*composición*' had been admitted; secondly because the whole process was suspended in New Spain during the political crisis beginning in the summer of 1808; thirdly because, as Arrangoiz, the chief administrator of the consolidation, himself admitted, there was much incorrect declaration of eligible capital; fourthly because there was much opposition, both among lessees of the funds and amongst clerics who benefited from pious works and chantries by living off the interest on the capital loaned.[1]

As the Bishop-elect of Michoacan, Abad y Queipo, had warned in 1805, resistance to the measure would be strong and widespread.[1] After his visit to New Spain, Humboldt remarked, concerning the procedure for the *Consolidación de Vales Reales*, that, 'The resistance was so strong on the part of the proprietors that, after the month of May 1805 up to the month of June 1806, the *Caja de Amortización* secured no more than the quite modest sum of 1,200,000 pesos'.[2]

Arrangoiz observed exactly such a recalcitrance. For: 'Each community, or rather each of its individual members, each lessee of cash, each tribunal, and even each individual on the Junta has been an opponent, a mortal enemy of the Consolidation. For, they have omitted no means by which they could delay the circulation of the despatches on the question.'[4]

Moreover, of the Oaxaca figure, given in the Consolidation account books, the sum of 161,924 pesos 6 reales 10 granos had not been at all secured from the expropriation of pious funds, but had been transferred from the *Caja de Bienes de Comunidad de Indios* (the treasury for Indian communally-owned funds) into the *Caja de Consolidación*. These sums had been delivered in two instalments, on 8 August 1806 and 25 November 1808. After their deduction, the sum of 501,647 pesos remained, that which had actually been consolidated in Oaxaca.[5] In short, then, for all the above reasons, the Crown failed to secure 1,200,000 pesos of the cash due to it under the provisions of the *Real Cédula* of 1804.

Abad y Queipo himself went from Valladolid de Michoacan to Madrid at the beginning of 1807 to petition in person before the Spanish Government that the *Real Cédula* of 1804 should be suspended. He was promised an interview with Godoy, but was kept waiting for four hours only to be

estimated 60,000,000 pesos. BM Add. MSS 13,978, Papeles varios de Indias (1784–1816), file 28, ff. 159–62, 'Calculo de las obras pías en Nueva España'.
1 BM Add. MSS 13,978.
2 See Mora, *Obras sueltas*: Abad y Queipo, 'Representación a nombre de los labradores y comerciantes de Michoacan, 214–30.   3 Humboldt, *Essai politique*, ii, 447.
4 BM Add. MSS 13,978.   5 AGN *Consolidación* 5.

told that the matter was too delicate to be broached. Through the intervention of the Secretary of the Council of the Indies, Antonio Porcel, he secured an interview with the Minister of Finance, Manuel Sixto Espinosa, who, while sympathising with the grievances of the injured parties, explained that the financial exigencies of the Spanish Government were such that under no circumstances could the Consolidation be abrogated. However, in the spring of 1808, the régime in Spain collapsed in the Motín de Aranjuez, the French began to occupy the Peninsula, and a Supreme Junta was set up in Seville. Abad y Queipo presented the memorandum he had prepared for Sixto Espinosa to the Junta a week after its installation, and he believed that it had some part in persuading the Junta to suspend the Consolidation under its Royal Order of 26 January 1809.[1] However, in New Spain, in the meantime, the measure had already been suspended unilaterally on 9 August 1808.[2]

The Spanish historian, Zamacois, considered that the inflexibility of Viceroy Iturrigaray in enforcing the *Real Cédula* of 1804, motivated by the commission he received from the revenues of the Consolidation, cast upon him the hatred of the merchants, landowners, mine-operators, and clergy.[3] Following the Spanish Liberal, the Conde de Toreno, moreover, stated that of the sums received by the Spanish Government, not all remained in Spain. For, a notable part went to France, since, on 10 May 1806, Godoy's special agent in Paris, Eugenio Izquierdo, handed over the sum of 5,000,000 pesos to the French as part of the Franco-Spanish Treaty of Subsidies of 1803.[4]

The Consolidation initiated a decade of political conflict and upheaval, between the years, 1805 and 1815, which culminated in the occupation of the Intendancy of Oaxaca from the Mixteca Alta to the Isthmus of Tehuantepec by the revolutionary forces under Morelos. After the withdrawal of the Insurgents, the Royalist Intendant, Brigadier Melchor Álvarez, took stock of the situation of the pious works and chantries. During the upheaval, interest on the sum of 318,496 pesos, which had been consolidated, had not been paid, and was, therefore, owed to the initial borrowers by the Royal Government. This had caused great financial hardship to owners of the local haciendas. To this was added the sum of 217,349 pesos, which, by the Intendant's estimate, had been the

1 Mora, *Obras sueltas*: Abad y Queipo, 'Sixto Espinosa', 240–1. AGN *Bandos* 25, no. 16.
2 Alamán, *Historia de Méjico*, 1.
3 Niceto de Zamacois, *Historia de Méjico* (21 vols.; Barcelona 1888–1901) vi, 16–19.
4 *Ibid.* 19, and see Conde de Toreno, *Historia del levantamiento, guerra, y revolución de España* (Madrid 1836), i, 6.

loss sustained by the Spanish-owned maize-producing haciendas of the Valley of Oaxaca out of funds borrowed from pious sources. Thus, the Oaxaca diocesan pious works had permanently lost a sum of 535,845 pesos, which would have, if the terms of the *Real Cédula* of 1804 had duly been observed by the Spanish Crown, rendered a total interest income to the initial borrowers of 35,723 pesos.[1]

It remains to discuss that state of trade and its effect on the merchants after 1800. Even after the annulment, by the *Reales Órdenes* of 20 April 1799, of the first series of concessions to neutrals, the amount of foreign products entering Veracruz still totalled 1,224,417¼ pesos, as opposed to a value of 1,963,577¼ for Spanish national products.[2] Apart from the 4 million pesos of coin and plate exported to Spain in 1800, the chief export was still the cochineal of Oaxaca, a total of 5,150 arrobas at 70–80 pesos per arrobas, giving a value of 379,256½ pesos.[3] Even so, these figures were a far cry from the previous heights the cochineal trade had reached, and reflected the consequences of the war, the flight of investment, and the abrogation of the 'neutral' concessions. Nevertheless, they do not include what quantities might have been exported in the contraband trade, chiefly to Jamaica.

Upon the restoration of peace-time conditions in 1802, the proportion of Spanish national goods, reflected in the trade balances meticulously recorded by the Consulado of Veracruz, rose in relation to those pertaining to foreigners. In that year, Spanish goods accounted for a value of 11,539,000 pesos, while foreign products came to a total of 8,851,000. The distance between the two values was considerably increased in the last peace year, 1804, when Spanish goods were valued at 10,412,000 pesos, as opposed to a value of 4,493,000 pesos for foreign goods.[4] When war returned between Spain and Great Britain, the figures for 1805 and 1806 showed a marked decline in Spanish national imports into Veracruz.[5]

The period of peace, however, had its effects on the Oaxaca dye trade. For, from the disastrous nadir of 1801, when only 96,400 pounds valued at 298,258 pesos had been exported, the export figures at Veracruz rose

---

[1] BM Add. MSS 17,557, Noticias de América, ff. 31–33, and see also Murguía's list for 1828 in Appendix 11. [2] AGI *Mexico* 2509.

[3] *Ibid.* 287,277 pesos' worth of sugar (87,570 arrobas at 23–9 reales), and 257,184 pesos' worth of indigo from Guatemala (124,393½ pounds at 12–20 reales) were the next highest figures.

[4] Lerdo de Tejada, *Comercio exterior*, números 15–17, 'Balanzas del comercio marítimo, 1802–1804.'

[5] *Ibid.* See also comments of the former Secretary of the Veracruz Consulado Vicente Basadre, in his Memoria of 1807, in AGI *Indiferente general* 2439, para. 22.

to a splendid height of 1,081,925 pounds, valued at 3,303,470 pesos, in 1802. This figure included the discharge of the large quantities of cochineal which had been accumulating in Veracruz warehouses during the British blockade. The figures for 1803 were still promising, with an export total of 681,275 pounds, valued at 2,191,399 pesos, indicating heavy demand for the dye, and a resulting high price.[1] From the time of the establishment of the Consulado of Veracruz, the price of cochineal in the port had been rising considerably in response to the vicissitudes of war. From between 71 and 72 pesos per arroba the price rose to a peak of between 103 and 104 pesos in 1804, the last year of peace, and before the issue of the second phase of concessions to neutrals.[2] After that year, however, the effects of both the war and the pressure of the Consolidation on the investors could be seen. For in the city of Oaxaca, the quantities registered dropped to 191,250 pounds in 1805, and hovered between 340,000 and 358,000 pounds during the years 1807–1809. The effect of the second phase of 'neutral' concessions, while it could not be seen in the levels of the Registry production figure in view of the crisis in the *partidos* of origin, could be detected in the continuing heavy demand for the dye, and the severe rise of its price in both the city of Oaxaca and the port of Veracruz. For in Oaxaca the price rose from 23 reales in 1805 to a peak of 33 reales per pound in 1809. This latter price level reflected a demand that could not be satisfied by supply.[3] In Veracruz, meanwhile, the price increased from 100 pesos per arroba in 1806 to 120 in 1809.[4]

On 21 July 1807, the former Secretary and Treasurer of the Veracruz Consulado, Vicente Basadre, presented a *Memoria* to Godoy, concerning the course of New Spain's trade since the initiation of *comercio libre*.[5] He stated, continuing the tradition of Viceroy Revillagigedo, that all the provinces of both the Metropolis and its colonies had benefited from the reform after 1778, and 1789 for New Spain. For foreign woollen and silk manufactures had disappeared like a lamp put out. Spanish national products had now replaced Genoese silk-stockings for women, Neapolitan

---

1 Lerdo de Tejada, *Comercio exterior*, Price figures calculated from número 14.
2 *Ibid.*
3 From the Oaxaca registry figures, which are presented in full in Appendix 1.
4 Lerdo de Tejada, *Comercio exterior*.
5 Basadre belonged to the school of Revillagigedo, and Saavedra (Minister of Finance at the end of 1797, and first Secretary between March 1798 and August 1798: he returned to influence after 1808.). Basadre had spent twenty years in continual voyages in Spanish America and Asia, reaching even the Chinese Empire. Between 1789 and 1795, he resided in Madrid as a *vocal* of the Junta de Comercio of the Royal Philippine Company. From there he had moved to New Spain as Secretary of the new Consulado of Veracruz, between 1795 and 1802. Both Saavedra and Basadre became Intendants of Venezuela.

ribbons, Italian velvet, French taffeta, Flemish carriages and inlaid work, Dutch and Genoese paper, Northern European wax, and English serges, flannels, and other cloths. Linens, however, slow to develop in Spain's industry, were still supplied by the foreigners. Despite all the changes, though, a commodity in especial esteem and with great consumption in the Indies were the English cotton textiles.

These had always strictly been forbidden in peace-time, but during the war they had been brought in on neutral ships, which thereby contributed the only grudgingly admitted benefit of reducing contraband.

The chief reasons for the progress of Spain's national industry in the latter part of the eighteenth century were the labour and industrious character of the Catalans, and the operation of the many cotton, woollen, and silk textile plants which, over the previous twenty-five years (i.e. since 1785) had been established in several towns of the Peninsula. Wise ministerial policies, and the Spanish nation's increased '*Ilustración*' also contributed. Unfortunately, five years of disastrous war had set back industry's progress. The reawakening had come with the restoration of peace in 1802—as we saw from the trade figures. This revival was especially evident throughout the Principality of Catalonia, where every class of manufacture down to wine and brandy was exported to Spanish America. In Mexico City itself there had been in that year great rivalry between the Barcelona painted cotton textiles and the fine chintz of England. The Catalan product had triumphed owing to its superior quality and design and more permanent colours. A decade of peace would then have driven the English out of the market altogether. A similar progress was observed in the woollen industries of Segovia and Escaray, and the silk textiles of Talavera, Toledo, Valencia, Granada, Málaga and Seville. In response to the revival of Spain's trade, a reciprocal development had been taking place in the most important products of Spanish American agriculture, namely cochineal, indigo, cotton, cacao, vanilla from Teutila and Papantla, sugar, and coffee.[1]

---

[1] AGI *Indiferente general* 2439, Memoria of Vicente Basadre to Godoy, Madrid 21 July 1807, paras. 13–20. See also James C. La Force, *The Development of the Spanish Textile Industry 1750–1800* (Berkeley 1966), 16–17: 'When peace returned in 1802, the thoughts of the Catalonian industrialists turned to their American markets, for the English had moved into the commercial vacuum during the blockade of Spain, and the colonials themselves had begun to manufacture calicoes in Mexico and elsewhere.' On 9 February 1788, the Consulado of Barcelona requested the Crown to prohibit and suppress the manufacture of painted cotton fabrics in Mexico City and Puebla, which not only supplied New Spain, but also reached Peru. For their continued existence threatened the reciprocal union between the Metropolis and her dependencies. The Catalan industrialists repeated this request on 15 June 1804, warning that it threatened home industry: *ibid.* and José María Quirós, *Memoria*

Finance, trade and merchants

These developments were rudely shattered by the outbreak of war at the end of 1804, and Spain's declaration of war on Great Britain on 12 December 1804. As soon as this news reached the merchants in New Spain, they proceeded to buy up all the Spanish Metropolitan products remaining in the ports as a speculative venture anticipating the great demand and the exorbitant price. As a result of such a move, the second phase of the concessions to neutrals came as a positive advantage to the consumer through the lowering of prices. For example the price of Spanish-made Silesian linens ('*pontibi*' or '*platillas reales*'), so much in demand among the lower classes, fell from a range of 25–30 *reales de vellón* in Veracruz (35–8 in Mexico City, and 45–8 in the interior) to 15 in Veracruz as a result of the increased competition.[1]

Such a contrast can also be seen from the fate of the forty-three Spanish blockade-runners which entered Veracruz from Cádiz between 3 January 1805 and 16 December 1806, which could not even cover their costs, and the fifty-four neutral ships, which rendered sizeable profits to their investors, and benefited both merchants and consumers in New Spain.[2] The impact of this second wave of concessions to neutrals resulted in a total import value of 3,485,655 pesos in 1806, of which 1,554,647 pesos represented the value of cotton textiles, and 1,079,714 pesos in linens.[3] This figure rose in 1807 to a startling level of 10,123,895 pesos, of which 6,351,464 pesos were in foreign cotton textiles.[4] Such figures indicated the clear threat of a change in the direction of New Spain's trade, to the disadvantage both of the industries of the Spanish Metropolis, and of the domestic *obraje* textile production, associated as it often was with the merchants of Mexico City and Puebla.[5]

Basadre pointed also to the serious division between the old-style merchants of the Consulado of Mexico, and the more enterprising new-style merchants of the Consulado of Veracruz. For, as soon as a neutral

---

de Instituto, 10 January 1814 (Havana 1814), 13. A similar complaint is recorded in J. López Cancelada, *Ruina de la Nueva España si se declara el comercio libre con los extrangeros* (Cádiz 1811), 24.

[1] AGI *Indiferente general* 2439, Basadre, para. 30.   [2] *Ibid.* paras. 31–2.

[3] Lerdo de Tejada, *Comercio exterior*, numero 19, 'Balanza del comercio, 1806'.

[4] *Ibid.* número 20.

[5] See Appendix 12 for a note on the *obrajes* of Oaxaca. For the rest of New Spain, see especially Richard E. Greenleaf, 'The Obraje in the Late Mexican Colony', *The Americas*, xxiii (Jan. 1967), no. 3, 227–50; Jan Bazant, 'Evolución de la industria textil poblana 1544–1845', *Historia Mexicana*, 52 (April–June 1964), no. 4, 473–516; and Robert A. Potash, *El Banco de Avío de México* (Mexico 1959), 23, who states that the Spanish Peninsular merchants' functions extended not only to the capitalization of the primary product and the distribution of the finished, but also to the very means of production.

ship would arrive in Veracruz, two parties would form, the old men and the young men. The former were ignorant of the basic elements and attitudes of commerce, in spite of their substantial capital of 200,000 or 300,000 pesos. They were not anxious to take the risk of investing in the 'neutral' trade, preferring to foretell the return of peace and the restoration of the old trade with Spain, and other such 'unfounded calculations'. The young men, on the other hand, entered mercantile partnerships, enjoyed a commercial predilection, and were generally those who purchased a whole cargo for a certain amount in order to resell it at a profit of 10, 12 or 15 per cent. The old men would attack these profits of the intermediary agents, representing to the Superior Government and the Metropolis, from the vantage point of their superior age, the dangers which were resulting from 'neutral' commerce.[1]

But their complaints, Basadre said, could be seen upon examination to be motivated solely by a too great love of their own interests. As such they were untrue, ill-founded, and illegitimate. It was their jealousy which made them decry measures indispensible in war-time conditions. For, the concessions to neutrals brought distinct advantages to the respective classes of society.[2]

Turning to the very controversial question of the import into New Spain of foreign cotton textiles, much of what Basadre had to say foreshadowed the tariff and protection controversies of the early Mexican Republic.[3] For the issue centred on the consequences for New Spain of importing the finished textiles of a foreign power, with great consequences for her own primary producing agriculture. In response to the import of British cottons on neutral ships, the precious products—cochineal, indigo, cotton, sugar—would pass to the Northern European powers rather than to Spain. The neutral trade contained within itself the threat that Catalan cotton manufacturers would be denied both a market and a raw material supply, whereas the dye trade in New Spain would secure a new outlet, and probably a better price in Britain, France, or Holland. In such a situation there would be no room for either the political authority of Old Spain or for the functions of the merchants of the Consulado of Mexico City. Moreover, a further factor operated, that of the Mexican *obrajes*. For, if the British cotton textiles found such a profitable market in the

---

[1] AGI *Indiferente general* 2439, Basadre, para. 33. [2] *Ibid.* 34.

[3] See Lerdo, *Comercio exterior de México*, 29–44 for details of Mexican import duties between 1821 and 1853. Also J. Reyes Heroles, *El liberalismo mexicano*, i (Mexico 1959), 169–82, where the conflicts between the protagonists of Free Trade and the artisan interests in Puebla are discussed. See also Potash, *Banco de Avío*, 29–58.

tropical and sub-tropical regions of the Spanish Empire, the technologic-
ally retarded, expensive *obraje* cottons of Mexico City, Puebla, Cholula,
Oaxaca, and elsewhere in New Spain, in which many Mexico City and
associated local merchants had invested, might face a pace of competition
that would in the long run prove too much for them. Basadre's report,
then, in this respect foreshadows the problems faced by Lucas Alamán
and Esteban de Antuñano in the 1820s, 1830s, and 1840s.[1]

This English cotton-textile import had increased with enormous
rapidity over the previous fifteen years, that is since 1792. At first, India
had provided the bulk of the painted cottons, calicoes, consumed in the
markets of Europe and the Indies, but the British had learned the tech-
niques, and their active and vigilant textile industry was discharging great
quantities through the 'neutral' concessions. This drive coincided with,
and stimulated, a change in taste from continental European and Spanish
linens in favour of India-style cottons.[2]

Basadre recommended that the Spanish Government should recognise
realities, and allow the import into New Spain of British cottons in order
to forestall their illicit import through the contraband trade. If they were
made legal, they could, at least, be taxed, and made thereby to earn
revenue for the Crown. At the same time, he advocated a difficult task for
Spanish industry, that it should respond to the changing tastes of the
market, and go over to the increased production of cotton textiles in order
to prevent the loss of valuable markets to the British. For, in view of the
'*estudiada previsión y sagaz política*' of the British industry, whose consumption in some parts was extending so rapidly that the taste for linens had
been forgotten, the Spanish national industry faced ruin if it could not
adapt.[3]

However, Spain and its American empire, Basadre concluded as a last
driving point, were hampered by four ancient Consulados—Cádiz,
Mexico, Lima, and Manila—all opponents of change, dreaming of the
restoration of the days of excessive profits before *comercio libre*. They were
in dire and urgent necessity of reform. For, 'that of Mexico is a monstr-
ous, tyrannical, oppressive, destructive body'. And, after two-hundred
years of Mexico's monopoly, Veracruz, the sole port of commerce, was
without a wharf, without fresh, running water, without a proper high-
way, and without bridges over its rivers.[4]

Little action could be taken on Basadre's report, however, owing to
its appearance in the very last months of the Godoy régime. The Motín

1 Especially Potash, *Banco de Avío*, 29–58.
2 AGI *Indiferente general* 2349, Basadre, paras. 36–8.   3 *Ibid.* 41–4.   4 *Ibid.* 50–3.

de Aranjuez of March 1808 presented an entirely different political environment to all parties within New Spain. It left the controversial Viceroy Iturrigaray dangerously exposed, and lacking the crucial support necessary from Spain in view of the unpopularity of the Consolidation. All these factors presented the merchants of the Consulado of Mexico with the opportunity to take matters into their own hands. The political events in Mexico City had parallel repercussions in Oaxaca, where the whole issue of the advisability of Gálvez's reforms and the establishment of the Intendancy again occupied the forefront of political discussion.

CHAPTER 7

THE POLITICAL CRISIS OF 1808-1821

The news of the fall of Godoy and Charles IV, and of the succession of Ferdinand VII reached Mexico City on 8 June 1808. A fortnight later came the news of the departure of the Royal family for Bayonne, and of the Dos de Mayo rising in Madrid against the French occupation forces. On 14 July the arrival of the Madrid newspapers brought word of the Bayonne renunciations in favour of Napoleon, and the circular order of the Council of Castile commanding recognition of French authority throughout the Spanish Indies.[1]

The knowledge of these events led to a power struggle in Mexico City between the Creole lawyers of the Ayuntamiento of Mexico, and the Peninsular lawyers of the Audiencia, and their allies, the Peninsular merchants of the Mexico Consulado.[2] When Viceroy Iturrigaray's unilateral suspension of the Consolidation on 9 August 1808 failed to quieten animosities, he was forced to adopt an increasingly more open position in favour of the Creoles.[3] As the Creole lawyers, Azcárate and Verdad, began to claim that sovereignty had returned to the people in default of a king, the Peninsulares believed that the ending of Spanish Metropolitan rule in Mexico was about to take place.[4]

Therefore, they conceived of a quick coup to remove the Viceroy and his Creole associates in the Mexico Ayuntamiento. This conspiracy centred on the Audiencia and Consulado of Mexico. It was known to the Inquisitor, Alfaro, to the Archbishop of Mexico, Lizana, and to the chief Peninsular merchants and land-owners. Its leader, Gabriel de Yermo, was a merchant of the Consulado, and sugar hacienda-owner of Cuernavaca. The success of the coup on the night of 15 September 1808 brought to

---

[1] Full details of the events of 8 June–15 September 1808 can be seen in Lucas Alamán, *Historia de Méjico* (1883 ed.), i, 173–245, in Carlos María de Bustamante, *Cuadro histórico de la Revolución Mexicana* (1961 ed.), i, 12–18; and Bustamante, *Suplemento a la historia de los tres siglos de México durante el gobierno español* (Mexico 1836), iii, 225–42.

[2] *Ibid.*   [3] Alamán, *Historia*, i, 180.

[4] Alamán, *Historia*, i, 93, states that the Síndico, Verdad, and the Regidor Honorario, Azcárate, owed their positions and influence to Iturrigaray, while Bustamante, *Cuadro histórico*, i, 13, adds that the Oidores, Aguirre and Bataller, believed the Viceroy was about to relieve them of their posts, and confer them on the Creole lawyers, Cristo, Verdad, and Azcárate. For, he knew of their secret meetings with members of the Consulado of Mexico, which, he said, was being egged on by the Consulado of Veracruz.

power an alliance of the Consulado and Audiencia under the aged Marshall Pedro Garibay as Viceroy. The régime was guarded by the Peninsular merchant-controlled Volunteers of Ferdinand VII. Iturrigaray was deported to Spain, and the Creole lawyers were conducted to the Archbishop's prison.[1]

According to Bustamante, the capital seethed with discontent the morning after the coup. The common people, in their fury, armed themselves so menacingly that it was necessary for the speedy march to the capital of the Mexico Regiment of Dragoons, under Oidor Aguirre's friend, Colonel Empara, for the restoration of order in conjunction with the city Grenadiers' column. This coup marked the road to the revolution of 1810. Bustamante wrote, 'from this time appeared the symptoms of a violent revolution, and of a general hatred which seethed in the hearts of everyone. The Kingdom was stirred by volcanic passions, and was on the point of breaking out into a horrible explosion'.[2]

Alamán considered that the real power in the new régime lay with the Peninsular merchant Volunteers of Ferdinand VII. They had bestowed upon themselves the name of the People, and their predilection was for extra-judicial action. They would enter the chambers of the Audiencia, and their captains would demand that whatever orders they considered necessary should be passed.[3] These Volunteers rapidly became too extreme for the Real Acuerdo, with the result that the Audiencia was forced to call in troops from Jalapa to discipline them. That, however, failed. Therefore, Garibay ordered them to confine themselves to their homes, on 15 October. This they considered an insult, and some of the wilder elements talked of removing Garibay in the same way that they had removed Iturrigaray.[4]

In Oaxaca, during the month before the coup against Iturrigaray, the chief citizens were expressing 'voices of distrust' in the Viceroy. According to the Peninsular merchant, Antonio de la Portilla, their object was to make it clear to Iturrigaray that he could not count on them for the execution of his plans. All of them would be ready to shed the last drop of their blood before being traitors to their King. The merchants were anxious that a formal oath of loyalty should be taken to Ferdinand VII. In view of the political implications of such an action, against the back-

[1] For Yermo, see Alamán, *Historia*, i, 232; Bustamante, *Cuadro*, i, 14; and Bancroft, *History of Mexico*, iv, 52–3, n. 27.

[2] Bustamante, *Tres siglos de México*, iii, 240, and *Cuadro histórico*, i, 16.

[3] Alamán, *Historia*, i, 262.

[4] José María Luis Mora, *México y sus Revoluciones* (3 vols.; Mexico 1965 ed.) ii, 307–8.

ground of events in Mexico City, the Intendancy authorities, the *Teniente Letrado*, Antonio Izquierdo, and the Creole *Promoter Fiscal*, Mariano de Castillejos, were anxious to avoid provoking a public commotion. They, therefore, approached *Regidor Decano* Diego de Villasante, also a Peninsular merchant, to stop the ceremony, and they called upon the powerfully placed Captain of the Militias of the Costa del Sur, Alonso Magro, to persuade 'his friends of the commerce' to desist.

Magro replied that it was impossible for him to do anything at all, whereupon Izquierdo threatened to report Magro to the Viceroy. Magro, however, referred the scene to his associates, Juan Pascual de Fagoaga, Castilian merchant of Oaxaca, Juan Carlos Barberena, Manuel de Iribarren both of the same description, Martin de Uranga, Basque merchant of Oaxaca, and Pedro Nieto de Silva, retired Lieutenant of the Provincial Battalion of Militias and Alcalde Ordinario (second category) of the Ayuntamiento of Oaxaca. They assembled other merchants, and in full defiance of the authorities, they swore the oath of loyalty to Ferdinand VII at 7.30 a.m. on 17 August 1808 in the house of Manuel del Solar Campero. Once taken, they proceeded to the Cabildos Eclesiástico and Secular, which then took the oath, followed by 'almost all the citizenry'. The Ayuntamiento then went to the interim-Intendant, Izquierdo, and his Secretary, Álvarez, as senior officials of their corporation, requesting that they also swear. They, however, hesitated, to the scandal of the merchants and councillors. Under public pressure they swore, but Castillejos did not.[1]

After the oath ceremonies, the Oaxaca merchants then vented their wrath on Izquierdo, Castillejos, and Álvarez, for their opposition to their political aims. On 23 September 1808, three of them, Goytia, Andrés de Larrazábal, and Patricio Saravia wrote to Archbishop Lizana, for passage to the Viceroy and the scrutiny of the Real Acuerdo, that the public of the city had made a prior representation to Iturrigaray against the conduct of Izquierdo and his colleagues. Such men had now opposed the oath-taking to Ferdinand VII. The merchants accused the Oaxaca administrators of declaring their hatred for Ferdinand in private conversations, and their affection for Napoleon and the French. Iturrigaray, they said, had hidden or disdained their petition. Therefore, they requested that the present government and the Real Acuerdo should order the arrest of the traitors, who, they said, had been in league with the plans of Iturrigaray.

This representation was followed by another, signed by such citizens

1 AGN *Intendentes* 12. See Glossary of Personnel.

of note as Colonel Juan Francisco de Echarri, Adrián de Cerain, Juan Carlos Barberena, Pedro Nieto de Silva and others, chiefly representatives and deputies of the Oaxaca commerce. They requested the concession of special powers of investigation to a lawyer of the Audiencia, Juan Martín de Juanmartiñena, who had been Juan Francisco de Echarri's financial agent in Mexico City. His rank on the Audiencia had been his reward for support of the coup against Iturrigaray, whose bitter opponent he had been.[1] Juanmartiñena's purpose was to bring the grievances of the Oaxaca merchants before the Real Acuerdo.

On 24 October, this lawyer requested the Real Acuerdo to allow the formation of armed patrols from among the Oaxaca merchants and militiamen in order to check any disorders that might arise in the city. For, there circulated a rumour that 1,800 rifles were hidden, and Regidor Sebastián González was already requesting full powers for searching houses. The Real Acuerdo granted the merchants' request on 9 November.[2]

The merchants then celebrated a junta on 27 September, against the wishes of both Izquierdo and Bishop Bergoza y Jordán. Izquierdo reported to Garibay on the 30th that he had been visited by Echarri, Cerain, and Joseph Riveiro de Aguilar on behalf of the merchants. They had said that *pasquinades* had been posted on street corners, and that they feared attacks on certain houses by seditious persons. They wanted a 10 p.m. curfew to accompany the patrols. Izquierdo, however, said he had been surprised at this, for, to his knowledge, the city was perfectly calm. A short time later, Izquierdo was informed by them that they intended to hold another junta for discussion with the Intendancy authorities. This they held, but, instead of a private meeting, the merchants had, to the surprise of both Izquierdo and Bergoza, convened a public meeting, attended by a large crowd at the door, in the corridors and rooms. The meeting place was the Episcopal Palace, for which Bergoza wished to receive an explanation. The Bishop estimated the total at 150—persons he had never seen before, he reported to Viceroy Garibay. He said in his letter of 4 October, that so far the lower elements in the city were calm and very silent, but this junta, which was supposed to have been private, had been political in nature and public, and as such constituted a veritable threat to public order.[3]

From this, we can see that Bishop Bergoza was caught between the

---

[1] AGI *Mexico* 2131, *Cuentas de la tesorería principal de Oaxaca*, 1790–6, Otras Tesorerías, 1796. This lawyer was author of *Verdadero origen, carácter, causas, resortes, fines y progresos de la Revolución de Nueva España* (Mexico 1820), a defence of the *Peninsulares* in general, and especially of the authors of the 1808 coup against Iturrigaray.

[2] AGN *Intendentes* 12.   [3] *Ibid.*

position of Izquierdo and that of the merchants. He was surprised to find such an extreme and rapid reaction to the events of 15 and 16 September in Mexico City taking place now in Oaxaca. He was unsure which way the movement of the merchants would lead. His wariness led him to seek momentary refuge in the defence of the *status quo*. For he was not anxious to precipitate events by taking up a conspicuous political position. Such a dangerous course might provoke the lower orders out of their apparent quiescence. Yet, as the course of events moved against the *Teniente Letrado*, Bergoza himself began to take his stand alongside the merchants, joining in the attack on the recalcitrant oath-takers, adding with it an indictment of the policies and character of the deceased Intendant, Antonio de Mora y Peysal. Through the events of 1808–10 Bergoza emerged as one of the key figures not only of the Intendancy of Oaxaca, but also of the Viceroyalty of New Spain, culminating in his supremacy in the ecclesiastical sphere as Archbishop-elect of Mexico, alongside Viceroy Calleja in the secular sphere.

On 24 March 1809, an anonymous letter was received by Garibay, attacking Mora, and calling for the reform of the political régime in the city of Oaxaca. The unknown writer accused Mora of indolence and a preference for the interests of the lower orders. Their arrogance had, as a result, led them to decline to present themselves for the labour which was due from them on the haciendas, and to ignore their obligations to their debtors. Izquierdo, Castillejos, and Álvarez were attacked. The government should be removed from the hands of Izquierdo. The attack extended to the Ministers of the Royal Treasury. Micheltorena was a 'creature of Godoy', while Villarrasa was a complete 'Machiavellian'. In the meantime, the merchants cried out for the payment of debts; the *hacendados* for their workers' debts; the artisans for their journeymen's debts; the priest for his dues; the chaplain for the livelihood he derived from the pious works; and the Indian for a redress of grievances petitioned with such sterile results and at such expense. The writer went on to denounce the deputy of justice for Zaachila, a nominee of Mora, and a man of low birth, who had encouraged the Indians to refrain from work on the haciendas. This man was also a reader of French books.[1]

Despite the anonymity of the charges, Garibay's Superior Order of 31 March 1809, demanded an investigation of their substance. One of the replies came from the long opponent of Mora, the former Villa Alta Subdelegate, Bernardino Bonavia, on 7 April. He charged Mora with

---

[1] *Ibid.*

great pride and excessive sloth in his dealings with the lower classes, in whom, as a consequence, he had tolerated every excess. *Hacendados* remained without workers. The price of food was rising, and cultivation had been cut back by half. Castillejos, Izquierdo, and Álvarez were all members of a '*juzgado corrompido*'. Royal revenues were in decay. The Subdelegate of Zimatlán, whom, presumably, the anonymous writer had meant, read French books, and had '*muy poca religión*'. Such was the tone of Bonavia's posthumous attack on his old adversary's administration.

Bergoza's reply was sent on 14 April. Having departed from his caution of September 1808, he had now come so far along the road with the merchant party that he demanded that not only the city of Oaxaca, but, indeed, the whole Realm should be reformed. It was clear from the tone and spirit of argument exactly what he meant by reform. For, following the line of both the Anonymous and Bonavia, he accused Mora, whom he had not attacked during his lifetime, of inaction and indolence, preferring, that is, the Indians against other subjects. Such protection was perhaps unjust, and, surely, had been prejudicial to the Indians, whom he had, thereby, rendered bold, idle, and indifferent. He had desired the estimation of the Indians in order to bask in the aura of popular approval. In consequence, he had not tried to remedy abuses, by which Bergoza meant that he had been little or never accessible to the just complaints of the hacienda-owners, who were suffering from shortage of day-labourers. Moreover, the former Intendant's belief that the poor possessed integrity had led him to favour them at the cost of harming the interests of the artisans. Worst of all was the ugly situation in Zaachila, where always the Indians had been ill-humoured, with a propensity towards rebellion and insubordination. In 1806, they had refused to work on the lands of Simón Camacho, one of the best haciendas of the Valley of Oaxaca. Bergoza went on to denounce Izquierdo, Castillejos, and Álvarez, and the cupidity of the Sub-delegates. Such a situation ensured that in Oaxaca neither God nor King were well served.[1]

The new régime in Mexico City, thereupon, decided to summon the accused to appear for trial. As the Oaxaca administrators were making their way to Mexico City, the Oidores of the Audiencia, Aguirre and Carvajal, prominent in the coup of 1808, and the Fiscal, Sagarzurrieta, recommended that Juan José de la Hoz, interim-Intendant of Havana, then on leave in Mexico, should take over the post in Oaxaca in place of Izquierdo. The order to Hoz was sent out on 19 May 1809.[2]

---

[1] *Ibid.*   [2] *Ibid.*

Political crisis

In the summer of that year, Izquierdo defended himself before the Viceroy. Powerful persons in Oaxaca were persecuting him in bad faith, and the Superior Government's actions were illegal, a violation of the Laws of the Indies, which forbade legal proceedings on the basis of anonymous letters. Instead of despising and burning such letters, the Government had examined witnesses, and collected information. His chief enemy at the Audiencia was Oidor Carvajal, and in Oaxaca it was Alonso Magro, Commander of the Costa del Sur Militias, who himself aspired also to become Intendant.[1]

On 5 August 1809, however, at the orders of the Supreme Junta in Spain, Marshall Garibay handed over the government to Archbishop Lizana.[2] Though Lizana had participated in the coup of 1808, his gradual realization of its implications, and its provocative nature as regards both the Creoles and the lower elements in the Viceroyalty, brought him, in fear, to attempt to reverse those events. He began by attacking his former associates. He hoped desperately to prevent the outbreak of the revolution he sensed was about to occur, but such efforts only precipitated it all the more by dividing and alienating the supporters of the 1808 coup at the critical moment when a show of strength might have preserved a precarious peace. As Spanish Peninsular opposition to him mounted, Lizana fortified the Viceregal Palace against them, and opened a political campaign against the Oidor, Aguirre.[3]

This reversal of policy by Lizana showed itself in the final verdict in the Oaxaca trials, on 19 November 1809. For, though Izquierdo, Castillejos, Álvarez, and the deputies of justice for Zaachila, Ocotlán, and Ejutla had been arraigned for '*crímenes de venalidad, baratería, omisión, negligencia*', the charges were now dismissed as founded in calumny, which, it was added, was the dominant vice in the Realm. The proceedings had been entirely illegal, and not one of the accusations from the twenty-four witnesses could be proved. Archbishop-Viceroy Lizana promised Izquierdo an indemnification, and ordered the whole affair to be archived under the Superior Order of 14 December 1809. The trials ended, but the Audiencia had the last word. Its *Regente* explained that there were no funds available to cover the indemnification promised by Lizana to Izquierdo.[4]

The accusers of the Intendancy administrators were those merchants with intimate connexions with the old *repartimientos*, with the merchants

---

[1] *Ibid.*   [2] AGI *Mexico* 1633, Correspondencia del Virrey Garibay (1809).
[3] L. E. Fisher, *The Background of the Mexican Revolution for Independence* (Boston 1934), 313, and Alamán, *Historia de Méjico*, i, 277–9.   [4] AGN *Intendentes* 12.

of the Consulado of Mexico, with whom they operated in political harmony, and with the principal Oidores of the Audiencia of Mexico. It was they who, by their pressure on Izquierdo and Bergoza, in the autumn of 1808 managed to secure political control in Oaxaca. Gradually Bergoza, though reluctant at first, associated himself with them, and assumed leadership as chief political figure in the Intendancy of Oaxaca after 1809 and until the Insurgent occupation of the city in November 1812. The whole movement of the *Peninsulares* in Oaxaca, a vigorous reaction against Iturrigaray's association with the Creoles, sought to reverse the consequences of the establishment of the Intendancy in 1786. The various letters of the spring of 1809, and in particular that of Bergoza, blamed the late Intendant Mora and his administration for the loss of their privileges and prestige, and demanded that, now the régime in Mexico City had been changed, order should be restored in the locality so that the indigenous population would once more respect the *hacendado* and merchant. This order, Bergoza said, had lapsed due to Mora's favour of the Indians, and his taking seriously of the articles of the Ordinance of Intendants.

In the middle of 1810, the Audiencia compiled a report on the state of the economy and on the news of increasing insubordination among the lower orders. The Fiscal de lo Civil, Ambrosio Sagarzurrieta, pointed to the decadence of Oaxaca's dye trade, and warned the Superior Government to take action to prevent its impending extinction. The Audiencia, as a result, circulated the chief political, ecclesiastical, and military figures of Oaxaca for their views.

The opinion of the new Intendant of Oaxaca, a Creole, Joseph María Lasso, appointed by the Seville Junta on 18 June 1809, was that the *repartimiento* should be restored. For, though he believed that the very abuses which Article 12 had sought to eradicate would most likely return, he considered that the sole method of ensuring the survival of the cochineal trade would be the *repartimiento*. The end of the cochineal industry would result in incalculable harm for the State. Lasso recommended a return to the policy of 1751, and a departure from the policies of the first Intendant.[1]

Bishop Bergoza, in his most thorough indictment of the régime of the Intendancy, described the period after 1787 as a decline for the cochineal trade from the period of prosperity before that year. The explanations

---

[1] AGN *Industria y comercio*, 20 (1788–1821), exp. 6, ff. 165 *et seq.*, Lasso–Venegas, no. 140, February 12, 1811. See Glossary of Personnel.

were several: the variability of the weather, the frequent sickness among both men and livestock, the delay of shippings due to the wars after 1779; but the principal cause was the Spanish Government's departure from the traditional system of government in the Indies. Moreover, for the past twenty years [*sic*], the Spanish Government had been in the hands of a 'vicious and inept favourite', Godoy. Though every corporation within the State had suffered, the restoration of wise government had now taken place under the legitimate sovereign, Ferdinand VII (who, of course, had never been near the government in Spain since his abortive reign of the spring of 1808, and was now a prisoner of Napoleon in France).

The introduction of the Intendancies had been combined with the ineptitude of Godoy. As a result of the prohibition of *repartimientos* by the Alcaldes Mayores, the Indian towns no longer received their *habilitación*, which was the chief cause of the decline of the dye trade. The removal of the Alcalde Mayor's coercion ensured that the Indians, naturally given to drunkenness, would flee from work. It had proved impossible to excite within them a love of the *Patria* (i.e. Spain), or any concern for their own material welfare. Such was the Indian left to himself.

Bergoza's point of view was exactly the opposite of Mora's. In contrast to the late Intendant, Bergoza believed that what was good for the Indians was the stick, not philanthropic philosophies. He went on to say, 'The establishment of the Intendancies has indirectly stimulated the indolence and sloth of the Indians. This has been grievously suffered on the larger Spanish haciendas, where they used to go to work.'[1]

Without the intervention of the Alcalde Mayor, the merchants were unable to secure the same financial guarantees from the Indians who traded with them. They lost, as a result, the greater part of their investments, and present commerce was reduced to small purchases of the dye in the Friday and Saturday markets. This was in contrast to the 200,000 to 300,000 pesos in *habilitación*, which former Alcaldes Mayores might have secured for the richest *partidos*, Jicayan, Villa Alta, Zimatlán, Teposcolula, and Nejapa, and even 30,000 to 40,000 in the poorer parts. The aspiration of the reformers had been that others than the Alcaldes Mayores should be able to enjoy the profits of the trade once it had been opened to free competition, but the result had only been more merchants and less cochineal. For, laws in practice did not always correspond to the good intentions of the legislator. Moreover, 'while the reign of Charles III was certainly the epoch of the great reforms in the nation, nevertheless, with-

[1] *Ibid.*

out offence to his glory, that of the Intendancies, at least in the Province of Oaxaca, has not produced the happiest results'.¹

As a remedy for the decay, and adjacent problems such as the decline of Villa Alta cotton-mantle production from 200,000 a year before 1787 to less than one-third, and the migration of Indians from the *partidos* of production into the city of Oaxaca, Bergoza recommended the removal of the prohibition of the *repartimiento*, and that the law should be employed to keep the Indians at their tasks. Violence and usury should, however, be duly punished. He went on to suggest that *hacendados* with land fit for the raising of *nopaleras* should be ordered to cultivate cochineal. Finally, the Bishop reaffirmed his faith in the laws of God and Church, and declared that no laws were more holy than the Laws of the Indies.²

These views were supported by the Deputies of Commerce in Oaxaca, Francisco Antonio Goytia, Juan Carlos Barberena, Antonio Sánchez, Josef Castañeda and Juan Francisco de la Vega. They attributed the decline of cochineal to three causes, the natural idleness of the Indians if not coerced, the absence of *habilitación* as a result of the establishment of the Intendancies, and the lack of an '*agente interesado*' with authority to put the Indians to work. In the days before the Intendancy the annual crop of cochineal had been 30,000 arrobas, but at present it had dropped to 16,000 to 18,000. In the same way, before 1787 the sum of $1\frac{1}{2}$, or 2 million pesos had entered the province in the form of *habilitación*. The merchants required that their interests be guaranteed by a restoration of social order, and the reduction of the Indians to their proper place as workers in the cochineal trade or on the haciendas. In order to persuade the Superior Government of this necessity, they used the argument that the Royal revenues would benefit, though as, Appendix 7 shows (p. 176), there is every evidence that they had improved very considerably since 1787.

The prerequisite for the restoration of the cochineal trade was, of course, the re-establishment of the *repartimiento* on the lines of the legislation of 1751, and under the proviso that the future *Alcabalas* Mayores should be men of good birth, education, and honesty.³

The call for the restoration of the old system was reiterated by the Administrator of the Royal Customs and *Alcabalas*, Saravia, and by the Subdelegates of Nejapa, Teposcolula, Jicayan, and others, and by the most powerful military chief in Oaxaca, the Commander of the Seventh Brigade, who was the former Subdelegate of Villa Alta, Bernardino Bonavia.⁴

¹ *Ibid.*   ² *Ibid.*   ³ *Ibid.*   ⁴ *Ibid.*

Political crisis

One of the candidates for election to the Spanish Cortes in August 1810, the parish priest of Tlalixtac, Joseph Victoriano de Baños, added his weight to the call for the restoration of the *repartimiento* in his *Dictamen teológico-político a favor de los repartimientos*, of 24 October 1810. He added that the collapse would have been even more extensive had not several Subdelegates, unable to subsist on their 5 per cent levy, been obliged to practise clandestine inobservance of Article 12, and had not some merchants continued to issue their own *repartimientos* in response to the more than doubling of the cochineal price in last few years. The priest advocated the 1751 style controlled *repartimiento*, the type which, as we saw, never came into effect.[1] For, it was this system that Viceroy Venegas had in mind when he issued the *Bando* of 5 October 1810, of which the cleric approved.[2]

This *Bando*, which Alamán dated as the 8 October, formed the corollary of the declaration of the suspension of the Indian tribute payment, issued in the Decree of 26 May 1810, by the Regency Council in Cádiz. This decree had reached Mexico City in the summer of 1810, but had been held up by the Audiencia Gobernadora to await the arrival of the new Viceroy, Venegas. In the meantime, a few days before his arrival, the Hidalgo revolution broke out in the Intendancy of Guanajuato on 16 September. In order to forestall Indian support for the revolution, Venegas issued the Regency Council's decree. Since, however, the salaries of the Subdelegates came from the 5 per cent levy from the Indian tributes, the Viceroy ordered on 5 October that the discussion on the question of payment of salaries to the Subdelegates was to cease, and that the old system of the *repartimiento* by the Royal justices was to be restored.[3]

However, the Regency Council, the Cádiz Cortes, and the régime brought to power in Mexico by the 1808 coup were all interim régimes, which subsisted only until the return to the throne of Ferdinand VII. When Ferdinand returned from his French captivity in May 1814, he annulled all the measures legislated in his absence. One of them was the Regency Council's decree for the ending of the Indian tribute payments, and with it the Viceregal *Bando* of 5 October 1810. Ferdinand's Royal Decree of 1 March 1815 restored Indian tribute payment. This was not greeted in Mexico with any enthusiasm. For, when Viceroy Calleja proposed the dispatch of the decree to the Intendants of the provinces where the revolution had been crushed, or which had been unaffected, the

---

1 *Ibid.* ff. 208–19, and see also, Genaro V. Vásquez, *Doctrinas y realidades en la legislación para los indios* (Mexico 1940), 433–54. See Chapter 1.
2 *Ibid.*   3 Alamán, *Historia*, i, 342.

Audiencia opposed the action, declaring that the Crown's decree was unenforceable. The Superior Government, thereupon, suspended it, and informed the Crown that it had done so. In this way, the Viceregal *Bando* of 5 October 1810 for the return of the *repartimiento* remained in force after the restoration of the legitimate government of Ferdinand VII in Spain.[1]

During the course of the Hidalgo and Morelos revolutions in New Spain, the Constituent Cortes in Cádiz, which opened on 24 September 1810 and continued in session until 20 September 1813, was attempting to introduce a constitutional system of government throughout the Spanish Indies. The extension of constitutional government to Spanish America and the Philippines stemmed from the Supreme Junta of Seville's Decree of 22 January 1809, that Spain's overseas kingdoms and provinces were integral parts of the monarchy, and enjoyed thereby the same political rights as those of the Peninsula.[2] The Decree of the Regency Council issued on 14 February 1810, invited the American territories to send deputies to sit in the Cortes. This decree reached Mexico City on 16 May, and the Audiencia Gobernadora commissioned the holding of elections, which were to be conducted by the Ayuntamiento in each of the provincial capitals. These bodies, most of which were closed corporations with large numbers of perpetual councillors who had either inherited or purchased their office, would select three natives of their province as nominees, from whom one candidate was to be chosen as the deputy to the Cortes. He would then proceed to Spain.[3]

On 10 August 1810, the Ayuntamiento of Oaxaca met to conduct its elections. Besides Bishop Bergoza and his Cabildo Eclesiástico, who had been invited to attend, the members present were the President the Intendant Lasso, and the following Regidores Perpetuos: Ordóñez Díaz, Andrés de Larrazabal, Diego de Villasante, Sebastián González, José Regules Villasante, Mateo Alonso Mansilla, Pedro de Estrella, and Miguel Alesón. All of them were well-known Spanish Peninsular merchants.[4]

---

1 AGI *Mexico* 1830, *Expedientes inventariados* (1817), Calleja–Crown, 31 July 1816.
2 For the Hidalgo and subsequent revolutionary movements, see especially, Luis Villoro, *La Revolución de Independencia—Ensayo de interpretación histórica* (Mexico 1953), and Hugh M. Hamill, *The Hidalgo Revolt. Prelude to Mexican Independence* (Florida, Gainesville 1966). For the constitutional periods, 1810–14 and 1820–3, see, Nettie Lee Benson (ed.), *Mexico and the Spanish Cortes, 1810–1822: Eight Essays* (Latin American Monographs, No. 5, Institute of Latin American Studies, University of Texas, Austin, 1966).
3 *Ibid.* See especially, 1. Charles R. Berry, 'The Election of the Mexican Deputies to the Spanish Cortes, 1810–1822', 10–42.
4 Archivo Municipal de Oaxaca, *Tesorería municipal*, 1 (1746–1829). See Glossary of Personnel.

Ordóñez Díaz had inherited his office from Jiménez Bochórquez in May 1788, who himself had been a son-in-law of Diego de Villasante.[1] Larrazábal was a Castilian merchant. Villasante, also a Castilian, was recorded as a Regidor Perpetuo in 1772, and in the later 1770s was at the same time Alcalde Mayor of the Cuatro Villas.[2] Regules Villasante, who had inherited his office in 1797, was a Castilian, and had married María Josefa Ibáñez, sister of Antonio Ibáñez de Corbera.[3] Estrella had inherited his office in 1798 for a fee paid to the Crown.[4] Two Regidores Honorarios, that is councillors chosen every two years by the Perpetuos, also participated: Manuel de Anievas, another Spanish Peninsular, and Lic. Juan María Ibáñez, a Creole, and brother of Antonio Ibáñez de Corbera.[5]

This Ayuntamiento, controlled by the Spanish Peninsular merchants, conducted the first election of the constitutional period. As they were not allowed to elect themselves, for they were not natives of the province of Oaxaca, their choice rested on those either most closely associated or most favourably disposed towards them. The names selected most were Antonio Ibáñez de Corbera, Lic. Juan María Ibáñez, Manuel María Mejía, parish priest of Tamasulapan, and José Victoriano de Baños, the priest of Tlalixtac, who was to call for the return of the *repartimiento* in his *Dictamen* of 24 October. Both Ordóñez Díaz and Regules Villasante mentioned Murguía y Galardi as a possible candidate. However, the priest, Mejía, was elected. He, nevertheless, declined the honour, and a further election, on 10 September, resulted in the choice of Lic. Juan María Ibáñez.[6] He was about to leave in January 1811, but never reached the Cortes.[7] Therefore, Oaxaca was unrepresented by a proprietary deputy in this first phase of the Cortes before the promulgation of the Constitution in 1812. Nevertheless, the implications of this first essay in constitutionalism were clear. There could be no proper representative government as long as elections of deputies to the Cortes were based on an unreformed Ayuntamiento.

Under the Constitution, promulgated on 19 March 1812, a new system of elections was prescribed on the basis of a tier system from parish to district to province. At the same time Article 312 provided for popular

---

1 AGN *General de parte* 74 (1793–9) and 71, f. 61.
2 AGN *Intendentes* 49 (1772), and AGN *Civil* 1468, exp. 18.
3 AGN *General de parte* 74 (1793–9), and AGI *Mexico* 1496, *Duplicados del virrey* (1818), Apodaca–Min. de Hacienda, no. 376, 21 March 1818.
4 AGN *General de parte* 74 (1793–9).
5 Archivo Municipal de Oaxaca, *Tesorería municipal*, 1.
6 *Ibid.* See also Alamán, *Historia*, i, doc. no. 15, App. 452, where a list of New Spain's deputies to the Cortes are given.   7 Benson, *Mexico and Spanish Cortes*, 1. Berry, 16.

election of municipal councils, and ordered the cessation of all perpetual and purchased offices. However, by the time these reforms were to become implemented, the city of Oaxaca had already fallen to the Insurgents under Morelos.[1]

The response of the authorities in Oaxaca to the revolutionary movements of Hidalgo and Morelos was one of vigorous opposition. On 6 November 1810, the Ayuntamiento wrote to Viceroy Venegas offering its funds for the struggle against the insurrection. The same small group of Peninsular merchants, and their associate, Juan María Ibáñez de Corbera, signed the letter. They denounced the revolutionary movements as 'diametrically opposed to Religion, to King, and to the State', and they reaffirmed their support for the rights of Ferdinand VII, and in the links between New Spain and the Peninsula.[2]

During the years 1811 and 1812, the revolutionary forces of Morelos penetrated the Intendancy of Oaxaca from the Pacific coastal regions and through the Mixteca Alta. The first signs of unrest had been a revolution in the cotton region of Jamiltepec, in the Pacific *partido* of Jicayan, but Bishop Bergoza had apparently been able to pacify the rising without recourse to bloodshed. As the Insurgents approached Oaxaca, Bergoza took the lead in the resistance by raising a patriotic loan of 300,000 pesos from his clergy, and exhorting his flock in sermons and pastorals, such as that of June 1811 ordering the clergy to denounce conspirators on pain of excommunication, to remain loyal to the Crown.[3]

On the death of Lizana, the Regency Council in Cádiz appointed Bergoza to the dignity of Archbishop of Mexico, on 23 November 1811, but Intendant Lasso and the Oaxaca Ayuntamiento begged him to remain

---

[1] Benson, *Mexico*, 66–8, 76–81. These municipal elections were entirely separate from the election of deputies to the Cortes. Though the status of 'citizen', the category eligible to vote in such elections, was only generally defined, including Spanish *Peninsulares*, Creoles, Indians, and mestizos, but excluding all groups of African origin, the deciding issue would be over who was a '*vecino*' (resident). The *vecino* had to be a head of the family, permanent resident of the region in which he voted. This specification would naturally favour the Creoles.

After the expulsion of the Insurgents from Oaxaca in 1814, these elections to the Ayuntamiento Constitucional were held, and that body installed. However, on 8 November, 1814, Viceroy Calleja published Ferdinand VII's decree for the restoration of the pre-1808 municipal councils, and the Ayuntamiento Constitucional was dissolved.

[2] Hernández y Dávalos, Juan Eusebio, *Colección de documentos para la historia de la guerra de independencia de México, de 1808 á 1821* (6 vols.; Mexico 1877–82), ii, doc. 119, 207.

[3] AHH (AGN), leg. 696, exp. 42, Consulado, año de 1816, Informe de los méritos del Ilmo. Sr. Obispo de Oaxaca, Dr. D. Antonio Bergoza y Jordán, que este tribunal hizo al rey Ntro. Sr. See Karl M. Schmitt, 'The Clergy and the Independence of New Spain', *HAHR*, xxxiv (1954), 289–312.

in the city because of the proximity of Morelos. This he agreed to do, and while there, he organised a special militia force from among the very clergy itself to aid in the defence of the city against the approaching Insurgents. However, as the rebels continued to advance through the Mixteca Alta and into the Valley of Oaxaca, Bergoza, in company with Intendant Lasso, decided to abandon the city, soon followed by the *Teniente Letrado*. They made their way to Chiapas, in the Kingdom of Guatemala, by way of Tehuantepec, and from there they passed to the Gulf coast on the journey to Veracruz and Mexico City. Bergoza arrived in the capital on 13 March 1813, and promptly took up his position as Archbishop-elect of Mexico. He had left Dr. Antonio Ibáñez de Corbera in charge of the administration of the Oaxaca diocese.[1]

Morelos and the Insurgents entered the city of Oaxaca on 25 November 1812, and remained in occupation until 29 March 1814, when the Royalist commander Brigadier Melchor Álvarez recovered it for Spain. The first task of the revolutionaries was to administer punishment to those who had openly opposed them. The Commander-in-Chief of the Royalist forces in Oaxaca, Regules, who had checked Morelos' general, Trujano, at the siege of Yanhuitlán in February 1812, was captured in the Convent of Carmen, and shot on 4 December. Other Royalist commanders were also shot, Lieutenant-General Antonio González Saravia, chief of Spanish forces defending the city, Bernardino Bonavia, former Villa Alta Subdelegate and Colonel Commander of the Seventh Brigade, and Nicolás Aristi, present Subdelegate of Villa Alta and Captain Commander of the Division.[2]

With the occupation of Oaxaca, and the dispatch of Morelos' lieutenants Miguel and Víctor Bravo to Jamiltepec at the end of December 1812 to secure the whole Pacific coast as far as Acapulco, the circumstances of the revolution entirely changed. With the defeat of the Royalist forces from Guatemala in the Isthmus of Tehuantepec, the task of organising the captured provinces under a national Mexican government really began. On 9 February 1813, José María Murguía y Galardi was chosen Insurgent Intendant of Oaxaca by popular election, an innovation of Morelos. When, therefore, on 1 March 1813, the rebel propagandist, Dr. Cos, drew up the list of those who were to form the Congress of Chilpancingo, Murguía as Oaxaca's Intendant was included.[3]

1 Eutimio Pérez, *Recuerdos históricos del episcopado Oaxaqueño* (Oaxaca 1888), 87; and Andrés Portillo, *Oaxaca en el centenario de la Independencia Nacional* (Oaxaca 1910), 55–6.
2 Portillo, *Oaxaca*, 59.
3 Alamán, *Historia*, iii, 250–2; Hernández y Dávalos, *Colección*, v, 296–7.

The Spanish *Peninsulares*, meanwhile, attempted to salvage what they could of their position by a direct appeal to the Insurgent commander, Benito Rocha. The petitioners, led by Ordóñez Díaz, Simón Gutiérrez, Fausto de Corres, José de Regules, and other frequently cited names, in their representation of 19 March 1813 entirely changed their tone from the days when the Insurgents had been far from the city. Now the capital had been conquered by the 'immortal General Morelos', from whom they requested a pardon for all the Europeans, even for 'those who, obliged by the former régime, had the misfortune to find themselves under arms'. They went on to praise Morelos' government for its respect of ecclesiastical immunity, which was in contrast to their previous denunciation of the revolution in 1810 as the enemy of religion. They praised its protection of orphans, its relief of widows, and poor clerics, and its wise edict establishing a tithe on cochineal, which they themselves and their predecessors had been vigorously resisting since the beginning of the eighteenth century.[1]

On 30 April 1813, Morelos ordered the election of the fifth member, or *vocal*, of the Congress of Chilpancingo from the province of Oaxaca. The elected candidate would join those of Valladolid, Guadalajara, Guanajuato, and Tecpan (Guerrero). In preparation of the organisation of the junta to decide this election, the Insurgent lawyer and journalist, Carlos María de Bustamante, himself a Oaxaqueño, arrived on 24 May 1813; immediately he took charge of the Insurgent newspaper, *Correo Americano del Sur*.[2]

The Insurgent advance on the city of Oaxaca had provoked the flight of the principal Peninsular civil and ecclesiastical leaders. The fall of the city ensured the execution of the military commanders. Morelos' own departure from Oaxaca for the Pacific coast, on 9 January 1813, ensured that, alongside the remaining Insurgent garrison, the chief powers in

---

[1] Hernández y Dávalos, *Colección*, v, 923–4. The cochineal tithe was established by Morelos, himself a cleric; see Alamán, *Historia*, iii, 250.

Morelos wrote to the Dean and Chapter of Oaxaca on 12 November 1812, before the fall of the city, informing them of a letter of the same date sent to Bishop Bergoza, in which, denouncing the 'three centuries of despotism', he affirmed his desire to defend ecclesiastical immunity. AGN *Infidencias* 108, ff. 272–3 *v*, no. 2.

For the attitude of the Insurgent clerics to the controversial issue of ecclesiastical immunity, see N. M. Farriss, *Crown and Clergy in Colonial Mexico 1759–1821. The Crisis of Ecclesiastical Privilege* (London, University of, Historical Studies xxi, 1968), 197–253, and Appendix, 254–265, *Ecclesiastical Participants in the Mexican Independence Movement 1808–20*.

[2] AHN, *Consejos* 21,390, Consejo de Indias, no. 2, Superior Gobierno, año de 1817, ff. 13–13 *v*; J. M. Miquel i Vergés, *La Independencia Mexicana y la prensa insurgente* (Colegio de México 1941), 156.

Political crisis

Oaxaca would be the Ayuntamiento, under the presidency of the Intendant, Murguía y Galardi, or his *Teniente Letrado*, Manuel María Mimiaga, both of whom were Creole hacienda-owners, and the Cabildo Eclesiástico, under Dr. Ibáñez de Corbera, also from a wealthy and propertied Creole family. It was from the Creole personnel of these bodies that the fifth *vocal* was selected. The candidate selected was Intendant Murguía, who secured twenty-nine out of eighty-five votes, followed by Castillejos, with twenty-four, and Carlos Bustamante with twenty-three.[1] On 18 August 1813, the *Promotor Fiscal*, Castillejos, requested from the protesting Cabildo Eclesiástico the sum of 7,000 pesos to pay for the expenses of the persons proceeding to Chilpancingo, and for the maintenance of Insurgent troops.[2] In fact, Castillejos himself was soon to proceed to the Insurgent National Congress as one of the fifteen members of its judiciary, representing Oaxaca, along with Lic. Nicolás Bustamante, brother of D. Carlos.[3]

Murguía duly attended the Congress of Chilpancingo, and actively participated in its sessions, which opened on 8 September 1813. He it was who presided over the Congress when, on 13 September, it elected Morelos to be Supreme General and Chief of the Executive of independent America, the 'Republic of Anáhuac'.[4]

However, as the tide of the revolution changed, and, under the firm direction of Viceroy Calleja, the Royalists once more gained the upper hand, Murguía returned to Oaxaca. On the approach of the Royalist commander, Brigadier Melchor Álvarez, before the city, on 29 March 1814, Murguía, as Intendant, went from the city to meet Álvarez, and hand over authority in person. He was then summoned before Viceroy Calleja to account for his apparent espousal of the Insurgent cause. His defence must have been well substantiated, for he was acquitted without punishment or disgrace, and appeared again in Oaxaca as one of the Ministers of the Royal Treasury under the Royalist régime, between 1814 and 1817.[5]

Ibáñez de Corbera, for his part, emphasised to Intendant Álvarez his devotion to the 'good cause' and denounced the 'cruel and bloodthirsty

---

1 AHN, *Consejos*, ff. 21–48 *v*. The elections were held between 3 and 9 August 1813, with eighty-five persons present from among the leading Creole members of the Ayuntamiento and the clergy.
2 *Ibid.* Consejo de Indias, no. 5, ff. 11 *v*.–12 *v*.
3 Hernández y Dávalos, *Collección*, v, 159–60.
4 *Ibid.* vi, 216. This assembly produced the Act of Independence on 6 November 1813, and the Constitution of Apatzingán on 22 October 1814.
5 Portillo, *Oaxaca*, 88; Archivo del estado de Oaxaca, unclassified legajos for 1814–17.

despot, Morelos'. Nothing he had done during the rebel occupation had been voluntary, nor had he ever mixed in public or private with the Insurgents. The witnesses to his good faith were precisely those who had benefited by supremacy in the Ayuntamiento under Insurgent rule, namely Murguía y Galardi, Mimiaga, Pedro José de la Vega, and Pedro Nieto de Silva, and two Spanish Peninsular merchants, traditional associates of the Ibáñez family, the Regidor Manuel Anievas, and Simón Gutiérrez de Villegas. Murguía, himself compromised, testified that Ibáñez had never been a partisan of the Insurgents, and had never shown himself to be. Ibáñez himself in the presence of Intendant Álvarez on 20 May 1814, described Morelos' rule as 'duress' and 'captivity'. Typical of it was an order from 'that infernal clique formed in Chilpancingo', of which his principal defendant, Murguía, had been an active member, for the celebration of a Mass of Thanksgiving, for the installation of the 'so-called Supreme Congress'. He had been forced to accede owing to the armed force surrounding him on all sides. The Oaxaca Ayuntamiento concluded after hearing that defence that Ibáñez 'was certainly martyr to a despotism that knew no limits'.[1]

The documents captured from the Insurgents at Tlacotepec contained the correspondence between Ibáñez and the Insurgent leaders. It was these that Bergoza, Archbishop-elect of Mexico, discussed in his letter to Viceroy Calleja on 12 July 1814. In his view, Ibáñez, though his conduct had been cowardly, was innocent of the charge of collaboration. Nevertheless, he condemned the ambiguity of the behaviour of both Ibáñez and Murguía. Similar behaviour, he pointed out, had been observed in the case of the citizens and cabildos of Valladolid de Michoacan and Guadalajara.[2]

The Fiscal de Real Hacienda, however, disagreed with Bergoza's conciliatory policy, and declared that the captured documents clearly showed that the Cabildo Secular was guilty of complicity, and that Ibáñez had been not merely servile but had both voluntarily and efficaciously desired to comply with the orders of Morelos. The witnesses in Oaxaca now were protesting their loyalty to the Crown, but they had not shown it on the day.[3]

In Oaxaca, there was great confusion over ecclesiastical appointments until the issues of Ibáñez's guilt or innocence had been settled. For the

---

[1] AHN *Consejos* 21,390, Consejo de Indias, Superior Gobierno año de 1817, no. 1, ff. 6–25 *v.* See also AGN *Infidencias* 157, Secretaría del virreinato, año de 1814, Buena conducta observada por el Dr. D. José Ibáñez Corvera; and AGN *Infidencias* 108, f. 165, no. 848, and f. 270.   [2] AHN *Consejos*, ff. 27–8 *v.*   [3] *Ibid.* ff. 29–32.

accused was awaiting news of Royal approval for his elevation to the rank of Dean.[1]

Late in 1814, however, Ferdinand VII failed to approve Bergoza's promotion to the rank of Archbishop of Mexico, for it had been an appointment of the Regency Council, whose measures Ferdinand had annulled in his Decree of 4 May 1814. On 7 January 1815, Canon Pedro Fonte of the Mexico Cathedral was selected Archbishop. Against the removal of Bergoza, the Consulado of Mexico protested on 4 April 1815, emphasising Bergoza's merits and loyalty to the Royalist cause.[2] Bergoza's illustration of this devotion was his defrocking of the captured Morelos in November 1815, and his handing over of him to the secular arm for execution on 22 December 1815.[3] Bergoza's last official act was his consecration of Pedro Fonte as Archbishop, a humiliating duty, on 29 June 1816. Before leaving for Spain, however, he came to agreement with Viceroy Apodaca over the Ibáñez case, handing over to the Viceroy the Royal documents appointing Ibáñez to the Deanship in October. On 20 October of the following year, Bergoza left for Spain, where Ferdinand VII had appointed him not to an Archbishopric, but to the Bishopric of Tarragona.[4]

The whole Ibáñez case dragged on before the Council of the Indies until its final verdict on 19 April 1819, when, optimistically agreeing with the Audiencia of Mexico, the Council declared that nothing in the file of documents before it was sufficient to darken the faithful and loyal conduct of Ibáñez and his Cabildo Eclesiástico either before or after the occupation of Oaxaca by the Insurgents, despite Viceroy Apodaca's doubts to the contrary. As a result, Ibáñez should be promoted to the Deanship he had been requesting since 1811.[5]

The Royalist Intendant, Melchor Álvarez, reporting to the Superior Government in 1814 on the state of Oaxaca after the Insurgent occupation, lamented the damage done to the cochineal industry. For, the dye had suffered through lack of sale, and from the flight of Spanish *Peninsulares*, who had taken their capital with them. His estimate of production loss came to 11,000 arrobas per year, and claimed that the total value of such losses during the three years, 1811, 1812, and 1813 amounted to 2,268,750 pesos.[6] In the last two years, the production figure registered

---

1 *Ibid.* ff. 33–4, 37–8.
2 AHH leg. 696, exp. 42.
3 See Schmitt, 'The Clergy and Independence'.
4 Pérez, *Recuerdos históricos*, 87.
5 AHN *Consejos*, 21,390, 1818, Oaxaca, no. 68, Apodaca–Min. de Gracia y Justicia, November 11, 1817. The Council's verdict is contained on ff. 38–9 *v*.
6 BM Add. MSS 17,557, ff. 31–3.

in the Oaxaca office had dropped to 199,800 pounds and 178,875 pounds respectively, and by 1813 the peak price reached in 1809, 33 reales, had slumped to 15 reales, and the value of the crop reached its lowest ever since the registry figures were first issued in 1758, the minimal sum of 335,390 pesos.[1] These developments were reflected in the export trade at Veracruz. For, in 1814, with the highest cochineal price since the establishment of the Consulado in 1796, a figure of 320 pesos per arroba, the amount of the dye actually shipped sank to only 74,825 pounds.[2]

Most other commodities had been seriously damaged also. Álvarez described how, before the revolution, 9,000 persons had been employed in cotton-spinning and between 500 and 600 in weaving in the city of Oaxaca.[3] The raw material had come from Jamiltepec, where a rebellion had broken out in 1811. This cotton had been transported to the *obrajes* of Oaxaca and the city of Puebla by mule-train. The provision of this essential service had been the particular profession of the inhabitants of the *partido* of Justlahuaca. This transport stopped when the Insurgents under Morelos began to push through the Mixteca Alta on their way to the Valley of Oaxaca.[4] In their advance through the sugar-producing regions of Tlaxiaco, Murguía wrote, the industry had by 1813 been annihilated. As a result, after the departure of the Insurgents, the province of Oaxaca was compelled to import its sugar from Cuautla and Tenango, and other regions, as it had been in the days before the flourishing of its own industry in the course of the eighteenth century.[5]

Álvarez pointed to a similar experience in the case of Teposcolula, which had been the source not only of the best sugar of the province but also of the best wheat. Upon the invasion of the region by the Insurgents, the masters of the mills and haciendas had abandoned their lands and properties. The greater part of their workers had risen to join the Insurgents, and some of the former overseers, probably mestizos, had become leaders of rebel bands. This 'revolutionary mob' had appropriated the funds and tools of the estates. They had eaten the oxen meant for labour in the fields, and the cattle of the haciendas and ranches. The estates, in that way, had been reduced to total extinction.[6]

In their anxiety to clear the province of the Royalists, and prevent a Royalist counter-revolution from Guatemala, where most of the Oaxaca

---

[1] See Appendix 1.
[2] Lerdo de Tejada, *Comercio exterior*, número 14. See Appendix 6.
[3] For Intendant Mora's report on the Oaxaca *obrajes*, see Appendix 12.
[4] BM Add. MSS 17,557, ff. 31-3.
[5] Murguía, *Estadística*, i, Appendix to Part 2, f. 33, Tlaxiaco.   [6] BM Add. MSS 17,557.

émigrés had found their way, the Insurgents had advanced as far south as the Isthmus of Tehuantepec. According to Álvarez, when they entered the indigo-producing regions, they sacked the plantations and production plants to the ultimate degree. The owners had fled, and the crop had been lost.[1] Murguía's figures placed the loss at a decline from 2,340 arrobas in 1811 to 97 arrobas in 1815.[1] This had been an especially serious blow, Álvarez lamented, because the indigo dye, the traditional crop of Guatemala, was assuming importance in Tehuantepec towards the end of the eighteenth century and in the first decade of the nineteenth. Before the revolution, Tehuantepec had exported 66,000 arrobas to the cities of Mexico, Puebla and Veracruz, without counting the contraband trade, which the Intendant estimated at another 16,000 arrobas, yielding in all a total of 82,000 pesos.[2]

The implications of the flight of Peninsular capital combined with the devastation of the revolutionary civil war can be seen in the case of the formerly rich cochineal-producing *partido* of Nejapa. In 1817 there occurred a suit between the Subdelegate, Rafael Azurmendi, and Benito Zavala, merchant of the Oaxaca *Diputación Consular*. Azurmendi wrote to Viceroy Apodaca on 13 September 1817, stating that since his appointment in February 1816, his first concern had been the promotion of agriculture. For, the Indians of the *partido* had not had a proper administrator for many years. They had been governed only by a series of deputies (*encargados*), the last of whom had been the local Captain of Royalist forces who had several estates in the area. Moreover, proper salaried officials could not be provided, because the Subdelegates lacked the funds to pay them.

Therefore, hoping to salvage both the bankrupt administration and the depressed economy at the same time, he had fallen back on the traditional resort of the former Alcaldes Mayores, and had made a contract for the financing of cochineal production with an English merchant by the name of Patrick Meek. Such a choice indicated the lack of availability of a Spanish Peninsular merchant to act as *aviador*, and an early and tentative entry of English capital into one small area on the production side of the Mexican economy.

The Subdelegate explained that formerly seventeen towns had produced the dye, but cultivation for the most part had been abandoned. The only way to restore production was by compelling the Indians to work. This, thirty years after the prohibition of the *repartimiento* by the Spanish

[1] *Ibid.*   [2] BSMGE, Murguía, *Estadística*, Dept. de Tehuantepec, añil, f. 5 *v*.
[3] BM Add. MSS 17,557.

Crown, he said he was doing, and with success. For, the English *aviador* had sent him 8,840 pesos to invest for the year, 1817. In return the Sub-delegate was to receive as his share 1 real for every pound of cochineal that did not exceed 24 reales in value, and ½ real for every pound that did.

In explaining to Viceroy Apodaca that his own poverty obliged him to accept this modest gratification, Subdelegate Azurmendi threw light on his own family connexions. He had to maintain his mother-in-law, Joaquina Iturribarría, who was the widow of Lorenzo Murguía, father of José María Murguía, by an earlier marriage to the Galardi family.[1] Apparently, even after Murguía's connexions with the Insurgents, Ferdinand VII and the Superior Government in Mexico were prepared to sanction the appointment to public office of persons with such Creole and rebel associations. The explanation, and it accounts for Murguía's own rehabilitation after 1814, was undoubtedly that these were the richest and principal families of Oaxaca, and that there was no one else to govern but they.

Despite the financial support of the English merchant, the dye trade was in such a decadent state that the Subdelegate was only able to secure 42 arrobas at the price of between 16 and 26 reales per pound, a considerably more expensive transaction than the old *repartimiento* rate of 12 reales. He, therefore, owed his backer the sum of 5,000 pesos.

The problem was, then, who was going to pay, since the Subdelegate could not. When Benito Zavala, Oaxaca merchant, agreed to cover the payment of the interest, there arose the further question of whether the *Diputación Consular* had jurisdiction in a case in which one of the parties was not a merchant. The *Diputado Consular*, Manuel del Solar Campero, complained to the Intendant of the Subdelegate's financial incapacity, but the Intendant rejected the intervention of the *Diputación*, denying its competence in the case.

The affair then went before the Viceroy and Audiencia, whose Fiscal de lo Civil said the whole matter should have been decided in Oaxaca. The Asesor General agreed, denouncing the Subdelegate for engaging in commercial transactions, and stating in his reply of 21 February 1818, that the case had nothing to do with the *Diputación Consular*. The Su-perior Government, thereupon, ordered the Intendant of Oaxaca to investigate the matter, in order to see whether the Subdelegate's contract with the English merchant had been *bona fide*, or was really the *reparti-miento* in disguise. If it were the latter, the Viceregal government would

---

[1] For the Iturribarría and the Murguía, see Glossary of Personnel.

Political crisis

have to take 'the necessary measures'.[1] It neither explained what these measures were, nor did it specify whether it regarded the *repartimiento* as illegal or not. Nothing was mentioned concerning Azurmendi's financial obligations to either Meek or Zavala, and no alternative method of financing the recovery of the trade was put forward. In such a way, the decision, so far as it was one, on the Azurmendi case could not have inspired confidence either among the Oaxaca merchants or among the Subdelegates if they attempted to take initiatives to break out of their financial deadlock.

The Secretary of the Veracruz Consulado, José María Quirós, in his *Memoria de Estatuto* for 1818, attributed the decline of the cochineal trade to the prohibition of the *repartimiento* after 1787, without the return of which it would be useless to discuss any project for its revival. He pointed out that the problem for present investors in the dye was the lack of guarantees, which had been enjoyed under the Alcaldes Mayores. In short, then, Quirós repeated the views of Bergoza and the other writers of 1810, indicating that the decline was so serious that even from Veracruz the cry for the return of the pre-1787 system was made. Quirós, however, went on to suggest means of reorganisation of the trade. He advocated the formation of a junta composed of the Intendent of Oaxaca, the Bishop, the Deputy of the Tribunal of Agriculture (if that body should be established), six venerable and worthy citizens chosen by the Ayuntamiento, and the city attorney (*síndico*). This junta would then advertise for subscribers to a fund from which the *repartimiento* would be conducted with the Indians, operated either by the Subdelegates or by the Indian governors. Security of repayment would be guaranteed by mortgaging the fund of the Indian *Cajas de Comunidad*, or by obliging the Indians to pay back the loan in the finished product.[2]

The dye continued to decline from its peaks of the 1770s, though after the poor year, 1815, some recovery could be detected in the following year, when production rose to 358,687 pounds. Nevertheless, the decline

---

1 AGN *Subdelegados* 54, año de 1817. Fearing the consequence of the incorporation of the Consulados of Veracruz and Guadalajara in 1795 might lead to a further reduction of its jurisdiction, the Consulado of Mexico proposed the establishment of Consular Deputations in the cities of Puebla, Oaxaca, Valladolid de Michoacan, and Guanajuato. These Deputations were to recognise the Consulado of Mexico in all governmental matters. The Consulado was to select the two merchants to act as Deputies and two as substitutes. The first elections for Oaxaca were held by the Consulado of Mexico's Junta of March 18, 1807. See Robert S. Smith, 'The Institution of the Consulado in New Spain', *HAHR*, xxiv (1944), 62–85, and AHH leg. 463, exp. 3, Consulado, año de 1807, Sobre Diputaciones foráneas, ff. 4–5, 7.
2 AGI *Mexico* 2518, *Expedientes del consulado y comercio* (1817–18), Memoria de Estatuto, 10–11.

set in again in 1818, and despite a leap to 493,200 pounds in 1819, the crop fell to 311,787½ pounds in 1821. The price figures continued to indicate however, that demand for the dye was still great, for, in 1816, the price rose to 32 reales per pound.[1] The bankrupt Spanish Crown, attempting both to secure revenue and to check the export of cochineal on foreign ships, further aggravated the situation by imposing a 4 per cent excess tax on all goods passing to Spain in foreign ships above that paid on goods proceeding in Spanish ships.[2] Finally, the *Reales Órdenes* of 17 January 1819, and 31 August 1819, extended the right to cultivate cochineal to the province of Yucatán and the Kingdom of Guatemala.[3] This competition, especially from Guatemala, was to prove greatly detrimental to the Oaxaca industry during the immediate decades after Independence.

With the revolt of Liberal officers in Spain on 6 March 1820, the second constitutional period opened throughout the Spanish dominions. The Riego movement forced Ferdinand VII to convoke the Cortes, and re-issue the Constitution of 1812. The *Real Decreto* of 9 March 1820, re-established the Ayuntamientos Constitucionales, which had been suppressed in 1814. The Cortes was scheduled to convene in Madrid on 9 July and meanwhile a junta selected seven *suplentes* (substitute deputies) to represent New Spain until the results of the elections there were made known. Among the Veracruz merchants, the return to the constitutional system was welcomed, and, without awaiting a Viceregal decree, they forced the Governor of Veracruz to publish the 1812 Constitution, and call elections for an Ayuntamiento Constitucional. On 31 May 1820, Viceroy Apodaca published the Constitution, and on 8 June the decree for municipal elections.[4]

On 7 June the Ayuntamiento of Oaxaca received news of the restora-

[1] See Appendix 1, and Lerdo de Tejada.
[2] Lerdo de Tejada, *Comercio exterior*, 23. As a result, the cochineal, the most valuable of the commodities then exported, was so burdened with taxes that the total paid from the time of its departure from Oaxaca and Veracruz until its entry into Spain, and its export from there to foreign countries, came to the extraordinarily high figure of 41 pesos 30 centavos per arroba in 1820.
[3] AGI *Mexico* 1500, *Duplicados del virrey* (1820), no. 960, Venadito–Min. de Hacienda, February 29, 1820. However, from *Instrucción para cultivar los nopales y beneficiar la grana fina, dispuesta por el R.P. predicador general, Fr. Antonio López, del S.O. de predicadores y cura de Cubulco; la da a luz la Real Sociedad Económica de Guatemala* (reimpresa a expensas del Real Consulado de dicha ciudad) (Guatemala 1818), it is evident that the cultivation of cochineal had already begun in Guatemala, at first near Tuxtla in Chiapas, in the years before the Real Orden of 1819. (Reference to this document was kindly supplied by Professor Ernesto Chinchilla Aguilar, State University of New York at Stony Brook.)
[4] Benson, *Mexico*, 29–33, 82–6.

tion of the constitutional system, and, under the presidency of Intendant Francisco Rendón, swore allegiance to it. The Regidores Constitucionales of 1814 were recalled, including Manuel Murguía, and in the municipal elections Mariano Castillejos secured the office of Regidor.[1]

In the elections for deputies to the Cortes, conducted on 30 September the six persons chosen were the prominent Creoles, José María Murguía y Galardi, Lic. Mariano Castillejos, Lic. Tomás Bustamante, Colonel Patricio López, whose father had been Alcalde Mayor of Teotitlán del Camino in the 1780s and whose mother was an Iturribarría, and finally two clerics, Lic. Luis Castellanos and Dr. Francisco Ramírez de Aguilar.[2] As deputy for Oaxaca to the Diputación Provincial, which resided in Mexico City, the electors sent another leading Creole, Lic. Francisco Ignacio Mimiaga.[3] Murguía, Castillejos, Ramírez, and López and the two other deputies, however, faced great difficulties before they had even left Oaxaca. For, Intendant Rendón reported to the Ayuntamiento that the Provincial Treasury was so bankrupt that 54,000 pesos were owing in arrears of salaries to the troops, and that the fares of the six deputies to the Cortes could not be paid.[4] Moreover, despite the grant of 3,000 pesos towards their expenses awarded by the Superior Government, the deputies stated on 3 November 1820, that the sum was inadequate to cover their needs in Spain. For, they had been promised half the annual revenue of 12,000 pesos from the internal customs duties by the Ayuntamiento. However, they had declined to accept the sum in view of the extrajudicial statement of the Ministers of the Treasury that there was insufficient revenue in the coffers to cover the defence of the province. Not even the Bishop could supply any cash, attributing the depletion of ecclesiastical revenues to the Consolidation of Pious Works and Chantries, and to the numerous sums lent to the Royal Government to pay for the struggle against the various European powers and against the revolutionaries within New Spain.[5]

Four of the deputies, nevertheless, managed to leave Oaxaca, though Mariano Castillejos died on the journey. López, Murguía, and Ramírez reached the Cortes, and participated in its sessions for 1821, where Murguía presented a *Memoria sobre el cultivo de la grana en la provincia de*

1 Archivo Municipal de Oaxaca, *Libro de acuerdos* (1820), f. 220.
2 AGI *Mexico* 1503, *Duplicados del virrey* (1820), no. 71, Venadito–Min. de la gobernación de ultramar, 30 September 1820.
3 *Ibid.*
4 Archivo Municipal de Oaxaca, *Libro de acuerdos* (1820), f. 407, Rendón–Ayuntamiento, 20 September 1820.
5 *Ibid.* ff. 448 and 459.

Oaxaca.[1] The deputies chosen in Oaxaca for the session of the Cortes to begin in March 1822 never reached Spain. For, New Spain had become independent in the previous year.[2]

On the news of Iturbide's Plan of Iguala of 24 February 1821, and of the Treaty of Córdoba of 24 August, Murguía left the Cortes in Spain, and returned to Mexico to take up the post of Intendant of Oaxaca in 1822 under the First Empire. When the Empire collapsed, Murguía was able to retain his office, and, on 4 December 1823, he was nominated Governor of the Free State of Oaxaca, a post he held until his resignation in November 1824.[3]

The revolutionary period, 1810–21, motivated the flight of Peninsular capital from New Spain. In February 1815, Viceroy Calleja complained of the extraction of capital from the Realm by its principal merchants to the detriment of industry and government finance.[4] On 12 February 1818, Viceroy Apodaca complained that the emigration of Spanish peninsular merchants along with their funds had not abated.[5] As to the actual amount of this capital, there were widely varying estimates. For example, the British consul in Veracruz in 1824, Mackenzie, stated that 'since 1810, nearly the whole of the opulent Spanish merchants have withdrawn their families and their capital from New Spain, and it is estimated that the amount of the latter does not fall short of 140 million pesos'.

Moreover, when, after the Plan of Iguala of 1821, the final move to independence was taken, Mackenzie said that the 'most hardy lost confidence, and transferred the great bulk of their convertible property to Europe'.[6]

1 Benson, *Mexico*, 1. Berry, Table 6, 34–7; AGI *Mexico* 1676, *Sección de fomento &c.* The Memoria was dated 29 October 1821.
2 Benson, *Mexico*, 1. Berry, Table 7, 38–9.
3 For Agustín de Iturbide's career, see W. S. Robertson, *Iturbide of Mexico* (Duke Univ. Press 1952), and for the events of 1821, in particular, see Nettie Lee Benson, 'Iturbide y los planes de Independencia', *Historia Mexicana*, 11, no. 3 (Jan.–March 1953), 439–46. BSMGE, Murguía, *Estadística*, introduction to Part 1 for details of the persons occupying civil, military, and ecclesiastical office throughout the centuries.

Iturbide's chief protagonist in the province of Oaxaca was Captain Antonio de León, a Creole of Huajuapan. León took Huajuapan and Yanhuitlán in late June 1821, and entered the city of Oaxaca on 31 July 1821. However, after the proclamation of the Empire, he joined Bravo and Guerrero to pronounce against it on 14 January 1823.
4 AGI *Mexico* 1145, *Consultas, decretos, y reales órdenes* (1810), and AGI *Mexico* 1827, *Expedientes inventariados* (1816), Calleja–Min. Universal de Indias, 9 February 1815.
5 AGI *Mexico* 1495, *Duplicados del virrey* (1818), no. 338, Apodaca–Min. de Hacienda, 12 February 1818.
6 R. A. Humphreys, *British Consular Reports on the Trade and Politics of Latin America, 1824–26* (London 1940), 302–3, 318–19.

The British chargé d'affaires, H. G. Ward, disagreed with the Mackenzie estimate, based as it was on rough estimates made by prominent Mexicans. Ward stated that two-thirds of the capital invested in New Spain had pertained to the Spanish *Peninsulares*, who had engaged in mining, agriculture, and industry. Almost all of these investors left the country as a result of the revolution, and the depressed state of the mines, agriculture, and trade after Independence was due, in great measure, to this withdrawal of the bulk of the capital which had previously sustained them. Ward's estimate of the total amount extracted came to $36\frac{1}{2}$ million pesos, for Mackenzie had included the total value of all exports between 1810 and 1825 to arrive at his figure.[1]

This extraction had been a gradual process. Ward explained: 'The Old Spaniards, who had survived the first years of the Revolutionary war (in the course of which many transferred the bulk of their convertible property to Europe), retained a sufficient portion of their funds in circulation to give a certain activity to trade, and to the mines, in which most of them were directly or indirectly engaged.'

However, the political changes in Spain with the Riego revolt in 1820, and the return of the Liberals to power, and their consequent extension of the Cádiz Constitution of 1812 to the Indies, ensuring once more the triumph of the Creoles in political office in New Spain, inspired considerable apprehension among the Spanish *Peninsulares*. When the repercussions of these events led to the Plan of Iguala, the final incentive to pull out their remaining capital came. Ward stated: 'In 1821, when these apprehensions were realised, and the separation from the Mother Country became inevitable, the whole disposable capital that had remained till then invested was withdrawn at once, and the coinage of Mexico sank to 5 million pesos, from which it fell to $3\frac{1}{2}$ million, at which it continued during the years, 1823 and 1824.'[2]

[1] H. G. Ward, *Mexico in 1827* (2 vols.; London 1828), i, 379, 381–2.   [2] *Ibid.* 384.

CHAPTER 8

CONCLUSION—OAXACA WITHIN THE CONTEXT OF MEXICAN POLITICS

Until the political changes of 1810–21 ensured the triumph of the Creoles, the province of Oaxaca had traditionally been dominated by a small group of Spanish Peninsular merchants. For the most part, they undertook mutual financial obligations, and had close contacts with the merchants of the Mexico City Consulado. They were represented on the Ayuntamiento of Oaxaca, a closed body which left most of the work of governing the province to the Royal and episcopal authorities, where they held both elective and hereditary or purchased offices. They farmed many of the principal revenues of both Church and State, were owners or lessees of landed property, particularly in the fertile regions of the Valley of Oaxaca and Teposcolula. Many of them were commissioned officers in the Provincial Militia, established in the 1760s, and enjoyed the juridical privilege of the *fuero militar* under the Ordinance of 1768.

The local merchants and those of the Consulado of Mexico were particularly interested in Oaxaca's scarlet dye, extensively produced only by the Indian population, and in great demand in the textile factories of France, Holland, Britain, and Spain. The merchants traded with the great Spanish merchant houses, the Casa de Uztáriz and the *Cinco Gremios Mayores de Madrid* and others.

The insolvency of the Spanish régime, and its failure to pay its local administrators, the Alcaldes Mayores, a proper salary ensured that they would fall into the financial power of the merchants. Since the Metropolitan Government required all its officials to guarantee the regular and exact receipt of the revenues put to their charge, under a *fianza*, it was generally the merchant who acted as *fiador*. In return for this favour, without which the Alcalde Mayor could not assume office, the administrator would be required to use his judicial position in his territory of jurisdiction in order to guarantee the commercial interests of the merchant. The merchant supplied the administrator with *habilitación* or *avío*, a sum of money for distribution among the Indians to ensure that they were able to produce the cochineal, cotton, or cotton mantles required. In this way the merchant acted as the Alcalde Mayor's *aviador*. The administrator, and often his legal lieutenant (*teniente letrado*), who was generally a nominee of the merchant-*aviador*, and their band of armed men used the Royal authority entrusted to them to conduct a *repartimiento* in the interests of the merchant, that was, until its tacit concession in 1751, totally contradictory to the Laws of the Indies. On several occasions in the diocese of Oaxaca, the pious funds of the Church would be used to finance these *repartimientos*.

Throughout the eighteenth century, the Crown and its Ministers were coming to the conclusion that Spain had not been deriving sufficient material benefits from her overseas territories. The chief reasons were believed to be the commercial monopoly of the Cádiz, Mexico, and Lima Consulados, and the corruption of the Alcaldes Mayores in New Spain and the Corregidores in Peru.

The moral and political attack on the Alcaldes Mayores came in the latter part of the century. Both the Visitor-General to New Spain, José de Gálvez, and Bishop Ortigoza of Oaxaca called for the extirpation of their very name. The Crown and Ministry, over a period of two decades, became convinced of the need for a new administrative structure in the Indies, on the basis of Gálvez's *Plan de Intendencies* of 1768, which came into effect for New Spain after 1786. At the same time, in order to enable other major Spanish ports to trade with the Indies, the Crown issued the *Reglamento de comercio libre* in October 1778, but this freer trade within the Empire did not fully apply to New Spain until 1789, due to the privileged position there of the Consulado of Mexico.

The Intendants were to act as the intermediary authority between Mexico City, with its Viceroy and Audiencia, and the locality. Subordinate to the Intendants, a new category of administrators, the Subdelegates, were to replace the Alcaldes Mayores. Article 12 of the *Real Ordenanza de Intendentes* of 1786 prohibited the issue of cash to the Indians by these new justices in *repartimientos*. Instead of the often substantial profits which had accrued to their predecessors, the Subdelegates were to receive their salaries from a 5 per cent levy from the Indian tribute revenue. As a result of the prohibition of the contracting between merchant-*aviador* and administrator, many Subdelegates failed to secure *fiadores* for the revenues to their charge.

The Crown encountered great difficulty in securing men of sufficient intellect and merit to act as Subdelegates, plagued as they would be by lack of proper payment. Therefore, throughout the 1790s and 1800s, the principal issue before the Metropolitan and Superior Governments, as far as the Intendancy of Oaxaca was concerned, was whether the *reparti-*

miento conducted by the Royal justices should be restored or not. The Intendant of Oaxaca, Antonio de Mora y Peysal, bitterly opposed a return to the old system, and defended the capacity of the Indians to take advantage of the new. Viceroy Revillagigedo, while aware of the problems involved, especially over *avío*, was anxious that both the administrative and the commercial reforms should be allowed to subsist, and come to fruition, despite the opposition of the Consulado of Mexico and its associates in Oaxaca.

In view of both the ambiguities of the Ordinance, and the fear that, without the justices' *repartimientos*, the industry and agriculture of such a valuable province as Oaxaca would lapse into decay, both the Metropolitan Government in Spain and the Superior Government in Mexico City were severely divided over the issue of the restoration of the *repartimiento*. One group in the bureaucracy favoured prohibition. They feared a return to the restrictive practices under the Alcaldes Mayores and their *aviadores*. This group tended to uphold Mora y Peysal's position. They saw that to concede a return to the old system would be an admission that the reform had failed. On the other hand, following Viceroys Flores and Branciforte, and reiterating the objections of Viceroy Bucareli back in the 1770s, the opposing group believed that the Subdelegations could never work unless the Subdelegates received a proper salary, and this, they considered should, most economically, come from their share of the profits of the *repartimiento*. In other words, they favoured the reestablishment of the Alcaldes Mayores, preserving only the name of Subdelegate.

The Intendant of Oaxaca faced great obstacles in his effort to implement the reform. One example was the case of the Subdelegate of the lucrative, cotton mantle-producing *partido* of Villa Alta, Bernardino Bonavia, in 1790. This bitter opponent of the Intendancy advocated a total return to the old system, and openly defied Mora in his *partido*. He met his end, however, before a firing squad set up by the victorious Insurgent general, Morelos, after his entry into Oaxaca in November 1812.

Subjected to an onslaught of criticism during his lifetime, and even more sharply after his death in 1808, Intendant Mora found he was powerless to prevent the gradual return of the old *repartimientos* in important areas of his jurisdiction, Cuatro Villas, Miahuatlán, Jicayan, Villa Alta, and Tehuantepec. The matter was not helped by the unilateral decision of the Junta Superior de Real Hacienda in Mexico City, on 28 November 1794, that Subdelegates could practice *repartimientos*, providing none of the old abuses committed against the indigenous population should recur. This decision, however, was vigorously repudiated by Madrid. In the New Ordinance of Intendant of 1803, the prohibition was once more maintained, but this legislation never came into full force owing to the outbreak of war with Great Britain in 1804, and the pressure of the military within Spain.

The attack on the prohibition of the *repartimiento* coincided with the bitter criticism of the newly established (1795) Consulados of Veracruz and Guadalajara, by the Consulado of Mexico, which had thereby lost its consular monopoly of jurisdiction in New Spain. As Revillagigedo had already pointed out in 1793, the smaller-scale, but more commercially conscious, merchants of Veracruz began to replace those of Mexico in their competition for the products of New Spain. The evidence of the Treasury accounts of Oaxaca showed that by the later 1790s, these newer merchants of Veracruz had gained supremacy in the financing of the Oaxaca trades, and that several new merchants within Oaxaca had, in consequence, taken up their positions alongside the traditional names like Alonso Magro, Felipe Ordóñez Díaz, and Colonel Juan Francisco de Echarri. The two 'neutral' concessions of 1797–9 and 1804–9 further diminished the Mexico merchant's share of the export trade, and reorientated New Spain's trade away from Spain, at precisely the time the Catalan merchants were about to achieve supremacy in the Mexican market for textiles. In this neutral trade, in which chiefly the British, through United States' channels, benefited, by sending their painted cotton textiles to New Spain in return for bullion, coin, and precious dyes like cochineal and indigo, the Veracruz merchants tended to assume the role of commercial agents for the foreign traders, intermediaries in a trade in which New Spain was the primary producer.

The interests of all merchants, and of the chief landowners and citizens of the Realm were threatened by the Godoy régime's attempts to finance Spain's war effort against Great Britain by the appropriation of the funds of pious foundations and chantries, under the '*Consolidación de Vales Reales*'. This measure was commissioned under the *Real Cédula* of 26 December 1804. These pious funds had, through the centuries, become the chief bank of credit for merchants, mine-operators, landowners, and all who could offer sufficient guarantees of repayment of the principal, either through *fianzas* or by mortgaging their own property as security. Between 1805 and 1808, the debtors were required to pay back the principal in instalments. This procedure took place amid great protests. As the Viceroy, Iturrigaray, and the Intendancy authorities were the chief instruments in the enforcement of the measure, the split within the ranks of the *Peninsulares* came to an ugly climax. For, in response to the collapse of the Godoy régime in March 1808, the Peninsulares of the Audiencia and Consulado of Mexico seized the opportunity of Iturrigaray's approaches to the Creoles to remove the Viceroy in September.

This event had serious repercussions in Oaxaca. For, attempting to salvage their position after two decades of the Intendancy, and fearing any moves on the part of the Creoles, the Spanish Peninsular merchants assumed control of affairs in the city, manning it with armed patrols on the lines of the Volunteers of Ferdinand VII in Mexico City. The three chief personnel of the Intendancy, one of whom was the Creole hacienda-owner, Mariano Castillejos, later to attend the Insurgent Congress at Chilpancingo, were summoned to Mexico for trial before the régime of Viceroy Garibay, on the grounds that they had participated in the designs of Iturrigaray.

Bishop Bergoza, at first reluctant to commit his episcopal authority, in the course of 1809 and 1810 placed himself alongside the merchants. His political position assumed an increasingly more hostile attitude towards the late Intendant Mora and his policies, which both Bergoza and his merchant allies attacked as too favourable to the indigenous population involved in the cochineal, cotton, cotton-mantle trades, and in day-labouring on the hacienda lands. Bergoza demanded that the Superior Government should use the opportunity of the 1808 coup to salvage the political and economic position of the merchants within the Intendancy of Oaxaca. Bergoza called for the return of a régime of order, which could guarantee that cochineal and mantle-producers paid their debt obligations, and that the indigenous communities supplied what labour the hacienda-owners demanded. The key to this would, of course, be the reconstitution of the Subdelegates on the lines of the former Alcaldes Mayores.

The incursion of the Insurgents into Oaxaca, and their occupation of its capital between November 1812 and March 1814 prevented the realisation of Bergoza's objectives. The Bishop, Intendant, and his *Teniente Letrado*, and many of the other *Peninsulares* fled to Guatemala. Though the constitutional system emanating from the Cortes in Cádiz had until that time failed to result in the political supremacy of the Creoles in Oaxaca, the victory of Morelos ensured that it would. The two most politically prominent Creoles, José María Murguía y Galardi and Lic. Mariano Castillejos, both attended the Insurgent Congress at Chilpancingo after September 1813, where another Creole of Oaxaca, the Insurgent Carlos María de Bustamante, organised the Insurgent newspaper, *Correo Ameri-*

cano del Sur, and acted as substitute deputy (*suplente*) for Mexico, which was still under Royalist control. Ecclesiastical affairs fell under the control of another local Creole, Dr. Antonio Ibáñez de Corbera, of a very prominent property-owning family with a dye trade background. All these persons were severely compromised when the Royalist régime was restored after March 1814.

This restored régime, however, was not, despite the military victories of Viceroy Calleja, the aggressive régime of Bergoza and his Peninsular merchant associates. The Constitution of 1812 applied to Oaxaca after its deliverance from the Insurgents and their abortive attempts at constitutional government. The elections to the Ayuntamiento Constitucional in 1814 only served to confirm the political victory of the Creoles. Calleja's implementation of Ferdinand VII's Valencia Decree of 4 May 1814, for the restoration of the *status quo* of 1808, only served to postpone the ultimate triumph of the Creoles. The power, both political and economic, of the Spanish *Peninsulares*, merchants and lawyers of the Audiencia, never recovered from the moral and financial shock of the revolutions of Hidalgo and Morelos, which motivated the flight of personnel and capital. The final supremacy of the Creoles came with the re-establishment of the 1812 Constitution, the election of six Creoles proprietary deputies to the 1821 Cortes in Madrid, including Murguía and Castillejos, and the restoration of the Ayuntamientos Constitucionales. These developments were supported by the merchants of the Consulado of Veracruz, some of whom, like Tomás Murphí, supported the Government of Independent Mexico. Murguía returned to Oaxaca to rally to Iturbide's régime, which had triumphed there due to the efforts of Antonio de Léon. When the First Empire fell in 1823, Murguía turned his support to the republican system, and occupied the role of Governor of the State of Oaxaca until November 1824.

The combination of the establishment of Intendants in the provincial capitals, with the inclusion of New Spain into the régime of *comercio libre* and the constitution of the two new Consulados of Veracruz and Guadalajara contributed to a severe weakening of the political and economic supremacy of Mexico City over the rest of the Viceroyalty of New Spain. The Intendancies, instituted at the peak of Bourbon Absolutism, introduced an official entrusted with the four functions (justice, finance, administration, and war) whose status in the bureaucratic hierarchy lay between that of the Viceroy in Mexico City and the local justices in the towns. As most of the capitals of the Intendancies were also the

F

episcopal sees of New Spain, for example Valladolid, Guadalajara, Oaxaca, and Puebla, the Intendant represented a rival power in the province to the Bishop. Despite the fact that within the context of the Spanish Imperial bureaucracy both Intendant and Bishop received their political power from the same source, the Crown, the Mexican environment of personalist power politics ensured that the Intendant would be seen as a rival *cacique* to the Bishop, a power baron of the temporal sphere to offset the power baron of the ecclesiastical sphere.

The establishment of a new rank of Royal officials in the provincial capitals combined with the new merchant guilds in areas distant from Mexico City to emphasize the regionalism that had emerged out of the Mexican colonial experience. While the new Consulados looked towards the peripheries of New Spain, as opposed to the Mexico Consulado's position within the central plateau region, the Intendancies for their part became the blueprint for the State system of the Mexican Federal Republic after 1824.

A third factor contributing to the weakening of Mexico City's traditional dominant role was the Constitution of 1812. This Constitution not only established a unicameral legislature, but also centred provincial government in the municipal councils, reconstituted as Ayuntamientos Constitutionales. Moreover, the provisions of the constitution so weakened the authority of the Viceroy that Calleja, to whom the implementation of the new system was entrusted, hardly knew what his own powers were. There was great suspicion of the Constitution in Mexico City, but in Veracruz the merchants greeted the news of the restoration of the constitutional system, brought about by a Liberal coup in Spain, with enthusiasm. Their position in 1820, thus marks the beginning of Veracruz's long position as a centre of Liberal support in the Mexican Republic.

The alliance of the forces we have seen operating in the politics of Oaxaca, namely the tacit accord between the Intendancy administrators, the 'new bureaucrats', with the aspirations of the beneficiaries of *comercio libre*, the 'new merchants' of the Veracruz variety, contributed to the formation of Mexican Creole Liberalism. One further factor was required to complete the picture, the tradition of the Creole lawyers, such as the Oaxaqueño, Carlos María de Bustamante, which transformed the Hidalgo revolution from a type of Marian crusade into the constitutionalist movement which produced the Constitution of Apatzingán in 1814.

The opposing forces foreshadowed what would become in the course of the nineteenth-century political struggles, Mexican Conservatism.

Context of Mexican politics

There was, despite differing emphases according to decade, a continuity in the position of the opponents of Gálvez's Plan and the opponents of Liberalism. That continuity revealed how much, in the eyes of the Conservatives, Mexican Liberalism owed to its Spanish Bourbon Absolutist past. For the main platform of the Conservatives was the defence of the *fueros*, rejecting both the Gálvez school's administrative rationalization and the Liberal derivatives from the 1812 Cadiz Constitution, in favour of the historic corporativism engrained in the Mexican past throughout the Hispanic period. This defence of the *fueros militar y eclesiástico* could be seen in Bishop Bergoza's alliance of 1809 with the Spanish Peninsular merchants, who enjoyed the rank of militia officers. Moreover, their position looked to Mexico City, with its Consulado and Audiencia, for guidance and as an example. Bergoza himself became Archbishop-elect of Mexico City between 1812 and 1815. Their position, then, represented an alliance between the ecclesiastical hierarchy and the 'old bureaucrats' of the Audiencia of Mexico and the 'old merchants' of the Consulado of Mexico. Moreover, in contrast to Veracruz' support for *comercio libre*, and even for free trade with foreign nations in the later 1810s and 1820s, the 'old merchants' of the centre region of New Spain warned of the consequences for Mexico's *obrajes* of the import of foreign textiles. They tended, then, as the careers of Lucas Alamán and Esteban de Antuñano, were to show, to demand protective tariffs for domestic industry, in order to transform the *obrajes*, particularly of Puebla, into machine-operated textile industries.

GLOSSARY OF PERSONNEL

I THE ADMINISTRATORS

ÁLVAREZ, Melchor, Brigadier of the Royalist Army, Colonel of the Regiment of Savoy, Commandant-General of the Third Division of the South, Governor-Intendant of Oaxaca and *Juez Político* from 29 March 1814 until 29 August 1816.

BONAVIA, Bernardino, merchant of Oaxaca and Subdelegate of Villa Alta between 1790 and 1795, where bitterly opposed to Intendant Mora's attempts to enforce Article 12. Order of Calatrava, and Colonel-Commandant of Seventh Brigade. Executed by Morelos in 1812.

CERAIN, Adrián de, long career as an official in the Marquesado del Valle. 1785 Corregidor of Toluca. 1794 Alcalde Mayor of the Cuatro Villas in the Valley of Oaxaca, in which post he was arraigned before the Intendant's court for violation of Article 12 of the 1786 Ordinance. In 1796, the Indian village of Soledad in Etla issued a suit against him concerning possession of lands claimed by them, in which the Indians accused him of favouring the Hacienda de Guadalupe. Owner of mines and haciendas in the Real de Oro of San Miguel de las Peras, in the Cuatro Villas, and lessee of the Hacienda de Montoya, owned by the Convent of the Soledad. Accuser of interim-Intendant Izquierdo in 1808.

CORRES, Francisco de, Alcalde Mayor and Subdelegate of Miahuatlán, from 1770s to end of 1790s, born in Burgos, Castile, of hidalgo parentage. Between 1753 and 1757 was an official of the Principal Accounting House of the Province of Burgos, and between 1757 and 1765 the same in Toledo. In 1765 went to New Spain with the party of Visitor Gálvez, and nominated accountant of the *visita* in Veracruz. In 1767 co-operated in the expulsion of the Jesuits, and in 1768 appointed General Accountant of the properties of the ex-Jesuit College-Seminary of San Ildefonso. The *Real Orden* of 1772 indicated he was a candidate for the post of Intendant. 1776, settled financial accounts of the Department of San Blas. Since his appointment as Alcalde Mayor of Miahuatlán in 1770s, became a principal dealer in the cochineal trade, and, despite his early associations with Gálvez, became one of the chief violators of Article 12 of the 1786 Ordinance.

IZQUIERDO, Dr. Antonio María, *Teniente Letrado* and *Asesor Ordinario* of the Intendancy of Oaxaca, under the Superior Order of 19 February 1799. Born 1764, in Villanueva del Ariscal, León, Spain. Studied grammar at Seville University, where received bachelor's degree, and master's degree in philosophy in 1784. Bachelor of laws in 1786. After arrival in New Spain, joined the Royal and Pontifical University of Mexico in May 1787, and secured the degree of Bachelor of Canons. 1794 Licenciado, and Doctor. 1796 nominated by the Mexico Inquisitors as lawyer for arrested persons. Rector of Mexico University. 18 March 1799, took up position in Oaxaca. On 3 July 1804, requested Intendant Mora for a transfer owing to his critical financial situation with his large family, who were short of food. Requested transfer to one of the lesser Audiencias of the Indies. Not granted. Became the centre of attack by the Spanish Peninsular merchants in 1808. Tried before Garibay in 1809, but acquitted under Lizana.

Glossary of Personnel

On 25 November 1812, fled before Morelos to Ciudad Real (Chiapas), in such haste that he left his wife and children in Oaxaca. Insurgents sacked his property, reducing him to poverty. Borrowed from the Royal Treasuries of Ciudad Real and Veracruz in order to return to Mexico City, where, after deduction of the debt to Royal finances, he was awarded his full salary from November 1812 until August 1813. Appointed to a legal post on the Audiencia of Quito, but after the recovery of Oaxaca, Calleja ordered him to return there. Protested on 4 May 1814, requesting an Audiencia post. Allowed to remain in Mexico City under S.O. of 27 May 1814.

LASSO, José María, Intendant of Oaxaca from 18 June 1809 until his flight before the Insurgents on 25 November 1812. Born 1744, son of a Captain of the Dragoon Company in Veracruz. Creole. 1753 entered Infantry Regiment of the Crown as a cadet, stationed in Veracruz. In 1767 went with the volunteers on the Agüero expedition from Tepic to California, and was commissioned to expel the Jesuits and occupy their temporal possessions. Went on the second Sonora expedition with Gálvez, in his secretariat. 1769, under orders from Gálvez, went to the port of San Blas for a nineteen-month interim charge of that Department. 1773 Oficial Mayor of the Jesuit temporal properties in Mexico. 1777 Administrator of Alcabalas in Guanajuato. 1781 Treasurer of the Royal Treasury in Veracruz. 1794 Minister-Accountant of the Army and Royal Finance. 14 September 1808, nominated Administrator General of the Customs in Mexico City by Iturrigaray, but, rescinded after his fall on the 16th. As Intendant of Oaxaca, advocated return of the repartimiento, on 12 February 1811. Fled before Morelos to Tuxtla, and, after the defeat of the Guatemalan forces at Tehuantepec, proceeded to Isla del Carmen, Veracruz, and Mexico City. Had fled with only the clothes he stood up in, and, in consequence, acquired debts to the Royal finances. Granted two-thirds of salary of 6,000 pesos in late 1813. Under Bando of 13 December 1813, nominated President of the Junta de Arbitrios in Mexico City. Calleja twice ordered him to return to his post in Oaxaca in May 1814, but requested relief, and concession of an appropriate post in Mexico, or retirement on full Intendant's pay. This request he repeated in March 1816. On 18 July 1817, the Crown appointed him Director General of Outlying Customs in New Spain with a salary of 6,000 pesos.

LÓPEZ CHACÓN, Manuel José, Alcalde Mayor and Subdelegate of Teotitlán del Camino (including Papalotipac and Cuicatlán), between 1782 and 1795. Born Granada 1733. 1746–51 Administrator of Provincial Rents of the Province of Málaga, without salary. 1751 went to New Spain with Viceroy Amarillas, in whose secretariat he served. 1752 from Acapulco to Callao, taking Mexican tobacco pertaining to the Royal Treasury to Peru in exchange for Peruvian mercury; in 1758 repeated this. Returned to Spain in 1760, and requested employment in Cádiz, but nominated to aid Gálvez on visita of New Spain. 1765 on arrival in New Spain appointed by Gálvez as Factor Administrator, Treasurer, Accountant of the Royal Tobacco Monopoly in the Bishopric of Oaxaca. Established the Monopoly of Gunpowder, Playing Cards, and Lottery. In these posts between October 1765 and December 1776. Ordered by Gálvez to report on the state of the cochineal trade. Set the Alcaldía Mayor of Huajuapan in order after a disturbance against its deputy. Received Juan Baptista de Echarri as aviador in Teotitlán del Camino. After 1787, as Subdelegate, he was as unable to find *fiadores*, as was the Superior Government in finding a successor to him. Removed by order of the Crown in March 1795. Father of Francisco López de Iturribarría, who requested one of the Oaxaca Subdelegations, while in Cádiz in 1811. Father of Creole deputy in the 1821 Cortes, Patricio López.

MORA Y PEYSAL, Antonio de, Intendant of Oaxaca from 1787 until death in March 1808, with salary of 6,000 pesos p.a. Requested permission to return to Spain, on 30 April 1795, in order to attend to interests in Málaga, where he had been a Regidor Perpetuo since at least 1780. On 26 February 1801, once more requested leave, this time for transfer to a second-class Peninsular Intendancy with adjacent military duties, or a post in the Secretariat of the Indies. On 27 May 1802, asked to proceed to Spain for two years to attend to personal affairs. Not granted on any occasion.

RENDÓN, Francisco, Intendant-interim of Oaxaca (for Lasso) between 29 August 1816 and 9 May 1817, and proprietary Intendant between 20 June 1818 and 30 July 1821, when Manuel Obeso, Commander of the Royalists, capitulated to the Oaxaca Iturbidistas under Antonio de León at Etla. In January 1779, nominated by the Captain-General of Cuba as secretary to the commission of Miralles in the U.S.A., upon whose death in April 1780 Gálvez nominated Rendón to succeed. Secured the dispatch of 6,000 quintales of flour from Maryland for provision of the Spanish armies and fleets operating against Great Britain, facilitating the conquest of West Florida and the British possessions on the Mississippi in 1780. In co-operation with U.S. diversionary action in South Carolina, Spaniards took Pensacola. In September 1784, Spanish Minister Gardoquí nominated him chargé d'affaires in Philadelphia, but ordered by Floridablanca, Foreign Minister, to continue his post in Cuba. November 1786 returned to Madrid. Between August 1787 and December 1793 worked in the Ministry of Finance for Spain and the Indies. Nominated Intendant of Louisiana and West Florida, where served between September 1794 and April 1796, when appointed Intendant of Zacatecas.

VILLARRASA RIVERA, Francisco, Treasurer of the Royal Treasury in Oaxaca after 1787, and until 1812. Spanish Peninsular. Opponent of the prohibition of *repartimientos* on the grounds that Royal finances and trade were suffering, see his report of 1793. Bitter rival of Micheltorena, Accountant of the Royal Treasury, with often public, and occasionally violent quarrels after the Accountant's appointment in 1804. Micheltorena was protected by *Promotor Fiscal* Mariano Castillejos (Creole), and continued in office during the Insurgent period. Villarrasa believed that Intendant Mora was his sworn enemy. Not sent to Mexico for trial during the events of 1808–9.

2 THE MERCHANTS

ALLES, Pedro Alonso de, merchant of Mexico City with large interests in the cotton of Jicayan and the cochineal of this and other regions of Oaxaca, in the pursuit of which acted as *aviador* of Alcaldes Mayores. Born in Inguanzo in the Bishopric of Oviedo, Spain, and was a resident of Mexico City. In 1778, married a Creole, whose parents resided in the Real de Oro of Durango. February 1784 appointed Honorary Minister of the Tribunal de Cuentas in Mexico. Possessed the Order

Glossary of Personnel

of Calatrava, and was Treasurer General of the *Cruzada* of the Archbishopric of Mexico. For his donations to the war expenses of the Crown, awarded a Title of Castile for himself and his heirs, as the Marqués de Santa Cruz y Inguanzo, with the right to found a *mayorazgo*, since his capital was above 300,000 pesos. (*Reales Cédulas* of 20 and 25 March 1792.) Died in Tacubaya 1802.

BARBERENA, Juan Carlos, born 1758 in Castile, was a protégé of Juan Baptista de Echarri, in whose house he initially resided. Opponent of Article 12 of 1786, and of interim-Intendant Izquierdo in 1808.

ECHARRI, Juan Baptista, Alcalde Mayor of Tehuantepec between 1762 and 1769, when successfully introduced cochineal cultivation, and maintained interests there for eighteen years. In 1766 involved in the protracted San Mateo del Mar land dispute with the Huave Indians, in which he favoured the position of the Hacienda of Guazontlán, turning the Indians off the land. Native of Aldaz in Navarra, and studied at Santiago University in Pamplona, followed by two years of theology at the Convent of San Pablo in Burgos. At the University of Oñate for five years. 1755 Bachelor of Canons there. 1756 on the Junta of Jurisprudence of the city of Valladolid, and became its president in 1760. After his term in Tehuantepec, for which the Audiencia approved his *residencia* in 1773, he was elected to the office of Alcalde Ordinario de Primer Voto of the Ayuntamiento of Oaxaca. Resident and merchant of Oaxaca in 1780s and 1790s. *Aviador* of Manuel López Chacón, Alcalde Mayor of Teotitlán del Camino after 1782. He and his two brothers were among the most successful mine-operators in Oaxaca, and when the miners of Oaxaca wrote to Intendant Mora on 12 March 1790, for the election of *Diputados de Minería*, Echarri was one of the petitioners. Responding to this, Mora recommended him as one of the deputies. In March 1789 and May 1792 acted as *fiador* for the collection of tithes in Teotitlán del Camino. Denounced Article 12 on 21 November 1794.

ECHARRI, Colonel Juan Francisco de, owner of copper mine in San Mateo Capulalpa, in Ixtepeji, and of the mines of Cerro, Barranca, and Dolores in Villa Alta, of which he took possession in 1782, finding them in an abandoned state. In co-operation with his brother, Captain Juan Felipe, he put them in working order by 1786. Together they became the two *Diputados Territoriales de Minería* for Oaxaca. Six of their mines in Villa Alta were of silver. Collector of the Royal revenue from gunpowder in 1804, and on 26 October 1804, issued a *libranza* for the total of the summer quarter, 7,168 pesos 2½ reales, against the Mexico Consulado merchant, Juan Fernando de Meoquí, who would then pay the equivalent into the Mexico City Treasury. Was Colonel of the Provincial Battalion of Oaxaca, which Viceroy Iturrigaray stationed in the cantonment of Córdoba between 1805 and 1808. Debtor to the *Ramo de Consolidación*. Opponent of Izquierdo in 1808, in which year he died. Brother of Juan Baptista de Echarri.

ESTRELLA, Pedro de, secured office of Regidor Perpetuo of the Ayuntamiento of Oaxaca in 1798 for 1,500 pesos. Clerk of the Ayuntamiento of Córdoba and of the Royal Tobacco Monopoly there in 1806. Debtor to the *Ramo de Consolidación*.

GARCÍA HENRÍQUEZ, Pedro, Lieutenant-Colonel of the Oaxaca Militia. Debtor to the *Consolidación*. Issued a *libranza* against Tomás de Ibarrola of the Mexico Consulado on 18 January 1804, for the sum of 1,424 pesos 6 reales due to the Crown from its Gunpowder Monopoly.

GONZÁLEZ NORIEGA, Pedro, Mexico City merchant, purchased five *sitios de ganado mayor* in San Pedro del Gallo, in San Luis Potosí, but disavowed by the Commandant-General of the Internal Provinces, Nemesio Salcedo, in July 1807, on the grounds that such excessive awards prevented a wider distribution of landownership.

GOYA, Manuel Ramón de, originated from the Basque Provinces, and held important mining interests in New Spain, besides his *aviador* functions in the Oaxaca *partidos* of Villa Alta and Zimatlán–Chichicapa. On 30 September 1788, sent '*Discurso dirigido confidencialmente a D. Vicente de Herrera y Rivero, regente de la real Audiencia de México, con motivo de la R.O. del 30 de octubre de 1787 despachada al real Consulado para que informara sobre varios puntos de comercio*', stating that the Consulado of Mexico had not been heard on the question of New Spain's inclusion into the régime of *comercio libre*. He claimed the merchants regarded the system of *comercio libre* not so much as a contribution to the prosperity of trade and the nation, but as a new device for increasing Royal revenues.

GOYTIA, Francisco Antonio, one of the four Oaxaca Deputies of Commerce, chosen by the Consulado of Mexico in 1807. Opponent of Izquierdo in 1808.

GOYTIA, Ignacio, Creole Regidor Constitucional in 1820, proposed by the *Diputado Consular*, Joseph Riveiro de Aguilar, as a candidate for Consular Deputy for the term 1821–2. Declined the honour when appointed after the refusal of the two primary candidates, on the grounds that he was already Alcalde de Primer Voto. One of the signatories of the Oaxaca State Constitution on 14 January 1825.

GUTIÉRREZ DE VILLEGAS, Simón, protégé of José Francisco Ibáñez in the 1770s. Oaxaca merchant, and associate of the Subdelegate of Miahuatlán in 1790. Debtor to the *Consolidación*.

IBÁÑEZ DE CORBERA, José Francisco, report on cochineal production in Zimatlán was cited by Alzate y Ramírez. In 1784 recorded as Regidor Honorario of the Ayuntamiento of Oaxaca. Covered a six-month *fianza* of Esteban Melgar, Alcalde Mayor of Teotitlán del Valle, in the same year. Representative of Veracruz merchant, Gaspar de Elías, in 1786. One of the five Consular Deputies in 1793, but not included in the formally constituted *Diputación Consular* in 1807. Received seven votes for the office of Deputy to the Cortes in 1810, but not elected.

ITURRIBARRÍA Y URQUIJO, Vicente de, became Alcalde Mayor of Jamiltepec. Treasurer of Papal Bulls in Oaxaca in 1770, and in 1783 was Factor and principal Administrator of the Royal Revenues from Tobacco, Gunpowder, and Playing Cards. Born in Spain in 1713.

MAGRO, Alonso, in 1776 was Alcalde Ordinario de Primer Voto, and in 1786 Regidor Honorario of the Ayuntamiento of Oaxaca. One of the two *fiadores* for Pablo de Ortega in his borrowings from pious funds in 1786. Was one of the agents of the Mexico Consulado in Oaxaca in 1793. Recorded in 1796–7 as majordomo of the Convent of Soledad. Captain of the South Coast Militia, and great opponent of Izquierdo in 1808.

MURPHÍ (or Murfí), Tomás, was the chief partner of the Casa de Gordón y Murfí, and was a Spanish merchant with great influence at the court of Charles IV through his friendship with Godoy. He was lieutenant to the Second Consul of the Consulado of Veracruz in 1795, and Consul on the Junta de Gobierno in 1807. Through his connections, he was able to obtain numerous licences to import North American goods into the port of Veracruz, under the *permisos de Azanza* of 1798–1800, which gave the right to trade with Jamaica. According to Mora (*México y sus revoluciones*, iii, 230–1), Murfí was one of three Veracruz merchants addicted to the cause of the Revolution of 1810. The other two were Creoles, but, Murfí, the Peninsular, was described as the most enthusiastic. Luis Chávez Orozco's edition of López Cancelada's, *Ruina de la Nueva España*, 57, n. 3, states that after Mexican Independence, Murfí offered his services to the new government to secure foreign loans.

MURGUÍA, Lorenzo, nominated Accountant of the Royal Customs House in Oaxaca in 1778, with a salary of 1,600 pesos per year. From this post he was promoted to that of Administrator of Alcabalas and Pulques in February 1796. Creditor of Pedro Viguera, Regidor of the Oaxaca Cabildo, who also owed 1,775 pesos to Luis Gramecón, Oaxaca merchant, of whose will Murguía was the executor. The Alcalde Mayor of Huamelula, Tomás Villans de Aguirre, deposited 1,000 pesos with Murguía, which in March 1786 the Superior Government ordered to be used in payment of a debt of 2,950 pesos which the Alcalde Mayor owed the Huamelula communal funds. In 1791, acted on behalf of the Marqués de Villa Alta and Captain José Saldívar y Murguía, both residents of Havana. Revillagigedo consented to their despatch of 250 cwt. of copper and 40 cwt. of tin for the construction of foundries for sugar production in the mills they possessed in Cuba. Under the Consolidation procedure, Murguía, between February and May 1806, acted as interim Lieutenant-Deputy of the Treasury of the *Consolidación*, to which he himself was also debtor. Died in 1806.

ORDÓÑEZ DÍAZ, Felipe, succeeded to titles of Regidor Perpetuo and Alférez Real of the Oaxaca Ayuntamiento, valued at 1,000 pesos, in May 1788, after the renunciation in his favour by the Creole merchant José Jiménez Bochórquez. Received his title from the Crown on 28 April 1795. Also *fiador* of Ortega. Renounced his offices in favour of the Royal Treasury in February 1811.

ORTEGA, Pablo de, Alcalde Mayor of Villa Alta until 1790. Financial connexions with Magro and Ordóñez Díaz, and also with Pedro Alonso de Alles.

REGULES, José María, from Villasante in the Archdiocese of Burgos, Old Castile. Married María Josefa Ibáñez of Oaxaca. Primary interests in Yanhuitlán-Teposcolula region. Managed all Royal revenues in Nochistlán, where was the local chief of justice and commander of militia. Inherited office of Regidor Perpetuo of the Ayuntamiento of Oaxaca in 1797. Also one of the newly created Alcaldes de Barrio, created in 1795 for the policing of the streets. Brother of Captain of Loyal Royalists, Marcos Regules. Ruined by the Insurgent occupation of the city.

SÁNCHEZ, Antonio, born in 1757 in Villa de San Millán, Rioja, Spain. Married María Barbara Bustamante in Oaxaca. In 1817, recorded as Regidor Provisional and Alguacil Mayor of the Ayuntamiento of Oaxaca.

SOLAR CAMPERO, Manuel del, born 1757 in Spain. Entered Royal forces in 1797 at the canton of Orizaba. Lent the Crown 35,610 pesos during the war against Great Britain. In 1807, selected as one of the four deputies of commerce in Oaxaca. Opponent of Izquierdo in 1808. Between August 1809 and July 1815, loaned or donated 17,419½ pesos to the Crown. Rank of Lieutenant-Colonel and Battalion Commander. Fled to Campeche on entry of the Insurgents into Oaxaca, and thence to Veracruz and Puebla. Returned to Oaxaca on 30 May

1814. Frequent concession of his salary to the Crown. Order of Isabella the Catholic. Alcalde Ordinario de Primer Voto in the Ayuntamiento Constitucional in 1820. Consular Deputy in 1820. Mercantile interests included the cacao of Guayaquil and Soconusco.

VILLASANTE, Diego de, one of the Regidores Perpetuos of 1772, a native of Castile. Alcalde Mayor of Cuatro Villas in later 1770s. Received the lease of the mills of San Agustín and San Gabriel in the Villa de Etla, in 1785, from his father-in-law, Captain Sanz Rasines. Heavily indebted to the pious foundations and chantries. Opponent of Izquierdo in 1808.

3 THE CREOLES

CASTILLEJOS, Lic. Mariano, lawyer matriculated at the Audiencia of Mexico, Creole, hacienda-owner of Hacienda de los Cinco Señores. Borrower from pious foundations, and debtor to the *Consolidación*. *Promotor Fiscal* (district attorney), of the Intendancy of Oaxaca between 1802 and 1814, without salary, not even the expenses of a clerk or of the paper he wrote on. Frequent donations to the Crown. Object of Peninsular attack in 1808 and 1809, and ordered by Hoz, Intendancy candidate of the merchants, to hand over his office. Attended Insurgent Congress at Chilpancingo, in 1813. Rehabilitated. Calleja appointed him Subdelegate of Teotitlán del Valle on 20 September 1814. Took office. Elected one of Oaxaca's deputies to the 1821 Cortes, but died *en route*.

IBÁÑEZ DE CORBERA, Dr. Antonio José, born in Oaxaca, son of Spanish Peninsular merchant, Captain Antonio Ibáñez de Corbera, native of the region of Santander, who had married a Creole in Oaxaca. Studied grammar and philosophy in Oaxaca. In 1764 went to Mexico City on a Royal grant to study Sacred Canons. Bachelor in Philosophy and Letters, and Doctor in Canons at the Royal and Pontifical University of Mexico. 1781 governor of the diocese of Oaxaca. After 1780s Treasurer of the Oaxaca Cathedral, Vicar-General of the diocese, Visitor of Legacies, Pious Works, and Chantries, and one of the *Jueces Hacedores de Diezmos*. *Juez Conservador* (corporate lawyer) of the Dominican Province of Oaxaca. 1795 Knight of the Royal Order of Charles III. 1801 requested the Deanship of Mexico. 1802 requested the Archdeanship of Puebla. 1804 requested a Bishopric of New Spain. Left in charge of Oaxaca by Bergoza after November 1812. Pursued an ambiguous policy of apparent collaboration with the Insurgents, which he repudiated after March 1814, when the Royalists re-entered the city of Oaxaca. Rehabilitated, and promoted to the Deanship of Oaxaca in 1819.

IBÁÑEZ DE CORBERA, Juan María, lawyer, and brother of the above, elected deputy to the Cortes in Cádiz in 1810, but did not take seat. Lieutenant of militia battallion.

ITURRIBARRÍA, Juan José de, elected Secretary of the Cabildo Eclesiástico of Oaxaca on 20 April 1790.

ITURRIBARRÍA, Luis, in 1810, when he was unsuccessfully proposed deputy to the Cortes, he was both Accountant of the Tobacco Revenue of Veracruz and Regidor Alcalde Provincial of Oaxaca.

ITURRIBARRÍA, Manuel Ignacio, Regidor of the Ayuntamiento of Oaxaca during the rebel occupation in 1813. Elected a member of the Junta which was to choose the fifth *vocal* for the Congress of Chilpancingo. In 1820, after his rehabilitation, he was Administrator of the Post in Oaxaca, and on 2 July was elected to the Junta choosing the Ayuntamiento Constitucional. After the fall of the First Empire in 1823, became one of the three members of the Governing Junta under Intendant Murguía, until its resignation in December 1823.

ITURRIBARRÍA, Pedro de, mine-owner, and signatory of petition of 12 March 1790, requesting the establishment of a Provincial Mining Deputation in Oaxaca. Married María Barbara Galardi.

MIMIAGA Y ELORZA, José Mariano, born 1738, cochineal merchant, brother of Lic. Antonio Justo Mimiaga y Elorza, senior rector of the sacristy of Oaxaca Cathedral. 1787 Regidor Perpetuo of Oaxaca upon the resignation of another brother, Ignacio Tomás de Mimiaga, who had purchased it for 3,500 pesos. All brothers born in Oaxaca, sons of *'cristianos viejos, nobles, y limpios de mala raza'*.

MIMIAGA Y ELORZA, Lic. Manuel María, Alcalde Ordinario de Primer and de Segundo Voto and Regidor Honorario of the Oaxaca Ayuntamiento, between 1803 and 1807. At end of June 1809, provisional Asesor Ordinario of the Intend-ancy of Oaxaca. In the siege of Yanhuitlán, under orders of the Royalist Com-mander, Regules, 10–15 March 1812. Tried to hide during the Insurgent occupation of Oaxaca, but claimed that the Ayuntamiento forced him to con-tinue his office as Asesor of the Intendancy. Forced to comply to avoid being shot by the rebels, but tried to use his office to mitigate the extremes of the rebel régime against the Europeans, city patricians, and those who had never adhered to the 'detestable régime', i.e. that of Morelos. Rehabilitated after March 1814, and continued in office. Promoted to Auditor de Guerra of the Province of Oaxaca. Since 1803 received no salary from the Crown.

MURGUÍA Y GALARDI, José María, born Oaxaca 1769, son of Lorenzo Murguía and María Agustina Galardi, whose sister married Pedro de Iturribarría. Debtor to the *Ramo de Consolidación*. Owner of three haciendas in Nejapa, purchased in 1803. May 1809, awarded tithe farm for Nejapa by the Cabildo Eclesiástico. Alcalde Ordinario of the Ayuntamiento in that year. Unsuccessful candidate for deputy to the Cortes in 1810. Collaborated openly with the Insurgents, and became Oaxaca's deputy at the Congress of Chilpancingo in 1813. Rehabilitated after 1814, and became one of the Ministers of the Royal Treasury between 1814 and 1817. Elected deputy to the Cortes in 1820, and took his seat in 1821. Intendant of Oaxaca under Emperor Iturbide in 1822. Governor of Oaxaca under republican system between December 1823 and November 1824. Wrote his statistical survey of the State of Oaxaca between 1826 and 1828.

4 THE EPISCOPACY

ORTIGOZA, José Gregorio Alonso, Bishop of Oaxaca from 1775 until 1792. Spanish Peninsular, born in 1720 in Viguera near Logroño. Studied the sciences in the Logroño seminary. Appointed Inquisitor General in the Holy Office in New Spain. Presented by Charles III to Pius VI for the see of Antequera de Oaxaca, and consecrated in Mexico City. Entered Oaxaca on 17 December 1775. On visitation of the diocese between 1776 and 1783, and became a vigorous opponent of the Alcaldes Mayores. Renounced his office in 1791, but continued the administration of the see until the Holy See had accepted. According to the

Gaceta de México for March 1794, he invested the sum of 299,386 pesos 5 reales in pious funds and chantries during his administration.

OMAÑA, Gregorio José de, Bishop of Oaxaca from 1793 until his death in Mexico on 11 October 1797. Creole, born in Tianguistengo in the Archbishopric of Mexico, in 1739. Studied theology, Latin, and philosophy in the University of Mexico, and was ordained in 1764. Archdeacon of Mexico Cathedral. Consecrated Bishop of Oaxaca by Archbishop Núñez de Haro y Peralta in February 1793.

BERGOZA Y JORDÁN, Antonio, Bishop of Oaxaca from 1800 until 1812. Spanish Peninsular, born in 1747 in Jaca, Aragon. Studied Thomist philosophy for two years at University of Salamanca, followed by Law and Canons. 1768 received his Bachelor's degree in Law at Salamanca, and became President of the Academy of Laws there. In 1771 Bachelor of Sacred Canons in the University of Valencia, followed by a Doctorate in the same. 1774 nominated Visitor-General of the Bishopric of Salamanca by the Inquisitor General. In August 1779 received title to the office of Apostolic Inquisitor of the Holy Office of the Inquisition in New Spain, a post he effectively retained until his departure for Oaxaca in 1802. On 2 April 1784, requested his transfer back to Spain, on the grounds that he had already been in Mexico over three years and on only one-third of his salary, and that ill health would cut short his life. This request was apparently denied. Appointed Knight of the Royal Spanish Order of Charles III, and received the Grand Cross of America of Isabella the Catholic. On 13 October 1800, appointed Bishop of Oaxaca, where he arrived on 3 May 1802. Began his *visita* on 21 October and continued it into 1804, reporting in detail on the population of the parishes of the diocese. Ardent defence of the Royalist cause during the Hidalgo and Morelos movements after 1810. On 27 August 1811, after the Royalist defeat at Chilapa, he drafted a proclamation calling the diocese to arms, but decided not to issue it, for fear of terrifying the inhabitants. Appointed Archbishop of Mexico, 23 November 1811. Fled from Oaxaca, November 1812.

PÉREZ SUÁREZ, Manuel Isidoro, Bishop of Oaxaca between 1819 and 1831. A Spanish Peninsular, born in Paso de Guadalajara in 1776. Seminary of the Archbishopric of Toledo. Ferdinand's candidate to replace Bergoza. Arrived in Oaxaca on 20 July 1820. Like Antonio Joaquín Pérez, Bishop of Puebla, he adhered to the Iturbide movement in 1821, and remained Bishop until his resignation in December 1831. Died 1838.

SOURCES

ACO Actas Capits. 7, 8. (Roll 73).
AEO 1804, 1817 (unclassified legajos).
AGI *Mexico* 1142, 1146, 1147, 1495, 1496, 1675, 1811, 1823, 1832, 1973, 1974, 1416, 1975, 1977, 1984, 2131, 2513, 2583, 1861, 2591, 1862, 3170, 1368, 1872; *Indiferente general* 1508.
AGN *Industria y comercio* 20.
AGN *Intendentes* 12, 13, 32, 34, 37, 39, 48, 49, 69, 20; *Subdelegados* 51, 65; *General de parte* 60, 65, 67, 69, 68, 74, 75, 76; *Civil* 1427, 1641; *Vínculos* 56; *Bandos* 18; *Alcaldes Mayores* 1; *Minería* 41; *Consolidación* 5; *Reales cédulas* (Dupl.) 156, 158, 160.

Glossary of Personnel

AHN *Consejos* 21,390.
AMO *Tes. Mun.* 1 (1746–1829); *Lib. de Acuer.* (1820).
BN (Mexico) MSS 58.
Dahlgren, *Nocheztli*, 166, 211.
Gay, *Historia de Oaxaca*, ii, 351–3.
Pérez, *Recuerdos históricos*.

APPENDICES

SOURCES AND BIBLIOGRAPHY

MAPS

INDEX

APPENDICES

APPENDIX 1

Cochineal registration figures in the city of Oaxaca

	Pounds	Price (reales)	Value pesos:reales
1758	675,562	16½	1,393,346:5
1759	686,812	16½	1,416,549:6
1760	1,067,625	16	2,135,250
1761	788,625	15	1,478,671:7
1762	823,500	14¾	1,534,921:7
1763	599,625	15½	1,161,773:3½
1764	898,875	19½	2,191,007:6½
1765	1,082,250	18½	2,502,753:1
1766	932,625	19½	2,073,273:3½
1767	849,375	19½	2,070,351:4½
1768	621,000	22½	1,746,562:4
1769	1,024,312½	24½	2,136,957
1770	1,043,437½	25	3,260,742:2
1771	1,050,187½	32	4,200,750
1772	839,677½	30	3,148,790:5
1773	782,437½	25½	2,494,018
1774	1,558,125	17½	3,408,398:3½
1775	837,000	16	1,674,000
1776	808,550	17	1,718,168:6
1777	1,244,812½	15	2,334,023:¾
1778	1,057,800	16	2,115,600
1779	842,625	15	1,579,921:7
1780	1,385,437½	17	2,944,054:½
1781	464,625	17	987,318:1
1782	1,035,675	17	2,265,539:½
1783	990,000	18	2,227,500
1784	535,900	16	1,171,800
1785	537,750	17	1,142,718:6
1786	610,875	16½	1,259,929:5½
1787	451,125	16	902,250
1788	317,662	16	635,324
1789	478,125	15½	926,367:1½
1790	471,150	16	942,300
1791	538,650	16½	1,410,340:3
1792	433,125	15½	839,085:7½
1793	334,250	13½	564,053:1
1794	655,550	10½	860,409:3

Appendix 1 (cont.)

	Pounds	Price (reales)	Value (pesos:reales)
1795	584,125	12	876,187:4
1796	207,450	17½	453,796:7
1797	493,425	15½	956,010:7½
1798	512,325	18	1,152,731:2
1799	452,675	19½	1,103,395:2
1800	374,400	19	889,200
1801	406,012½	18	913,528:1
1802	433,550	19	1,029,681:2
1803	559,350	21	1,468,229:6
1804	346,500	28½	1,134,406:2
1805	191,250	23	549,843:6
1806	251,550	27	848,981:2
1807	341,550	29	1,143,118:6
1808	358,200	29	1,298,475
1809	343,350	33	1,416,318:6
1810	545,727½	29	1,298,475
1811	478,912½	28½	1,706,069:4
1812	199,800	20	449,500
1813	178,875	15	335,390:5
1814	327,937½	25	1,024,804:5½
1815	283,275	24	849,825
1816	358,687	32	1,410,748
1817	315,000	29	1,141,875
1818	250,412	28½	892,092
1819	493,200	27½	1,695,375
1820	...	...	...
1821	311,787½	23	896,389:½

Figures from Murguía, *Estadística*, tome VIII, Miahuatlán, f. 18. Also cited in B. Dahlgren de Jordán, *Nocheztli. La grana cochinilla* (Mexico 1963), App. II, no page number.

APPENDIX 2

Ten Year period registration figures, 1758–1826

1758–67	8,413,874	pounds valued at 18,157,924:4 pesos
1768–77	9,809,540	27,122,412:5½
1778–87	7,911,812½	16,452,162:4
1788–97	4,513,512	8,136,267:6
1798–1807	3,869,162½	10,428,179:5½
1808–17	3,383,764½	11,661,338:6:¼
1818–26	3,025,674½	7,857,797:6:¾

BSMGE, Murguía, *Estadística*, Miahuatlán, tome VIII, f. 18.

APPENDIX 3

Oaxaca cochineal dye (grana fina) *exports on the fleets from Veracruz, 1760–1772*

1760	24,089½ arrobas	at	64 pesos	1,541,728 pesos
1762	29,569 arrobas 15½ pounds	at	64 pesos	1,892,455
1765	20,827 arrobas 14¾ pounds	at	70 pesos	1,457,943:6
1769	19,038 arrobas	at	104 pesos	1,979,952
1770	19,037 arrobas 21 pounds	at	90 pesos	1,713,405:4:9
1772	32,261 arrobas 20 pounds	at	85 pesos	2,997,253

Figures from Lerdo de Tejada, *Comercio exterior de México*, numbers 3, 4, 5, 7, and 8.

The figure for 1770 is derived from AGI *Mexico* 1369, *Duplicados del virrey, 1769–70*, no. 673, Croix–Arriaga, 2 May 1770.

Appendix 4

Cochineal trade at Cádiz, February 1783–November 1786

1 Imported on private ships:

	arrobas	pounds
1783	69	8
1784	8,946	12½
1785	20,810	12½
1786	20,806	22¼

= 50,633 arrobas 5¼

2 Imported on ships of the Royal Armada:

1783–6 = 69,005½ arrobas

3 Exported from Cádiz:

	arrobas	pounds
1783	21,108	6½
1784	25,405	7¾
1785	24,184	8½
1786	17,743	19

= 88,441 arrobas 16¾

4 Destination of the dye after reaching Cádiz:

	pounds
To France	805,693½
To Spain	779,925
To Britain	580,175

out of a total of 2,674,525 pounds registered in the city of Oaxaca, 1783–6 inclusive

5 In the following way:

	arrobas	pounds
Marseilles	26,661	21¼
London	22,583	10
Amsterdam	20,717	8
Genoa	5,982	8
Ostend	2,809	11
Rouen	2,356	13¾
Le Havre	1,682	13½

Figures from AGI *Indiferente general* 2435, Relación de la grana entrada en esta ciudad de Cádiz en embarcaciones mercantes procedentes de América, bajo las reglas del libre comercio, &c.

Año de 1787, Expediente sobre la grana que entró en Cádiz después de la última guerra, en buques del rey y mercantes, y su extracción para otros reynos.

APPENDIX 5

Cochineal of Oaxaca within the context of Spanish American trade in 1786 to the port of Cádiz

		(reales de vellón)
1	Coined silver pesos	238,687,185
2	Indigo of Guatemala	49,840,000
3	Royal Tobacco Monopoly	46,418,880
4	Cochineal (all grades)	30,057,754
5	Coined gold pesos	24,981,145
6	Venezuelan cacao, (Caracas, Magdalena, and Cúcuta)	22,253,940
7	Hides of Buenos Aires	16,420,544
8	Peruvian quinine	12,375,904
9	White sugar	10,615,131
10	Cacao of Guayaquil	9,870,169
11	Indigo of Caracas	4,825,890
12	Palo de Campeche	4,711,992
13	Unclarified sugar	4,707,717
14	Copper	3,065,344
15	Unseeded cotton	2,601,354
16	Brazil wood	1,953,420
17	Gold disc coined pesos	1,671,835
18	Tabasco pepper	1,460,870
19	Purge of Jalapa	1,220,544
20	Cedar wood	1,210,080
21	Crafted silver	1,146,210

Total value of trade from the Indies: 501,001,664 reales de vellón.

Figures from AGI *Indiferente general* 2435, Estado general de la carga y sus valores a los precios corrientes de la plaza, que condujeron las embarcaciones del comercio libre, despachadas de los puertos de América, que entraron en esta bahía en todo el año de 1786.

Appendix 6

Export figures at the port of Veracruz, 1796–1821

1796	6,112 arrobas at	71–2 pesos	439,609 pesos
1797	838	65	54,471
1798	12,220	65–6	804,903
1799	40,602	66½	2,703,471
1800	5,150	70–80	379,256
1801	3,848	77½	298,258
1802	43,277	76–7	3,303,470
1803	27,251	80	2,191,399
1804	11,737	103–4	1,220,193
1805	. . .	. . .	. . .
1806	4,254	100	425,400
1807	2,823	100	282,300
1808	7,374	100	737,400
1809	21,569	120	2,587,200
1810	20,415	120	2,449,800
1811	11,215	108	1,211,220
1812	7,664	100	766,400
1813	6,381	113–14	724,080
1814	2,993	320	959,160
1815	21,006	120	2,520,720
1816	11,434	129–30	1,476,420
1817	14,640	130	1,903,200
1818	4,961	110	545,710
1819	21,704	112	2,430,848
1820	15,956	105	1,675,380

Lerdo de Tejada, *Comercio exterior de México*, número 14, Estado o balanza general del comercio recíproco hecha por el puerto de Veracruz, &c.

APPENDIX 7

Revenue and expenditure of the Oaxaca treasury 1790–1819

	Cargo	Data	Existencias
1790	101,428:6:7½	49,042:5:1	52,386:1:6½
1791	387,248:5:5½	301,443:2:9	85,805:2:8½
1792	407,206:5:2	380,630:0:9	26,576:4:5
1793	457,081:6:2	325,407:3:6	131,674:2:8
1794	475,982:6:11	401,724:3:6	74,258:3:5
1795	402,120:4:3	368,545:6:7	33,574:5:8
1796	340,370:4:1½	193,382:3:7	146,988:0:6½
1797	609,134:7:9¾	427,287:7:9	181,847:7:9
1798	543,738:3:4½	470,634:3:10	73,103:7:6½
1799	597,020:2:4¾	456,596:4:9	140,423:5:7¾
1800	515,918:6:0¼	326,689:5:5¼	189,229:0:7
1801	644,080:5:2½	278,075:6:3¾	366,004:6:10¾
1802			
1803			
1804	538,990:6:1	398,649:3:9½	140,341:2:3½
1805	645,416:5:3	379,749:0:10¾	265,667:6:8¾
1806	752,446:0:10	687,043:2:3¾	65,402:6:6¼
1807	637,724:4:5¾	610,476:5:2¼	27,247:7:3½
1808			
1809			
1815	634,271:5:1	637,013:0:6	2,741:3:5 (Deficit)
1816	682,516:0:9	680,597:4:2	1,918:4:7
1817	594,236:2:7	592,821:0:2	1,415:2:5
1818	630,346:0:9½	632,276:7:5½	1,930:6:3 (Deficit)
1819	555,392:5:0	557,861:0:11	2,468:3:11 (Deficit)

Notes:

1 After a thorough search no records for 1802 and 1803, and 1808–14 inclusive have been found. In any case records for 1812, 1813, and 1814 would have been either incomplete or lost in the course of the Insurgent occupation of the city.
2 Sums are presented in pesos, reales, and granos.

Sources:

1 For 1790–6, see AGI *Mexico* 2131, Contaduría general de Indias, cuentas pe Real Hacienda de Oajaca, 1799–6.
2 For 1797–1800, see AGI *Mexico* 2132, Cuentas de Real Hacienda de Oaxaca, 1797–1800.
3 Figures for 1797–1806 are found in AGI *Mexico* 2034, Estados, cortes y tanteos de las cajas reales de Hacienda, 1770–1820, Oaxaca, Estados, 1797–1806, nos. 6, 13, 15, 9, 3, 6, 7, and 5.
4 The accounts for 1807 are found in AGI *Mexico* 2374, Expedientes de Real Hacienda, 1807–1810, Iturrigaray–Cayetano Soler, no 1507, 27 April 1808.
5 For 1815–19, see Murguía, *Estadística*, ii, f. 17 *v*.

Appendix 8

APPENDIX 8

Table to illustrate the relationship between the Oaxaca merchants, and those of Mexico City and Veracruz, 1790–1800

1790

40,000 pesos were paid by the Principal Treasury of Oaxaca to the Oaxaca merchant, Alonso Magro, to reimburse him for the same amount, which his financial backer (*aviador*) in Mexico City, Francisco Ignacio de Iraeta, had already paid into the Mexico Treasury General.

1791

13,000 pesos to Juan María García for the same paid into the Mexico Treasury by Matías Gutiérrez de Lanzas, merchant of the Mexico Consulado.

69,000 to the same for that paid in by his other *aviador*, José Rafael de Molina, also a Mexican merchant.

50,000 to Francisco Antonio Goytia, Oaxaca merchant, for the same paid into the Mexico Treasury by the Marqués de Sierra Nevada.

19,214 pesos 5 reales 6 granos to the same, for that paid in by Francisco Ignacio de Iraeta, in Mexico.

5,000 pesos paid to Tomás López de Ortigoza, Oaxaca merchant, for the same paid in by his *aviador*, Pedro Alonso de Alles, merchant of Mexico.

29,000 paid to Juan Ramón López de Sagredo, Oaxaca merchant, for that paid into the Mexico Treasury by Matías Gutiérrez de Lanzas.

40,000 paid to Alonso Magro for the same paid by the Mexico merchant, Francisco Iraeta.

19,341 paid to Francisco Monterrubio, Oaxaca merchant, for that paid in by Gutiérrez de Lanzas.

10,000 paid to Pablo Ortega, former Alcalde Mayor of Villa Alta, for that handed into the Mexico Treasury by his *aviador*, Pedro Alonso de Alles, Mexico merchant.

6,000 to Felipe Ordóñez Díaz, Oaxaca merchant, for the same handed in by Alles in Mexico.

Of the gross total revenue of the Oaxaca Treasury for that year, a sum of 387,248 pesos 5 reales 5¼ granos, the large quantity of 266,555:6:6 was paid to local merchants to reimburse them for the sums their financial backers in the Consulado of Mexico had placed in the Royal Treasury General there.

1792

10,509½ pesos paid to Juan María García for the same paid in Mexico by Gutiérrez de Lanzas.

63,000 to the same for that paid by Molina.

20,000 to Goytia for the same paid by Iraeta.

14,000 to López de Ortigoza for that paid in Mexico by the merchant, Francisco Antonio Pesquera.

30,827 pesos 6 reales to López de Sagredo for the same paid into the Mexico Treasury by Lanzas.

11,000 to the same, paid in by Juan José de Oteyza, merchant of Mexico.

70,000 to Alonso Magro for that which Iraeta had paid into the Mexico Treasury.

25,000 to the same, for that paid into the Provincial Treasury of Veracruz by Pedro de Cos, merchant of that port.

25,000 to Antonio Moreda, Oaxaca merchant, for that paid in Mexico by the Marqués de Sierra Nevada.

80,000 to Ordóñez Díaz paid into the Mexico Treasury by Pedro Alonso de Alles.

Of the gross total revenue of 407,206:5:2, the quantity of 335,607:2:0 was paid to the merchants.

1793

15,000 pesos paid to Bernardino Bonavia, Subdelegate of Villa Alta, to reimburse him for the same amount due from the Tribute income, which his *aviador*, Iraeta, paid into the Mexico Treasury.

30,000 to Leonardo del Castillo, Oaxaca merchant, in the name of Militia Colonel Juan Francisco Echarri for whom the same was paid in Mexico by Martín Angel Michaus.

33,881 to Goytia, for the same paid in by Iraeta.

20,000 to Manuel del Solar Campero, Oaxaca merchant, paid into the Mexico City Treasury General by the commercial agent of the *Cinco gremios mayores de Madrid*, Pedro Basave.

Of the total gross revenue of 457,081:6:2, the quantity of 285,990:4:6 went to reimburse the Oaxaca merchants.

1794

1,500 to Lic. Luis Acosta for the same paid in Mexico by the merchant, José Antonio Otaegui.

12,000 to Juan María García, for the same paid in Mexico by the merchant, José Martín Chávez.

15,000 to Pedro García Henríquez, Oaxaca merchant, for that paid into the Treasury of Veracruz by the Veracruz merchants, Pedro Miguel de Echeverría and Francisco Guerra y Agreda.

25,000 paid to Goytia for the same paid into the Veracruz Treasury by Pedro Miguel de Echeverría and Francisco Guerra y Agreda, both Veracruz merchants.

5,500 to the same, paid into the Mexico City Treasury by Juan Baptista Iturriaga, on behalf of the Jalapa merchant, Juan Esteban Elías.

5,000 to the same Goytia for what Iraeta had paid into the Mexico Treasury.

46,000 paid to López de Sagredo for what Lanzas had handed over to the Mexico Treasury.

60,000 to the same for what Juan José Oteyza, merchant of Mexico, had paid into the Mexico Treasury, with the object that Juan Manuel Muñoz, merchant of Veracruz, should collect it and hold it at his own disposition.

20,000 to Alonso Magro for what Pedro de Cos, Veracruz merchant, had paid into the Veracruz Treasury.

6,000 to Ambrosio Martínez de Lejaiza for the same paid in Mexico by the Mexico merchant, Gaspar Nicario.

5,000 to Antonio Moreda, for what Iturriaga had paid in Mexico, on behalf of Elías.

9,000 to Ordóñez Díaz for that paid in Mexico by Joaquín Alonso de Alles.

2,000 to Diego de Villasante for what his *aviador*, Manuel Prieto y García, had paid in Mexico.

Appendix 8

Out of the gross total revenue of 475,982 pesos 6 reales 11 granos, the sum of 352,900 was paid by the Oaxaca Provincial Treasury to local merchants to reimburse them for what their *aviadores* had paid into the Mexico or Veracruz Treasuries. For the first time, the number of Veracruz merchants involved in these transactions is significant.

1795

10,000 pesos paid to Antonio García for what the Casa de Unanué y García paid into the Veracruz Treasury.

25,000 to Goytia and Magro for what Echeverría had paid into the Veracruz Treasury.

40,000 in the same category.

35,000 to Goytia for what Echeverría had paid in Veracruz.

33,000 to Gregorio López de Novales for the same paid in Mexico by Lanzas.

7,300 to López de Sagredo for that paid in Mexico by Pablo Jáuregui.

59,000 to Magro for the same paid by Echeverría in Veracruz.

13,000 to Magro for that paid into the Veracruz Treasury by the Casa de Cos y Arvizuri.

8,000 to Victores de Manero for the same paid in Mexico by Nicolás Antonio del Puerto, merchant of Mexico. Manero was a dependent of Juan María García.

6,000 to Francisco Monterrubio for what Echeverría had paid in Veracruz.

8,000 to the same for what Iturriaga had paid in Mexico.

7,000 to Moreda for what Iturriaga had paid in Mexico, on behalf of Elías.

12,000 to José María Murguía y Galardi for the same paid in Mexico by the Mexico merchant, Juan Martín de Chávez. Murguía had received the sum initially from Juan María García.

8,400 to Diego de Villasante for what Manuel Prieto y García had paid into the Mexico Treasury.

Out of the gross revenue of 402,120:4:3, the sum of 299,949:5:9 was paid by the Oaxaca Treasury to cover sums paid by other treasuries. In 1795 the Consulado of Veracruz was established, and in these figures Veracruz merchants appear more prominently than their rivals in Mexico City.

1796

10,000 pesos paid to Colonel Juan Francisco Echarri for what his commercial agent, Juan Martín de Juanmartiñena, had paid into the Treasury General of Mexico City.

27,782 to Goytia for what Francisco Guerra y Agreda, of the Consulado of Veracruz, had paid into the Treasury there.

40,000 to Magro, received by Tomás López de Ortigoza, for what Echeverría had paid in Veracruz.

3,600 to J. M. Murguía for what Prieto y García paid in Mexico.

18,000 to Antonio Sánchez for the same paid in Veracruz by the Casa de Unanué y García.

1,000 to Diego de Villasante for the same paid in Mexico by Prieto y García.

Of the gross total of 340,370:4:1½ entering the Oaxaca Provincial Treasury, the sum of 100,474:2:6 was paid to the merchants.

1797

50,000 to Colonel Juan Francisco Echarri for what Gabriel de Iturbe paid into the Mexico Treasury.

12,000 to retired Lieutenant-Colonel Pedro García Henríquez for that paid in Mexico by Iraeta. The sum originally had been lent by Echarri.

28,000 to Goytia for the same paid in Veracruz by Juan Lázaro de Unanué.

15,000 to Goytia for what Antonio de Couto y Avalle, resident of Orizaba, had paid provisional Treasury of the Army there for maintenance of the troops encamped at Orizaba.

30,000 to López de Ortigoza for the same paid in Mexico by Diego de Agreda of the Mexico Consulado.

28,200 to López de Sagredo for what Lanzas had paid in Mexico.

55,000 to Antonio Sánchez for that paid in Mexico by Diego de Agreda.

20,000 to the same for what Juan de Unanué paid in Veracruz.

20,000 to Manuel del Solar Campero for what Lanzas paid into the Mexico Treasury.

8,000 to Francisco de la Torre Marroquín for the same paid into the Treasury of Veracruz by Elías, of the Veracruz commerce.

15,000 to Francisco López y García for the same paid in Mexico by Pedro González Noriega.

Of the total of 609,134:7:9¾, the sum of 288,553:2:9 was paid to merchants of Oaxaca.

1798

12,048 pesos paid to Juan Garay for the same paid in Mexico by Victor Moreda.

70,000 to Cristóbal García Velarde for what Juan Ignacio Campero paid into the Mexico Treasury.

5,000 to the same for the sum paid into the Veracruz Treasury by Felipe de la Quintana.

100,000 to Goytia for what Echeverría paid into the Veracruz Treasury.

20,000 to the same for what Lieutenant-Colonel Iturbe paid in the Mexico Treasury. Sum originally lent by Echarri.

10,000 to Esteban Melgar, Subdelegate of Teotitlán del Valle, for the same paid in Veracruz by Domingo de Lagoa.

45,257:7 to J. M. Murguía for that paid in Veracruz by the Veracruz merchant, Pedro Antonio Garay.

7,000 to Antonio Rodríguez for the same paid in Veracruz by Gregorio García del Corral.

11,000 to Manuel Saenz Pardo for the sums paid into the Veracruz Treasury by Miguel González and Francisco Pérez Muñoz.

44,000 to Antonio Sánchez for the same paid in Veracruz by Juan de Unanué.

60,000 to the same for that paid in Veracruz by Juan Manuel Muñoz.

Of the total of 543,738:3:4½, the sum of 428,096:3:0 was paid to the merchants. The year, 1798, established the clear supremacy of the Veracruz merchants over those of Mexico City in the financing of the Oaxaca trades.

1799

36,767:2:0 to Juan Carlos de Barberena for the same paid in Veracruz by Martín de Olagasti.

23,558:7:9 to Bernardino Bonavia, ex-Subdelegate of Villa Alta, for what he had paid into the Mexico Treasury between December 1794 and February 1796.

6,900:3:0 to Vicente Domínguez for that paid in Veracruz by Nicolás Manuel de Enales.

Appendix 8

30,000 to Colonel Echarri for the same paid into the Mexico Treasury.

17,228 to Andrés Fernandez de Larrazábal for the same paid in Mexico by José de Castro.

18,325:6 to the same for what Juan Manuel Muñoz had paid into the Treasury of Veracruz.

25,000 to Goytia for what Juan Fernando Meoquí handed into the Mexico Treasury, at instructions of Colonel Echarri.

10,000 to José Gutiérrez Villegas for the same paid in Veracruz by Joaquín del Castillo, of the Ayuntamiento and commerce of Veracruz.

1,437:4:6 to Mariano de Heredia for what Captain Ramón de Arriaga had paid into the Mexico Treasury.

9,000 to Tomás López Cavada for the same paid in Veracruz by Pedro Antonio Garay of the Consulado and Ayuntamiento there.

4,311:1:6 to Melgar for the same paid in Veracruz by Domingo Lagoa.

29,478:2:9 to Monterrubio for the same paid by P. A. Garay in Veracruz.

12,000 to the same for the sum paid in Veracruz by Juan Manuel Revueltos.

14,056 to Victor Moreda for the same paid in Mexico by Pedro Barros.

12,068:2:3 to Murguía for the same paid in Veracruz by P. A. Garay.

4,819:1:6 to the same for the sum paid in Veracruz by Enales.

30,000 to Andrés Riveiro de Aguilar for the same paid in Veracruz by Miguel de Garfías y Zúñiga.

40,000 to Antonio Rodríguez for the same paid in Veracruz by Gregorio García del Corral.

1,082:2 to José Rodríguez Nieto for the same paid in Veracruz by Pedro del Puerto Vicario.

8,000 to Joaquín Ruiz de Ballesteros for the same paid in Veracruz by Juan Antonio Serrano.

6,500 to Antonio Sánchez for the same paid in Veracruz by Unanué.

5,550 to Juan de Siga for the same paid in Veracruz by Juan Manuel Muñoz.

20,000 to Manuel del Solar Campero for the same paid in Veracruz by José Ignacio de la Torre.

1,100 to Francisco Villarrasa Rivera, Minister of the Oaxaca Royal Treasury for the same paid in Mexico in the name of Colonel Echarri.

Of the gross revenue of 597,020:2:4¾, the sum of 371,474:5:9 was paid to the Oaxaca merchants and various others. The supremacy of Veracruz was clearly maintained.

1800

8,734:1 to V. Domínguez for that paid into the Veracruz Treasury by Enales.

25,000 to Echarri for the same paid in Mexico by Meoquí.

20,853:6:0 to Fernández de Larrazábal for what José Martín de Chávez paid in Mexico.

7,760:3:6 to Goytia on behalf of Echarri for the same paid in Veracruz by Olazagasti.

6,000 to López Cabada for that paid in Veracruz by Enales.

2,485:7:6 to the same for what Pedro González Noriega paid into the Mexico Treasury.

25,102:4 to López de Sagredo for the same paid in Mexico by Lanzas.

9,254 2:9 to Francisco Maza for the same paid in Veracruz by Enales.

5,720:6 to the same for the sum paid in Mexico by Domingo Zapiain.

5,000 to the same for what Felipe de Quintana paid in Veracruz.

3,500 to Melgar for the same paid by Domingo Lagoa in Veracruz.

12,000 to Antonio Sánchez for what José Mariano de Almanza paid into the Veracruz Treasury.

50,000 to Manuel del Solar Campero for what José Ignacio Uriarte and José Salazar, commissioners of the *Casa de los cinco gremios mayores de Madrid*, paid into the Veracruz Treasury.

1,383 paid to Villarrasa for the same handed into the Veracruz Treasury by Rómulo Ramírez.

11,929:6 to Fernández de Larrazábal for what Juan Antonio Gutiérrez paid in Veracruz.

Of the total revenue of 515,918:6:0¼, the sum of 279,915:0:3 was paid to merchants and others.

AGI *Mexico* 2131, Cuentas de la tesorería principal de Oaxaca, 1790–6.
AGI *Mexico* 2132, Cuentas de Real Hacienda de Oaxaca, 1797–1800.

Appendix 9

Personnel involved in the Oaxaca Consolidation, years 1806, 1807, and 1808

ALESÓN, Regidor Miguel, paid into the Royal coffers 2,000 pesos on 21 April 1807 and 26 April 1808, which he had borrowed from chantries (ff. 183 and 212 *v.*)

ARRIAGA, Miguel de, deceased, paid in 4,000 pesos, on 2 March 1807, which he had invested in his Haciendas de Tapanala and Lachipi, borrowed from the *Obra Pía de Dotar Huérfanas.* (f. 182 *v.*)

BARBERENA, Juan Carlos de, paid in 6,000 pesos on behalf of the Subdelegate of Tehuantepec, Vicente Lelo, as part payment for a sum of 6,000 pesos, borrowed from the *Obra Pía de Fiallo* and the Colegio de Niñas Educandas. Paid on 23 May 1807 and 23 May 1808. (f. 214)

CALDELAS, Francisco, paid in 2,000 pesos in the name of a resident of Tututepec, who was acting as *fiador* of the Subdelegate of Jamiltepec, borrowed from the same sources as Lelo. Paid on 12 February 1808. (f. 210 *v.*)

CAMACHO, Simón, on 25 June 1806 and 9 April 1808 this *hacendado* paid in 3,162 pesos, as an instalment towards a larger sum, borrowed from chantries. (ff. 167 and 212)

CARRASQUEDO, Pedro, merchant of Tlaxiaco, on 15 June 1808, paid in 500 pesos towards a 6,000 pesos debt, for 4,000 of which he was eligible as *fiador* of Francisco de la Torre Marroquín, taken in September 1794 from the *Obra Pía de Fiallo.* At the same time, he also paid in 2,000 pesos as *fiador* of Antonio de Lavanda y Garcés, taken from a chantry in May 1800. (f. 214 *v.*)

CASTILLEJOS, Lic. Mariano de, on 22 March and 28 July 1808, paid in 4,000 pesos, as a contribution to a larger sum, borrowed from funds set aside in the will of Regidor José Lara, and invested in his Hacienda de los Cinco Señores. (ff. 211 *v.* and 215–15 *v.*)

CORRES, Fausto de, ex-Subdelegate of Miahuatlán, paid in 4,000 pesos as an installment on 27 September 1806, borrowed from a pious foundation. (f. 168 *v.*)

DÍAZ, Juan Antonio, owner of the sugar-mill, Santa Ana, in Zimatlán, paid in 1,000 pesos as a contribution towards a sum of 13,000, borrowed from the *Obra Pía de Fiallo.* Paid on 21 May 1807. (ff. 184–4 *v.*)

ECHARRI, Lieutenant-Colonel Juan Francisco, paid in 1,024 pesos on 6 August 1806, borrowed from a pious work founded by Fiallo in the Oaxaca Seminary College. (f. 167 *v.*)

ESTRELLA, Pedro de, Regidor Perpetuo, paid in 4,000 pesos on 26 February and 2 July 1806, borrowed from the Colegio de Niñas, the *Obra Pía de Huérfanas*, and the *Obra Pía de Sermones del Carmen.* (ff. 166–7)

GARAY, Juan José, Oaxaca merchant, paid in three sets of 1,000 pesos, the first on 3 March 1807 as *fiador* for the larger sums borrowed by Antonio Labanda y Garcés from the Convento de Religiosas Agustinas of Oaxaca; the second on 18 June 1807 as *fiador* of the same for the sums borrowed from the Convent of the Soledad, and the last on 22 February 1808, as *fiador* of the Oaxaca merchant, Francisco de la Torre Marroquín, for the sums borrowed from the Hospital de SS. Cosmé y Damián. (ff. 182 *v.*, 185–5 *v.*, 210 *v.*)

Politics and trade in Southern Mexico

GONZÁLEZ, Sebastián, Regidor Perpetuo and merchant of Oaxaca, paid in 32,000 pesos on 19 July 1806, and 28 April and 21 August 1807, borrowed from five pious foundations, and from the revenues of the Convent of the Conception, the Colegio de Niñas, the *Obra Pía de Huérfanas*, the Colegio de San Bartolomé, the Seminary College, and funds of the Oratory of San Felipe Neri. (ff. 167, 183 v.)

GOYTIA, Francisco Antonio, paid in 4,350 pesos on 19 September 1806, borrowed from a chantry in the Oratory of San Felipe Neri. (f. 168)

GÜENDULAIN, Manuel Dionisio, paid in 2,000 pesos on 10 June 1807 (for a sum of 3,000 pesos, borrowed from the revenues of the Colegio de San Bartolomé, under *fianza* of the Oaxaca merchants, Alonso Magro and José Fernández), and 5 May 1808 (for a sum of 3,280 pesos, borrowed from the same college and from the *Obra Pía de Huérfanas*). (ff. 184 v. and 213)

GUTIÉRREZ VILLEGAS, José and Simón, paid in 12,827 pesos, on 24 December 1806, borrowed from a chantry and thirteen pious foundations. (f. 109 v.)

MARISCAL, Francisco, Oaxaca merchant, paid in 13,980 pesos, on 9 April 1808, borrowed from a patronage fund. (ff. 212–13 v.)

MURGUÍA Y GALARDI, José María, on 17 March 1807 paid in 300 pesos as a contribution to the repayment of a loan taken from the *Obra Pía de Dotar Huérfanas*, and on 1 March 1808 a sum of 300 pesos from the *Obra Pía de Fiallo*, applied to his three haciendas in Nejapa. Also paid in were 600 pesos, on 22 July 1807 on behalf of his brother, Manuel, militia sub-lieutenant, borrowed from the parish funds of Cuilapan in May 1800, and 5,000 pesos, on 26 and 29 October 1807, on behalf of his deceased father, D. Lorenzo, who had borrowed from pious works and the funds of the city's Convent of San Juan de Dios, for application to his town house. (ff. 182 v.-3, 211, 185 v.-6)

REGULES, Marcos, resident of Yanhuitlán, on 31 May 1808, paid in 500 pesos, part of a loan of 2,000, owed as *fiador* of Francisco de la Torre Marroquín, from pious foundations, totalling 12,000 pesos, borrowed in 1794. (ff. 214–14 v.)

RIVEIRO DEL AGUILAR, José, Oaxaca merchant, paid in 2,100 pesos on 16 June 1806, borrowed from a pious foundation. (f. 166 v.)

SOLAR CAMPERO, Manuel del, Oaxaca merchant, paid in 8,800 pesos on 2 July 1806 (from two pious works), and October 9 1807 (from several chantries, pertaining to the Oratory of San Felipe Neri). (ff. 167 and 186)

From AGN *Consolidación* 5.

Appendix 10

Sums collected during the Consolidation in Oaxaca

1805 (20 August–31 December)	25,869:0:9
1806	143,248:4:11¾
1807	135,780:1:3
1808	272,885:6:2
1809 (till 30 April)	28,271:4:9
	606,055:1:10¾

Figures from AGN *Consolidación* 5, *Cuenta general de cargo y data de los cargos introducidos en la tesorería principal de Oaxaca, 1805–9.*

APPENDIX II

Debts of the Oaxaca Treasury to the Pious Foundations, *1828*

	Principal	Interest
Chantries	115,308:7:0	5,755:5:10
Pious Funds of the Cathedral	40,764:0:11	2,038:2:4
Obra Pía de Dotar Huérfanas	55,266:5:4	2,663:2:7
Revenues of College of Santa Cruz and San Bartolomé	30,813:7:0	1,540:5:5
Funds for the Souls in Purgatory	4,887:0:0	244:2:8
Revenues of Colegio de Niñas Educandas	48,533:0:0	2,426:5:2
Convent of Monican Nuns of the Soledad	15,123:2:8	756:1:4
Convent of Dominican Friars	4,100:0:0	205:0:0
Convent of Catherine Nuns	7,200:0:0	360:0:0
Convent of Nuns of the Conception	18,225:0:0	911:2:0
Convent of San Juan de Dios	2,300:0:0	115:0:0
Parish of the city of Oaxaca	2,300:0:0	115:0:0
Convent of Bethlemite Friars	30,000:0:0	1,500:0:0
Pious Works administered by the Sacred Mitre	17,704:1:6	885:0:7
Hospital of SS. Cosmé y Damián	13,030:5:0	651:4:3
Oratory of San Felipe Neri	18,800:0:0	940:0:0
Lay Patronages	19,780:1:0	989:0:0
	442,136:6:5	22,097:0:2

Note: Interest had been paid for the first third of the year, 1812, a sum of 3,882:6:8, leaving the total amount of interest due to be paid reduced to 18,414:1:4. To this should be added the sum of all the interest that should have been paid, but which had not been, for the fifteen years between the remainder of 1812 and 1827, which came to a total of 331,455:2:6. The full total due from interest was, therefore, 349,869:3:10. Added to the amount due on the principal, the total debt of the *Ramo de Consolidación* came to 792,006:2:3.

Source: BSMGE, Murguía, *Estadística*, ii, ff. 25–5 *v*.

Appendix 12

APPENDIX 12

The Obrajes in Oaxaca

1 The cotton weavers of the city of Oaxaca received their guild ordinances in 1757, from the superior weavers guild of Mexico City.
2 Intendant Mora reported that, in 1793, there existed 500 looms for cotton textile manufacture, and 7 for silks in the city. The former produced *rebozos* (shawls), striped mantles of all colours, blue ribbon, *chiapanecos*, (Chiapas-style mantles), and table cloths.
3 Between 1793 and 1796, little progress in quality took place, but the number of looms increased from 500 to 800, because of the outbreak of war. Certain types of striped cotton cloths had also been developed. The only woollen goods produced were hats, which had improved in quality to such an extent that superficially it was impossible to tell them apart from the Spanish product.
4 In 1828, Murguía reported that the number of cotton textile looms in the city had fallen to 50, due to the import of foreign machine-produced cottons, which, while of good quality, sold for a lower price than the local product.

Legislación del trabajo en los siglos XVI, XVII y XVIII, Historia del movimiento obrero en México, tomo I (Mexico 1938), 151; AGN *Historia* 74, exp. 10, and 122, ff. 18–29; BSMGE, Murguía, *Estadística*, i, App. to Pt. II, f. 58.

Politics and trade in Southern Mexico

APPENDIX 13

Oaxaca—Population estimates of the Intendancy and State

1 The Revillagigedo Census of 1793, (AGN Historia 523).

	Spanish/Creole	Indian	Mixed	Total
Oaxaca City	10,970	5,333	2,528	19,069
Corregimiento	1,147	35,549	974	37,703
Villa Alta	38	58,088	120	58,280
Teposcolula	4,388	38,974	184	43,591
Huajuapan	483	25,524	4,746	30,770
Jicayan	2,787	20,568	5,379	28,749
Teutila	25	23,825	44	23,906
Tehuantepec	2,226	16,189	3,316	21,746
Teotitlán del Camino	455	18,506	301	19,367
Zimatlán	460	16,548	960	17,984
Cuatro Villas	328	17,249	152	17,740
Miahuatlán	314	14,745	928	16,003
Nejapa	212	12,885	950	14,060
Teococuilco	65	12,782	85	12,938
Teotitlán del Valle	89	12,159	177	12,432
Justlahuaca	1,205	6,890	70	8,171
Chontales	18	7,283	89	7,398
Nochistlán	325	5,615	5	5,955
Ixtepeji	84	5,469	85	5,642
Huitzo	177	5,281	123	5,585
Huamelula	203	3,250	376	3,833
Jalapa del Estado	6	368	37	413
Total	25,805	363,080	21,729	411,336

2 Humboldt, Essai Politique, op. cit, ii, bk. iii, 91.
   1803   534,800

                                    Total Viceregal population: 5,837,100
3 Navarro y Noriega, Fernando, Memoria sobre la población del reino de Nueva España (Mexico 1820).
   1810   595,604 (of which 526,466 were Indians, 37,694 white, and
                   31,444 mestizo and mulatto)
                            Total Viceregal population 6,122,354
4 Murguía y Galardi, Estadística, I, Pt. 2, appendix, ff. 27 v.–38.

                          1827 Population Estimates
Department 1.   Oaxaca: partido: Oaxaca   15,429
                                              Etla   30,013
                                              Zimatlán   30,800
                                              Tlacolula   22,988
                                                            _____
                                                            99,230

Appendix 13

Department 2.	Villa Alta:	*partido*:	Yalalag	30,317
			Chuapan	14,317
			Ixtlán	11,585
				56,219
Department 3.	Teotitlán del Camino:	*partido*:	Teotitlán	17,319
			Teutila	27,972
				45,291
Department 4.	Teposcolula:	*partido*:	Teposcolula	24,984
			Nochistlán	18,928
			Tlaxiaco	20,598
				64,510
Department 5.	Huajuapan:	*partido*:	Huajuapan	24,470
			Justlahuaca	22,536
				47,006
Department 6.	Jamiltepec:	*partido*:	Jamiltepec	26,436
			Juquila	11,067
				37,503
Department 7.	Miahuatlán:	*partido*:	Miahuatlán	25,708
			Pochutla	6,129
			Ocotlán	24,123
				55,960
Department 8.	Tehuantepec:	*partido*:	Tehuantepec	27,246
			Nejapa	14,581
			Chontales	8,990
				50,817
		Total Population of the State:		456,536

SOURCES AND BIBLIOGRAPHY

MANUSCRIPT SOURCES (*only those cited in the text*)

Archivo del Estado de Oaxaca (unclassified and in chaos):
legajos for 1804, 1814–17.

Archivo de Notarías, Oaxaca:
Protocolos, legajo 19 (1786).

Archivo del Tribunal de la Federación, Oaxaca:
legajo 1.

Archivo General de Indias, Seville, Spain (AGI):
Audiencia de México, legajos 19, 600, 634, 635, 871, 877, 1128, 1141, 1142, 1144, 1145, 1146, 1147, 1300, 1368, 1369, 1400, 1416, 1495, 1496, 1500, 1503, 1633, 1675, 1676, 1780, 1811, 1818, 1823, 1827, 1830, 1832, 1861, 1862, 1868, 1872, 1890, 1973, 1974, 1975, 1977, 1984, 2034, 2131, 2132, 2374, 2506, 2508, 2509, 2512, 2513, 2518, 2583, 2585, 2587, 2588, 2591, 2693.
Indiferente General, legajos 666, 1508, 1713, 2439, 2466, 2485.

Archivo General de la Nación, Mexico City (AGN):
Bandos 18.
Civil, legajos 26, 1427, 1641, 1866.
Consolidación 5.
Correspondencia de los virreyes (1st series) 1.
General de parte 60, 65, 67, 68, 69, 72, 74, 75, 76, 77, 78.
Historia 74, 122, 523.
Industria y comercio 9, 20.
Infidencias 108, 157.
Intendentes 12, 13, 20, 23, 33, 34, 37, 39, 48, 49, 69.
Minería 41.
Reales cédulas (origs.) 71, 72.
Reales cédulas (duplics.) 156, 158, 160.
Subdelegados 20, 21, 34, 35, 47, 51, 54, 65.
Tributos 6, 14.
Vínculos 56.

Archivo Histórico de Hacienda (AHH) (included in AGN):
legajos 276, 463, 696.

Archivo Histórico Nacional, Madrid (AHN):
Consejos 21,390.

Archivo Municipal de Oaxaca:
Tesorería municipal 1 (1746–1829).
Libro de acuerdos (1820).

Biblioteca de la Sociedad Mexicana de Geografía y Estadística (BSMGE):
MSS José María Murguía y Galardi, *Estadística del Estado de Oaxaca* (1826–8), 5 tomes containing 9 volumes.

Biblioteca Nacional, Mexico City (BN):
MSS 58, 1378, 1385, 1407.

British Museum, London (BM):
Add. MSS 13,978, 17,557, 38,345.

Bibliography

Museo Nacional de Anthropología, México (MN):
Microfilm Collection, Oaxaca, Roll 24: Archivo del Juzgado de Teposcolula, Civil 12; and Roll 73, Archivo de la Catedral de Oaxaca, Actas Capitulares 7 and 8.

PUBLISHED DOCUMENTS, COLLECTIONS OF DOCUMENTS, AND WORKS OF REFERENCE

Alba, Rafael (ed.), La constitución de 1812 en la Nueva España (Publicaciones del Archivo General de la Nación, no. 5, 2 vols.; Mexico 1913).

Archivo Histórico de Hacienda, Colección de documentos publicados bajo la dirección de Jesús Silva Herzog,vol. i, La libertad del comercio en la Nueva España en la segunda década del siglo XIX (Mexico 1943), and vol. iii, Relaciones estadísticas de Nueva España de principios del siglo XIX (Mexico 1944).

Banco Nacional del Comercio Exterior, Colección de documentos para la historia del comercio exterior de México (Introducción por Luis Chávez Orozco), primera serie, vol. ii, Controversia que suscitó el comercio de Nueva España con los países extranjeros (1811–1821) (Mexico 1959), and vol. v, El comercio de la Nueva España y Cuba (1809–1811) (Mexico 1960); segunda serie, vol. i, El comercio exterior y el artesano mexicano (1825–1830) (Mexico 1965).

García Carraffa, Alberto y Arturo, Diccionario heráldico y genealógico de apellidos españoles y americanos (86 vols.; Madrid 1919–63).

García Cubas, Antonio, Diccionario geográfico, histórico y biográfico de los Estados Unidos Mexicanos (5 vols.; Mexico 1888–91).

García, Genaro (ed.), Documentos inéditos o muy raros para la historia de México, tomo ix, El clero de México y la guerra de independencia (Mexico 1906).

Hernández y Dávalos, Juan Eusebio, Colección de documentos para la historia de la guerra de independencia de México de 1808 a 1821 (6 vols.; Mexico 1877–82).

Humphreys, Robin A., British Consular Reports on the Trade and Politics of Latin America (London 1940).

Instrucciones que los Virreyes de Nueva España dejaron a sus sucesores (2 vols.; Mexico 1867–73).

Klarvill, Victor von, The Fugger News-Letters. Being a Selection of unpublished letters from the Correspondence of the House of Fugger during the years, 1568–1605 (2 vols.; London, 1925–6).

Konetzke, Richard (ed.), Colección de documentos para la historia de la formación social de hispanoamérica 1493–1810 (3 vols.; Madrid 1953–62).

Lerdo de Tejada, Miguel, Comercio exterior de México desde la Conquista hasta hoy (Mexico 1853).

López Cancelada, Juan, El Telégrafo mexicano (Cádiz 1811, 1813).

Ruina de la Nueva España si se declara el libre comercio con los extrangeros (Cádiz 1811).

Navarro y Noriega, F., Memoria sobre la población del reino de Nueva España (Mexico 1943 edition).

Ordenanza general formada de orden de Su Magestad para el gobierno é instrucción de intendentes, subdelegados y demás empleados de Indias (Madrid 1803).

Quirós, José María, Memoria de Instituto (Havana 1813).

Memoria de Estatuto (Veracruz 1817).

Memoria de Estatuto (Mexico 1818).

Pérez y López, A. X, Teatro de la legislación universal de España é Indias por orden cronológico de sus cuerpos y decisiones no recopilados (28 vols.; Madrid 1791–8).

191

Politics and trade in Southern Mexico

Real Ordenanza para el establecimiento é instrucción de intendentes de exército y provincia en el reino de la Nueva España (Madrid 1786).

Recopilación de leyes de los reynos de las Indias (3 vols.; Madrid 1943 edition).

Revillagigedo, Viceroy, 'Informe sobre el estado del comercio de Nueva España', (31 August 1793), in AGN *Correspondencia de virreyes* (reservada) 26, f. 42 *et seq.*; reprinted in *Boletín del Archivo General de la Nación*, i (Nov.–Dec. 1930), and ii (Jan.–Feb. 1931).

Velasco Ceballos, R. (ed.), *La administración de D. Frey Antonio María de Bucareli y Ursua* (2 vols.; Publicaciones del Archivo General de la Nación, Mexico 1936) xxix and xxx.

Zamora y Coronado, J. M., *Biblioteca de legislación ultramarina en forma de diccionario alfabético* (6 vols.; Madrid 1844–9).

Zavala, Silvio A. and Castelo, María, *Fuentes para la historia del trabajo en Nueva España* (8 vols.; Mexico 1939–46).

SECONDARY SOURCES I: CONTEMPORARY WORKS

Alamán, Lucas, *Historia de Méjico desde los primeros movimientos que prepararon su Independencia en el año de 1808 hasta la época presente* (5 vols.; Mexico 1883–5 edition).

Alzate y Ramírez, J. A., *Gacetas de literatura de México* (4 vols.; Puebla, 1831).

Antúñez y Acevedo, R., *Memorias históricas sobre la legislación y gobierno de los españoles con sus colonias* (Madrid 1797).

Beleña, Eusebio Bentura, *Recopilación sumaria de todos los autos acordados de la Real Audiencia y Sala del Crimen de esta Nueva España*, (2 vols.; Mexico 1787).

Bustamante, Carlos María, *Cuadro histórico de la Revolución Mexicana* (4 vols.; Mexico 1961 edition).

Suplemento a la historia de los tres siglos de México durante el gobierno español (3 vols.; Mexico 1836).

Memoria estadística de Oaxaca, y descripción del valle del mismo nombre, extractada de la que trabajó en grande José María Murguía y Galardi, Intr. by Ernesto Lemoine Villicaña (Mexico 1963 edition).

Fonseca, Fabián, y Urrutia, Carlos de, *Historia general de la Real Hacienda* (6 vols.; Mexico 1845–53).

Humboldt, Baron Alexander von, *Essai politique sur le royaume de la Nouvelle Espagne* (5 vols.; Paris 1811).

Maniau, Joaquín, de, *Historia de la Real Hacienda* (Mexico 1914).

Mier y Noriega y Guerra, Fray Servando Teresa de, *Historia de la Revolución de Nueva España, antiguamente Anáhuac, ó verdadero orígen y causas de ella con la relación de sus progresos hasta el presente año de 1813* (2 vols.; London 1813).

Pinkerton, John, *A General Collection of the Best and Most Interesting Voyages and Travels in all parts of the World* (17 vols.; London 1808–14), vol. xiii, Thierry de Ménonville, M. Nicolas Joseph, *Travels to Guaxaca Capital of the Province of the same name in the Kingdom of Mexico 1777*.

Raynal, Abbé G. T. F., *Histoire philosophique et politique des établissements et du commerce des européens dans les deux Indes* (5 vols.; Paris 1820).

Toreno, Conde de, *Historia del Levantamiento, Guerra, y Revolución de España* (Madrid 1835).

Ward, H. G., *Mexico in 1827* (2 vols.; London 1828).

Bibliography

Zavala, Lorenzo de, *Ensayo histórico de las Revoluciones en México 1808–1830* (Paris 1831–2).

SECONDARY SOURCES 2: OTHER BOOKS AND ARTICLES

Aguirre Beltrán, Gonzalo, *La población negra de México 1519–1810* (Mexico 1946).
Aiton, Arthur S., 'Spanish Colonial Reorganization under the Family Compact', *Hispanic American Historical Review (HAHR)* xii (1932), 269–80.
Altamira y Crevea, Rafael (ed.), *Contribuciones a la historia municipal de América* (Mexico 1951).
Arcila Farías, Eduardo, *El siglo ilustrado en América, reformas económicas del siglo XVIII en Nueva España* (Caracas 1955).
Artola, Miguel, 'Campillo y las reformas de Carlos III', *Revista de Indias*, no. 50 (1952), 685–714.
Armytage, Frances, *The Free Port System in the British West Indies, A Study in Commercial Policy 1766–1822* (London 1953).
Bancroft, Herbert H., *History of Mexico* (6 vols.; San Francisco 1883–8).
Bayle, Constantino, *Los cabildos seculares en la América española* (Madrid 1952).
Bazant, Jan, 'Evolución de la industria textil poblana 1544–1845', *Historia Mexicana*, 52 (April–June 1964), 473–516.
Benson, Nettie Lee, *La diputación provincial y el federalismo mexicano* (El Colegio de México 1955).
Mexico and the Spanish Cortes 1810–1822, Eight Essays (Latin American Monographs, No. 5, Institute of Latin American Studies, University of Texas, Austin 1966).
'The Contested Mexican Election of 1812', *HAHR* xxvi (1946), 336–50.
'Iturbide y los planes de Independencia', *Historia Mexicana*, 11 (Jan.–March 1953), 439–46.
Bernstein, Harry, *The Origins of the Inter-American Interest, 1700–1812* (New York 1965).
Bobb, Bernard, E., *The Viceregency of Antonio María Bucareli in New Spain, 1771–1779* (Texas Panamerican Series, University of Texas, Austin 1962).
Boletín del Archivo General de la Nación, México, tomo II, no. 4, primera serie (July–August 1931), 493–506.
Borah, Woodrow, W., *Silk Raising in Colonial Mexico* (Ibero-Americana 20, California 1943).
'The Collection of Tithes in the Bishopric of Oaxaca during the Sixteenth Century', *HAHR* xxi (1941), 389–409.
'Tithe Collection in the Bishopric of Oaxaca 1601–1867', *HAHR* xxix (1949), 498–517.
Brown, V. L., 'Contraband Trade as a Factor in the Decline of Spain's Empire in America', *HAHR* vii (1928), 178–89.
Calderón Quijano, José Antonio, *El banco de San Carlos y las comunidades de indios de Nueva España* (Escuela de Estudios Hispano-americanos, Seville 1963).
Capella, M. and Matilla Tascón, A, *Los cinco gremios mayores de Madrid, estudio crítico-histórico* (Madrid 1957).
Cappa, Ricardo, S. J., *Estudios críticos acerca de la dominación española en América* (Madrid 1888–97), vols. i–xix and xxvi.
Carrera Pujal, Jaime, *Historia de la economía española* (5 vols.; Barcelona 1943–7).

Carrera Stampa, Manuel, *Los gremios mexicanos, La organización gremial en Nueva España 1521–1861* (Mexico 1954).

'El Obraje Novahispano', *Memorias de la Academia Mexicana de la Historia*, xx (April–June 1961), no. 2, 148–71.

'Los obrajes de indígenas en el virreinato de la Nueva España, *Vigésimo-séptimo Congreso Internacional de Americanistas* (Actas de la Primera Sesión celebrada en la Cuidad de México en 1939), ii, 555–62.

Castañeda, Carlos E., 'The Corregidor in Spanish Colonial Administration', *HAHR* ix (1929), 446–70.

Céspedes del Castillo, Guillermo, 'Lima y Buenos Aires. Repercusiones económicas y políticas de la creación del virreinato del Plata', *Anuario de Estudios Americanos,* iii (1946), 669–874.

'La visita como institución indiana', *Anuario de Estudios Americanos* iii (1946), 984–1025.

Chevalier, François, *La formation des grands domaines en Mexique* (Paris 1952).

Christelow, Allan, 'Contraband Trade between Jamaica and the Spanish Main and the Free Port Act of 1766', *HAHR* xxii (1942), 309–43.

'Great Britain and the Trades from Cadiz and Lisbon to Spanish America and Brazil 1759–83', *HAHR* xxvii (1947), 2–29.

Costeloe, Michael P., *Church Wealth in Mexico. A Study of the 'Juzgado de Capellanías' in the Archbishopric of Mexico 1800–1856* (Cambridge Latin American Studies no. 2, Cambridge University Press, 1967).

Dahlgren de Jordán, Babro, *Nocheztli, la grana cochinilla* (Mexico 1963).

Davis, R., 'English Foreign Trade 1660–1700', *Economic History Review*, series II, vol. vii (1954–5), 150–66.

'English Foreign Trade 1700–74', *Economic History Review*, series II, vol. xv (1962–3), 285–99.

Deustua Pimental, C., *Las intendencias en el Perú 1790–6* (Seville 1965).

Farriss, N. M., *Crown and Clergy in Colonial Mexico 1759–1821, The Crisis of Ecclesiastical Privilege* (London, University of, Historical Studies xxi, 1968).

Fisher, L. E., *The Background of the Mexican Revolution for Independence* (Boston 1934).

Champion of Reform, Manuel Abad y Queipo (New York, 1955).

The Intendant System in Spanish America (Berkeley 1929).

Viceregal Administration in the Spanish American Colonies (Berkeley 1926).

Flores Salinas, B., 'En busca de la grana mexicana, 1777', *Memorias de la Academia Mexicana de Historia*, 19 (Jan.–March 1960), no. 1, 5–18.

Floyd, Troy, S., 'The Guatemalan Merchants, the Government, and the "Provincianos" ', *HAHR* xli (1961), 90–110.

Fugier, André, *Napoléon et l'Espagne 1799–1808* (Paris 1930).

Gamio, Manuel, *Legislación indigenista de México* (Mexico 1958).

Gay, Padre José Antonio, *Historia de Oaxaca* (2 vols.; Mexico 1881).

Gibson, Charles, *The Aztecs under Spanish Rule. A History of the Indians of the Valley of Mexico 1519–1810* (Stanford 1964).

Tlaxcala in the Sixteenth Century (Yale 1952).

Giménez Fernández, Manuel, *Las doctrinas populistas en la Independencia de Hispanoamérica* (Seville 1946).

Goebel, D. B., 'British Trade to the Spanish Colonies 1796–1823', *American Historical Review*, xliii (1938), 288–303.

Bibliography

González Obregón, Luis, 'Las sublevaciones de indios en el siglo XVII: iii. Las sublevaciones de indios en Tehuantepec, Nejapa, Ixtepeji, y Villa Alta', *Anales del Museo Nacional* (Mexico), segunda época, tomo IV (1907), 145 *et seq.*

Grandmaison, Geoffroy de, *L'Espagne et Napoléon 1804–1809* (Paris 1908).

Greenleaf, R. E., 'The Obraje in the Late Mexican Colony', *The Americas*, xxiii (1967), 227–50.

Griffin, Charles C., *Los temas sociales y económicas en la Independencia* (Caracas 1962).

Hale, Charles A., *Mexican Liberalism in the Age of Mora, 1821–1853* (Yale 1968).

Hamilton, Earl J., 'Monetary Problems in Spain and the Spanish Empire 1751–1800', *Journal of Economic History*, iv (1944), 21–48.

Hamill, Hugh M., *The Hidalgo Revolt, Prelude to Mexican Independence* (University of Florida, Gainesville 1966).

Hamnett, Brian R., 'The Appropriation of Mexican Church Wealth by the Spanish Bourbon Government— The "Consolidación de Vales Reales"', 1805–1809', *Journal of Latin American Studies*, i, no. 2 (Nov. 1969), 85–113.

Haring, C. H., *The Spanish Empire in America* (Oxford 1947).

Trade and Navigation between Spain and the Indies (Harvard 1918).

Herr, Richard, *The Eighteenth Century Revolution in Spain* (Princeton 1958).

Howe, Walter, *The Mining Guild of New Spain and its Tribunal General 1770–1821* (Harvard 1949).

Humphreys, Robin A., 'Historiography of the Spanish American Revolutions', *HAHR* xxxvi (1956), 81–93.

'British Merchants and South American Independence', (Raleigh Lecture, British Academy, London 1965).

'Tradition and Revolt in Latin America', (London University, Athlone Press 1965).

King, J. F. 'The Coloured Castes and American Representation in the Cortes of Cádiz', *HAHR* xxxiii (1953), 33–64.

Konetzke, Richard, 'La condición legal de los criollos y las causas de la Independencia', *Estudios Americanos*, 11 (1950), 31–54.

'El mestizaje y su importancia en el desarrollo de la población hispano-americana durante la época colonial', *Revista de Indias*, vii (1946), 7–44, and 215–37.

La Force, James C., *The Development of the Spanish Textile Industry 1750–1800* (Berkeley 1966).

Lafuente Ferrari, Enrique, *El virrey Iturrigaray y los orígenes de la Independencia de Méjico* (Madrid 1941).

Lavrín, Asunción, 'The Role of the Nunneries in the Economy of New Spain in the Eighteenth Century', *HAHR* xlvi, No. 4, (nov. 1966), 371–94.

Lee, Raymond L., 'Cochineal Production and Trade in New Spain to 1600', *The Americas*, iv (1947–8), 449–73.

'American Cochineal in European Commerce 1526–1625', *Journal of Modern History*, xxiii (1951), 205–24.

Lerdo de Tejada, Miguel, *Apuntes históricos de la heroica ciudad de Vera-Cruz* (3 vols.; Mexico 1850–8).

Lohmann Villena, Guillermo, *El corregidor de indios en el Perú bajo los Austrias* (Madrid 1957).

López Cámara, Francisco, *La Génesis de la conciencia liberal en México* (El Colegio de México 1954).

López Sarrelangue, Delfina E., 'Población indígena de la Nueva España en el siglo XVIII', *Historia Mexicana*, xii (April–June 1962), 516–30.

Lynch, John, *Spanish Colonial Administration, 1782–1810. The Intendant System in the Viceroyalty of the Rio de la Plata* (London: University of, Historical Studies 5, 1958).

McAlister, Lyle N., 'Social Structure and Social Change in New Spain', *HAHR* xliii (1963), 349–70.

The *'Fuero Militar'* in New Spain 1764–1800 (University of Florida, Gainesville 1957).

Medina, José Toribio, *La imprenta en Oaxaca 1720–1820* (Santiago de Chile 1904).

Miquel i Vergés, J. M., *La Independencia Mexicana y la prensa insurgente* (Mexico 1941).

Miranda, José, *Las ideas y las instituciones políticas mexicanas 1521–1821* (Mexico 1952).

Mora, José María Luis, *México y sus revoluciones* (3 vols.; Mexico 1965 edition).

Obras sueltas (Mexico 1963 edition).

Navarro García, Luis, *Intendencias en Indias* (Escuela de Estudios Hispano-americanos, Seville 1959).

Ots Capdequí, J. M., *El Estado español en las Indias* (Mexico 1941).

'Apuntes para la historia del municipio hispano-americano del período colonial', *Anuario de Historia del Derecho Español*, i (1924), 105–49'.

'Las instituciones económicas hispano-americanas del período colonial', *Anuario de Historia del Derecho Español*, xi (1934), 211–83.

'Instituciones sociales de la América española en el período colonial' (La Plata 1934).

Parry, J. H., *The Sale of Public Office in the Spanish Indies under the Habsburgs* (Ibero-Americana 37, California 1953).

Pérez, Eutimio, *Recuerdos históricos del episcopado oaxaqueño* (Oaxaca 1888).

Phelan, John L., *The Kingdom of Quito in the Seventeenth Century, Bureaucratic Politics in the Spanish Empire* (Wisconsin 1968).

'Authority and Flexibility in the Spanish Imperial Bureaucracy', *Administrative Science Quarterly*, v (1960), 47–65.

Pike, Fredrick B., 'The Municipality and the system of Checks and Balances in Spanish Colonial Administration', *The Americas*, xv (1958), 139–58.

Portillo, Andrés, *Oaxaca en el centenario de la independencia nacional* (Oaxaca 1910).

Potash, Robert A., *El Banco de Avío de México, El fomento de la industria 1821–1846* (Mexico 1959).

Priestley, H. I., *José de Gálvez, Visitor-General of New Spain 1765–1771* (Berkeley 1916).

Ramírez, A. F., *Hombres notables y monumentos coloniales de Oaxaca* (Mexico 1948).

Reyes Heroles, Jesús, *El liberalismo mexicano* (3 vols.; Mexico 1957, 1959, and 1961).

Robertson, W. S., *Iturbide of Mexico* (Duke Univ. Press 1952).

'The Juntas of 1808 and the Spanish Colonies', *English Historical Review* (1916), 573–85.

Rodríguez Casado, Vicente *La política y los políticos en el reinado de Carlos III* (Madrid 1962).

Rojas, Basilio, *La rebelión de Tehuantepec* (Mexico 1964).

Rousseau, F., *Le règne de Charles III d'Espagne* (2 vols.; Paris 1907).

Bibliography

Rubio Mañé, J. Ignacio, *Introducción al estudio de los virreyes de Nueva España 1535–1746* (4 vols.; Mexico 1959–61).

Ruiz Guiñazú, E., *La magistratura indiana* (Buenos Aires 1916).

Sarrailh, Jean, *L'Espagne éclairée de la seconde moitié du XVIIIe Siècle* (Paris 1954).

Schaefer, Ernesto, *El Consejo real y supremo de las Indias* (2 vols.; Seville 1935–47).

Schmitt, Karl M., 'The Clergy and the Independence of New Spain', *HAHR* xxxiv (1954), 289–312.

Sierra, Justo, *Evolución política del pueblo mexicano* (Mexico 1950 edition).

Simpson, L. B., *The Encomienda in New Spain. The Beginning of Spanish Mexico* (California 1950).

Smith, Donald E., *The Viceroy of New Spain* (Berkeley, 1913).

Smith, Robert S., 'Indigo Production and Trade in Colonial Guatemala', *HAHR* xxxix (1959), 181–211.

'The Institution of the Consulado in New Spain', *HAHR* xxiv (1944), 62–85.

'Sales Taxes in New Spain 1575–1770', *HAHR* xxviii (1948), 2–37.

'Shipping in the Port of Veracruz', *HAHR* xxiii (1943), 5–20.

Torre Villar, Ernesto de la, *La Constitución de Apatzingán y los creadores del Estado mexicano* (Mexico 1964).

Vásquez, Genaro V., *Doctrinas y realidades en la legislación para los indios* (Mexico 1940).

Velázquez, María del Carmen, *El Estado de Guerra en Nueva España 1760–1808* (Mexico 1950).

Vilar, Pierre, *La Catalogne dans l'Espagne Moderne, recherches sur les fondements économiques des structures nationales* (3 vols.; S.E.V.P.E.N. Paris 1962).

Villoro, Luis, *La Revolución de Independencia, ensayo de interpretación histórica* (Mexico 1953).

Zamacois, Niceto de, *Historia de Méjico desde sus tiempos más remotos hasta nuestros días* (21 vols.; Barcelona 1888–1901).

Zavala, Silvio, *La encomienda indiana* (Madrid 1935).

Zimmerman, A. F., 'Spain and its Revolted Colonies 1808–1820', *HAHR* xi (1931), 439–63.

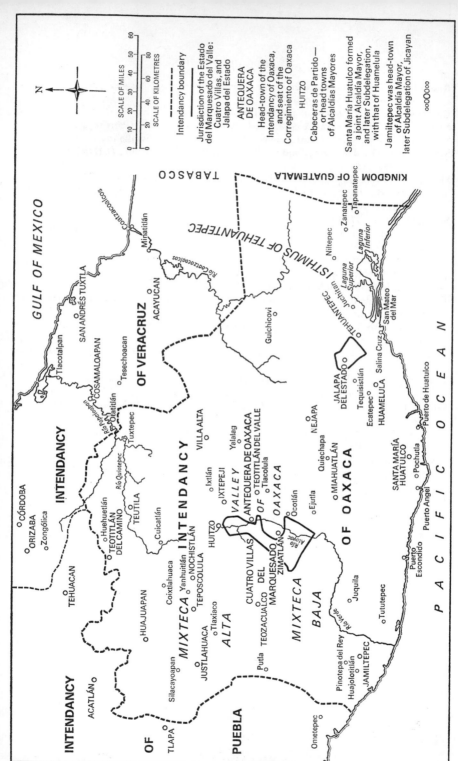

Map I. *The Intendancy of Oaxaca*

Map 2. *Valley of Oaxaca*

NOTE: The boundary given for the Alcaldía Mayor of the Cuatro Villas is based on that presented in Bernardo García Martínez, *El Marquesado del Valle, Tres siglos de régimen señorialen Nueva España* (El Colegio de México 1969), 136.

INDEX

Index

Index

Index

Index

Index

Index

Index

Index

Index

Index

Index

Index

Index

Index